ALSO BY GILES WHITTELL

*Lambada Country*

*Extreme Continental*

*Spitfire Women of World War Two*

[illegible] hittell is Washington correspondent for *The Times*, having [illegible] or them in Los Angeles and Moscow.

*A True Story of the Cold War*

# BRIDGE OF SPIES

GILES WHITTELL

SIMON & SCHUSTER

London · New York · Sydney · Toronto · New Delhi

A CBS COMPANY

First published in Great Britain by Simon & Schuster UK Ltd, 2011
This edition published in Great Britain by Simon & Schuster UK Ltd, 2012
A CBS COMPANY



1 3 5 7 9 10 8 6 4 2

Simon & Schuster UK Ltd
1st Floor
222 Gray's Inn Road
London
WC1X 8HB

www.simonandschuster.co.uk

Simon & Schuster Australia, Sydney
Simon & Schuster India, New Delhi

A CIP catalogue copy for this book is available
from the British Library.

ISBN: 978-1-84983-327-1

Designed by Elina D. Nudelman
Printed and bound by CPI Group (UK) Ltd, Croydon, CR0 4YY

*For Bruno, Louis, and Enzo*

# CONTENTS

# DRAMATIS PERSONAE

*THE PRINCIPALS*

*William Fisher,* aka Rudolf Abel, Emil Goldfus, Martin Collins, Robert Callan, Frank, Milton, and Agent Mark: KGB colonel and the most senior undercover Soviet agent in North America from 1948 to 1957

*Francis Gary Powers:* U-2 pilot trained by the U.S. Air Force and employed by the CIA to fly reconnaissance missions over Soviet Russia; shot down May 1, 1960

*Frederic Pryor:* PhD student at the Free University of West Berlin who was arrested by East German secret police on suspicion of spying but released to his parents as part of the Glienicke Bridge exchange on February 10, 1962

*KGB*

*Reino Hayhanen,* aka Eugene Maki and Agent Vik: Fisher's KGB subordinate in New York from 1952 to 1957 and the man who would betray him to the United States

*Pavel Sudoplatov:* KGB general who masterminded the assassination of Leon Trotsky in 1940 and adopted Fisher as his protégé later in World War II.

*Yuri Drozdov:* KGB officer assigned to correspond with James Donovan from East Germany in hopes of arranging an exchange of Powers for Abel

*Alexander "the Swede" Orlov:* prewar Soviet "illegal" agent who defected to the United States, where he was the only person who knew Fisher's true identity

*Ivan Shishkin:* senior KGB officer who posed as second secretary at the Soviet embassy in East Berlin to represent Moscow in negotiations for the Powers-Abel swap

### *CIA*

*Marty Knutson:* U-2 pilot whose July 1956 photographs of Engels Air Force Base in Russia helped to demolish the theory of a "bomber gap" threatening U.S. national security

*Bob Ericson:* U-2 pilot who flew the penultimate Soviet overflight of April 9, 1960, and was Powers's backup pilot on May 1

*Richard Bissell:* civilian head of the CIA's U-2 program from 1954 to 1962 as the agency's deputy director and then director of plans

*Allen Dulles:* Director of Central Intelligence from 1953 to 1961; lobbied President Eisenhower for authorization for U-2 overflights of the Soviet Union and was responsible for the timing of Powers's flight on May 1, 1960

*Stan Beerli:* air force colonel who joined the CIA to become civilian head of Detachment B, the U-2 unit based in Adana, Turkey, where he designed the Operation Quickmove security procedures for Soviet overflights

*Joe Murphy:* CIA security officer in Adana who was later assigned to identify Powers on Glienicke Bridge in Berlin on February 10, 1962

### *SOVIET LEADERSHIP*

*Nikita Khrushchev:* Soviet premier from 1958 to 1964; abandoned bold plans for nuclear disarmament and walked out of 1960 Great Power Summit meeting in Paris after the Gary Powers overflight of May 1, 1960

*Roman Rudenko:* Soviet prosecutor general and veteran of the Nuremberg Nazi war criminal trials who presided at the trial of Gary Powers in August 1960

*Sergei Biryuzov:* marshal of the Soviet Air Defense Forces who coordinated efforts to intercept Gary Powers and told Khrushchev once the shoot-down was confirmed

*Yevgeni Savitsky:* colonel-general in the Soviet Air Defense Forces who ordered Igor Mentyukov to ram Powers in his Sukhoi Su-9 fighter, knowing the mission would be suicidal if successful

### *U.S. LEADERSHIP*

*Dwight D. Eisenhower:* president of the United States from 1953 to 1961; authorized the U-2 program but bitterly regretted the flight of May 1, 1960

*John F. Kennedy:* president of the United States from 1961 to 1963; promised as a candidate to close a "missile gap" that did not exist and declined to meet Powers on his return to the United States

*William F. Tompkins:* U.S. attorney assigned to prosecute "Rudolf Abel" (William Fisher) in 1957; called Fisher's espionage "an offense directed against our very existence"

*James Donovan:* former U.S. prosecutor at Nuremberg trials of Nazi war criminals assigned to defend Fisher at his trial; later brokered the Glienicke Bridge exchange in Berlin

*Llewellyn Thompson:* U.S. ambassador to Moscow from 1957 to 1962; learned of Powers's survival minutes too late to prevent the release of a false cover story by NASA

*Frank Meehan:* U.S. diplomat assigned to assist the family of Frederic Pryor in Berlin in 1961; subsequently became the last U.S. ambassador to East Germany

## SUPPORTING ACTORS

*Burt Silverman:* Brooklyn artist and friend of "Emil Goldfus" (William Fisher) whose typewriter was used to help convict Fisher of espionage against the United States

*James Bozart:* Brooklyn newspaper delivery boy who picked up a "hollow nickel" dropped by Reino Hayhanen containing a microfilm eventually decoded and traced to Fisher

*Oliver Powers:* miner, cobbler, and father of Gary Powers; requested an exchange of "Abel" for his son in a letter to Khrushchev and traveled to Moscow for his son's trial in 1960

*Millard Pryor:* businessman and father of Frederic Pryor; traveled to Berlin in 1961 to seek his son's release from the notorious Stasi Investigation Prison at Hohenschönhausen

*Wolfgang Vogel:* East German lawyer who served as go-between in Millard Pryor's efforts to contact East German authorities

*Carl McAfee:* Virginia lawyer who traveled with Oliver Powers to Moscow for the Gary Powers trial and pleaded unsuccessfully for leniency to Leonid Brezhnev, the future Soviet premier

*Kelly Johnson:* founder of Lockheed's secret "Skunk Works" hangar in Burbank, California, designer of the U-2, and employer of Gary Powers after he parted ways with the CIA

*Dave Clark:* pioneer of the use of stretch fabrics in women's underwear and designer of the pressure suits worn by all U-2 pilots including Powers at the time of his last flight over Russia

*Marvin Makinen:* American student at the Free University of West Berlin who was sentenced to eight years in prison for spying on Soviet military installations in 1961 but released after two years at the urging of James Donovan

# AUTHOR'S NOTE

Wherever possible I have traced and interviewed those still alive who played roles in this story as it unfolded fifty years ago. Remarks from these interviews are related in the present tense to distinguish them from material found in documents, diaries, or secondary sources.

# PROLOGUE

*February 10, 1962*

The road out of Berlin was practically deserted. It was a Saturday morning, and cold. The forecast was for snow and the rumors were keeping people in town. All the news bureaus had sent reporters to Checkpoint Charlie because it seemed the obvious place. But the forecast was wrong, and so were the rumors.

At about nine thirty a lone taxi cleared the last traffic lights in Wilmersdorf and headed west on Königstrasse, picking up speed. For a while it barreled through pristine woodland across a big, diamond-shaped island formed by the Wannsee and the river Havel. Then it crested a rise, descended for half a mile in a gradual left curve, and stopped at a traffic barrier. Beyond the barrier were a watchtower and a bridge—a solid span of green-painted steel girders across the Havel, bisected by a thin white line. Beyond the bridge was another watchtower and another barrier, beyond them a free-fire zone for the East German frontier police, and beyond that the wall—not the short section that divided the heart of Berlin but the long one that sealed off the Allied sectors from the East. At the white line the American sector ended and the Soviet empire began. It was the closest thing on the planet to a land frontier between the world's two nuclear superpowers.

The taxi turned to be ready to head back into town. Out of it stepped a young woman with a notebook. She had fair hair and blue eyes and was shaking with nerves.

She glanced over at the military police guarding the barrier and thought better of approaching them. Instead she settled on an officer walking toward her in the uniform of the regular West German police. He carried a briefcase and a thermos and looked young, like her.

"Help me, please," she said.

He stopped long enough to hear her say that this was the chance of a lifetime, that her career would stop before it started if she went back with an empty notebook. He replied that he couldn't simply stand there and talk to her. The MPs were watching.

"Walk with me, then," she said.

To the north of the road a triangular grassy slope descended to the water, with a track on the uphill side leading to a cream-colored summer house. The MPs had a clear view along the track but not of the whole slope. Trees and shrubs marked it off from the road, and the woman found that the farther down the slope she walked, the better cover they gave her. She set off down it, and the young police officer followed.

"Maybe he felt pity for me," she says half a century later. "I took him for a walk behind the bushes and he told me the whole story."

It had been early—soon after dawn, he said. He had seen a small convoy of cars approach the bridge from the American side and another from the East German side. Groups of men had spilled out at each end and waited. Then three from each group had walked to the white line and exchanged a few words. There had been a delay, and then a shout, and then two figures had crossed the line, one in each direction.

Annette von Broecker wrote it all down. It was not the full story, but it was better than anyone else would get that day, including the American networks. She wanted more detail, and there was some that she could add herself—a hole in the cloud above the bridge, sunlight pouring through it, two swans gliding back and forth below.

"My heart was pounding," she remembers. "I kept telling myself what to put in. 'Swans, sun, spies. Swans, sun, spies.'" Then she ran back up the slope to a pay phone and called the bureau. Her editor told her to calm down and fed in some background as she went along, but the swans stayed in.

At 3:00 a.m. Washington time, President Kennedy's press secretary briefed him on what the police officer had seen. That left Kennedy better informed than von Broecker's readers, but not by much and not for long. The story she filed that morning made the front page of every paper in the free world with an interest in the unfree world. It recorded a kind of spy swap that had not been tried before, in which the protagonists had to be brought to the same place at the same time and bartered with utmost care under the quiet gaze of snipers hidden in the forests on each side. This was human trafficking with the blessing of two superpowers.

It was a story that started with a search for weapons of mass destruction. Its main players were its foot soldiers. They followed orders, but not ordinary orders. For the best part of seven years they had been drawn deep into the race between the United States and the Soviet Union to establish which was closer to acquiring the means to annihilate the other. When they ran out of luck, the consequences could be beyond disastrous. Just by being human they could change the course of history, and one of them did.

What the policeman told von Broecker that morning centered on three men, not two. The youngest, at that moment, was with his parents for the first time in three years, struggling to grasp that he was free and that he could stop thinking about suicide. He was a twenty-eight-year-old Yale postgraduate student interrogated by the East German secret police—the Stasi—every day for the preceding five months on suspicion of espionage, of which he was entirely innocent. He was a young man with an inquiring mind and a serious case of wanderlust who had driven blithely into the vortex of Berlin's paranoia in a bright red VW sports car. His personality type was not one that the Stasi, a monster sustained by suspicion and obsessed with conformity, found easy to comprehend. He was a joker, a thinker, a free spirit. His name was Frederic Pryor.

The next youngest had crossed the bridge from the East German side to the American in a cheap Russian suit, carrying a cardboard suitcase. It was a strange homecoming for a pilot, especially this pilot. He had entered Soviet airspace two years earlier wearing a custom-fitted pressure suit from the David Clark Company of Worcester, Massachusetts, to prevent his bodily fluids evaporating in the event that his cockpit sprang a leak. His mission was known only to the White House and a small team of CIA operatives scattered between Langley and the wilder fringes of Eurasia. His aircraft, a Lockheed U-2, had crossed the Kazakh steppe at two and a half times the height of Everest, then broken up and tumbled onto Russian soil not far from Sverdlovsk.

Falling from seventy thousand feet, there are no standing orders. To begin with there is only the hiss of oxygen, the slowly tilting blue black dome of the stratosphere, and the deathly quiet realization that the altimeter is starting to unwind. That is all this pilot had to work with. That and the time it takes to drop thirteen vertical miles at an average speed of a hundred miles an hour, which is about ten minutes. He was not supposed to live. If it was a rocket that hit him, the blast should have taken him out with the plane. Even if it was something else, there was almost no chance that his pressure suit would save him. At seventy thousand feet, blood boils in ten seconds. It was regrettable, they all agreed—the tight handful that knew—but the pilot was a goner.

He survived the blast. As he fell, he forced himself to think. As his cockpit began to spin, he ruled out the strategies that would definitely kill him. As he fell through thirty thousand feet, he calmly popped his canopy. As he kept on spinning, he cut his oxygen supply and floated free. He breathed what air there was six miles up, and five, and four. He thanked whoever packed his parachute when it opened. He looked at the countryside below him and thought it looked a bit like Virginia. He picked a spot and landed hard. In Washington, they had no way of knowing, but he survived it all.

His name was Francis Gary Powers, Frank to his friends, the son of a Virginia coal miner who defied his father's ardent wish that he become a doctor and became a fighter jock instead. He had never contemplated suicide, though there was no shortage of people back home who wished he had. His long fall to earth on May 1, 1960, led swiftly and directly to the worst rupture in U.S.-Soviet relations since the Berlin airlift of 1948. It wrecked the Paris summit later that month at which Eisenhower and Khrushchev had hoped to launch a new era of détente. It threw into high gear the arms race that took the world to the brink of nuclear war during the Cuban missile crisis of 1962 and did not end until the collapse of the Soviet empire nearly three decades later. From the moment Powers was reported missing, there were well-placed skeptics on both sides of the cold war who suspected that his entire mission had been planned to fail, and in doing so to prevent the outbreak of superpower peace. It is a theory that lingers to this day.

The oldest player in von Broecker's story walked away from the American sector toward the death strip and the wall and his idea of freedom. He stooped a little and smoked too much, which gave him a bad cough and a worse case of sinusitis. According to the *New York Times,* the CIA, and the Supreme Court of the United States, he was a Soviet master spy. It was a description that delighted his handlers and went with him to his grave. His name, allegedly, was Rudolf Abel. His aliases from nine years spent roaming North America under deep cover included Emil Goldfus, Martin Collins, Robert Callan, Frank, Mark, and Milton, shortened to Milt by coconspirators and admirers. In retirement and death he has acquired an aura as the last of the great Soviet "illegals"—not that Russia stopped trying to smuggle people like him into the United States. His professional heirs include the ten "unregistered agents" of Moscow uncovered by the FBI and sent briskly home in 2010, among them the bewitching redhead known as Anna Chapman and instantly immortalized by New York's tabloids. They and the courts quickly found out most of what there was to know about Miss Chapman. They were less thorough with Abel. Despite five years of exhaustive American due process, no one in the West knew who he was or where he came from, or what he spied on. Some of that is still not known, but this much is: his real name was William Fisher. He was exceptionally good at shrinking coded messages onto microdots, and he was British.

* * *

Thirty years later—in 1992—I hitched a ride in a Russian army truck across the roof of the world. That was what the driver called it, but Western cartographers know it as the Pamir plateau. It is a moonscape of thin brown grass and permanent snow, none of it lower than fifteen thousand feet. Across it winds a four-hundred-mile road built by Soviet frontier guards for no other reason than to defend their frontier. To the east of the plateau lies Tibet, to the south, a thin strip of Afghanistan, and beyond that the unspeakably jagged peaks of northern Pakistan.

Three hours along the road the truck stopped. The soldiers with me in the cab pointed toward the Afghan border and a tiny cluster of white domes just inside what had, only a few months before, been Soviet territory. The domes were a radar station. "That's where we detected Powers," the soldiers said. They used the word "we" even though the oldest of them would have been a baby at the time. Their inherited pride was as memorable as the freezing desolation of the place.

On the same trip I took a taxi halfway across Kazakhstan to Baikonur, the Soviet Cosmodrome, to watch a night launch by a Proton rocket with a German satellite in its nose. Later I trundled north over the steppe, along a lonely spur of the Trans-Siberian railway line, and pestered a sleepy crew of bureaucrats to let me into the Semipalatinsk nuclear test site. Eventually they relented. A charity had stuck a four-sided post in the dirt at the entrance with MAY PEACE PREVAIL ON EARTH in a different language on each side. Inside the site, an irritated Russian army colonel accused me of "radiophobia" for taking out a Geiger counter.

Times had changed. In 1960 the only way for a foreigner to see Baikonur or Semipalatinsk was via the inverted periscope through which U-2 pilots peered down on their targets from seventy thousand feet. Only Powers and a handful of others had that privilege. The same was true of Chelyabinsk, a grotesquely polluted arms metropolis in the Urals that was one of the last places Powers photographed before being shot down—and one of the first places I visited as a Moscow-based reporter in 1999. We were taken there by Green Cross International (chairman: Mikhail Gorbachev). Before that, covering show business and equally serious topics from Los Angeles, I interviewed women who had, they said, been abducted by aliens a few miles from where Powers trained in the Nevada desert, and I played cricket where he died in the San Fernando Valley. Wherever I went, his ghost seemed to have gotten there first.

The legacy of Francis Gary Powers is haunting enough anyway for how it changed the world. It gave us thirty years of cold war that might very well have been avoided. But it also gave us what the young policeman witnessed on Glienicke Bridge—a faint echo of the three-hour truce on Christmas Day in 1916, when troops from the opposing armies in the Flanders mud emerged from their trenches for a surreal game of football. Before and after those moments, human folly reigned supreme. Pryor, Powers, and Fisher bore more than their share of it. This is their story.

# BRIDGE OF SPIES

# part one

# MISSIONS IMPLAUSIBLE

# 1

# THE WATERSPOUT

Shock and awe was not invented for Saddam Hussein. It was invented for Joseph Stalin, and it worked pretty well.

On July 24, 1946, as most of Russia slept, a team of U.S. Navy frogmen guided a heavy steel container to its final resting place in the clear waters of Bikini Lagoon, 2,500 miles west of Honolulu. They stabilized it with cables ninety feet below an anchored amphibious assault ship that gloried in the name *LSM-60*. The container was made from the conning tower of the USS *Salmon,* a scrapped navy submarine, and inside it was a working replica of the plutonium bomb that had killed eighty thousand people at Nagasaki the previous year. That evening, on a support vessel outside the lagoon, the frogmen ate T-bone steaks with all the trimmings.

Around the *LSM-60,* like giant moon shadows on the water's calm surface, a target fleet of eighty-five more ships spent that night emptied of crew and supplies, with no role left except to sink. One of the closest to the bomb was the USS *Arkansas,* a 27,000-ton battleship that had carried President Taft to Panama before the First World War and bombarded Cherbourg and Iwo Jima in the Second. For most of her life the only way for a battleship to go down had been with guns blazing, but the nuclear age had changed that. It turned out that with the help of an atom bomb a battleship could go down like a toy in a bath. It could be flicked onto its bow and rammed into the seabed so that its superstructure fell off as if never even bolted on.

Shortly after breakfast time on the morning of the twenty-fifth, the *Arkansas* was photographed from every angle as the bomb in the steel container was detonated 170 yards from her hull. Cameras in a B-29 bomber twenty-five thousand feet above the lagoon and a little to the south captured the sight of a huge disc of ocean turning white in an instant. That was the water beneath the *Arkansas* being vaporized.

The shockwave from the initial blast rolled the ship onto her side and ripped off her propellers. A six-thousand-foot column of spray and water, created in about two and a half seconds, then heaved her into a vertical position in which two thirds of her length were clearly visible ten miles away, dwarfed by the largest man-made waterspout in history. She has lain upside down on the floor of the lagoon ever since.

The *Arkansas* was one of ten ships sunk outright by what came to be known as the Baker shot. It was the second of two nuclear tests conducted at Bikini with undisguised panache as the world adjusted to an awesome new technology (and to the daring swimsuit it inspired; the first-ever bikini, presented in Paris that month, was called *l'atome,* and the second was a buttock-baring thong described by one fashion writer as what the survivor of a nuclear blast could expect to be wearing as the fireball subsided).

Participation in the tests by U.S. military personnel was voluntary but popular. In shirtsleeves and sunglasses, 37,000 men extended their wartime service for a year to help set up the tests and to see for themselves the power of the weapon that had brought Japan to its knees.

Pat Bradley was there, up a tree with a movie camera on Bikini atoll to film the blast and the tsunami it produced—a single ninety-foot wave that subsided before it hit the island, then three smaller waves. “It took a couple of minutes before the first wave came in to the atoll,” he remembered. “The second came in higher, then the third completely covered the island four to six feet deep.”

A lean and thoughtful young air force captain named Stan Beerli was there too. He had survived the world war in B-17 bombers over Italy and would survive the cold war in the regulation dark suit of the CIA. His tasks would include trying to keep Gary Powers and the U-2 in the shadows where they belonged, but for the time being the cold war was pure spectacle.

The foreign and domestic press were welcome at Bikini. The Baker shot was witnessed by 131 reporters, including a full Soviet contingent. With Warner Bros.' help, the Pentagon released a propaganda film of the blast for anyone who had missed the initial coverage, and Admiral William "Spike" Blandy, who oversaw the operation, posed with his wife cutting an angel food cake in the shape of a mushroom cloud.

Responding to public anxiety before the blast, Blandy promised that he was "not an atomic playboy" and that the bomb would not "blow out the bottom of the sea and let all the water run down the hole." This was true, but it could still do a lot of damage. In the summer of 1947 *Life* magazine published a long article based on official studies of the intense radioactive fallout from the Baker bomb. It concluded that if a similar weapon were to explode off the tip of Manhattan in a stiff southerly wind, two million people would die.

America had finished the war with a pair of atom bombs and started the peace in the same way. President Truman's message to Stalin could not have been clearer if written in blood. It was a warning not to contemplate starting a new war in Europe trusting in the Red Army's old-fashioned strength in numbers. And it signaled more concisely than any speech that Truman had accepted the central argument of George Kennan's famous "Long Telegram," sent from the U.S. embassy in Moscow six months before the tests: the Soviet Union had to be contained. As Truman himself put it: "If we could just have Stalin and his boys see one of these things, there wouldn't be any question about another war."

Stalin refused to be intimidated. He had not sacrificed twenty million people to defeat Fascism only to be told where to set the limits on Stalinism. And yet he had a problem.

At the time of the Bikini tests, the Soviet Union was still three years and a month from exploding its first nuclear weapon. Its efforts to build one were under way on a bend in the Shagan River in eastern Kazakhstan, under the direction of a bearded young hero of Soviet science (and tightly closeted homosexual) named Igor Kurchatov. Stalin had deemed the bomb "Problem Number One." He had created a special state committee to ensure that no expense was spared in solving it. Whole mountains in Bulgaria had been commandeered to give Kurchatov the uranium he needed. But Kurchatov was not an innovator. He was a nuclear plagiarist, almost completely dependent on intelligence from left-leaning scientists in the Manhattan Project in Los Alamos.

As he admitted in a 1943 memo to the Council of People's Commissars, this flow of intelligence had "immense, indeed incalculable importance for our State and science"—but in 1946 the flow had slowed suddenly to a trickle.

Just a year earlier, not one but two descriptions of the first bomb tested at Los Alamos were in the Kremlin nearly two weeks before it even exploded. After that test, more detailed diagrams of the device reached Moscow than were provided in the first official nuclear report to Congress. One was smuggled out of Albuquerque in a box of Kleenex. Atomic espionage was never more bountiful than this. But on November 7, 1945, Elizabeth Terrill Bentley, a thirty-seven-year-old graduate of Vassar and a paid-up Soviet agent, went to the FBI with a 107-page description of Soviet intelligence activities in North America. The following day J. Edgar Hoover sent a secret memo to the White House based on Bentley's material. It produced few arrests because she offered scant supporting evidence, but her defection forced Moscow to shut down most of the channels feeding nuclear secrets to Kurchatov.

There were other reasons why Soviet espionage in the United States was grinding to a halt. Victory in the war had removed the most compelling reason for scientists at Los Alamos to share designs with their former Soviet allies—the defeat of Nazism. And the U.S. Army had at last begun decoding encrypted Soviet cable traffic, code-named Venona, that corroborated many of Bentley's allegations.

Without vital intelligence from the true pioneers of nuclear fission in New Mexico, Kurchatov would not be able to complete the bomb. Without the bomb, the most that the Soviet empire could hope to do was defend its interminable frontiers. As the Bikini lagoon erupted, the outlook for international Communism looked bleak indeed. Yet from the bowels of the Lyubianka—headquarters of the KGB and the true engine room of the revolution—there came a glimmer of hope.

# 2
# THE AGENT

*"There are many countries in our blood, aren't there, but only one person."*

Graham Greene (via Mr. Wormald in a cable to MI6 headquarters in *Our Man in Havana*)

Shortly before midday on November 14, 1948, an aging Cunard liner laden with immigrants picked up a pilot for the last few miles of its transatlantic crossing. It nosed up the Saint Lawrence Seaway beneath the lowering darkness of the Plains of Abraham and docked in Quebec at five past one. A cold wind raked the quayside. The SS *Scythia* had been nine days at sea since leaving Cuxhaven on the north German coast. Most of its passengers were in family groups being met by those who had made the journey before them. Most were refugees from the joyless austerity of a country destroyed by war and occupied by its victors. They stepped cautiously down the *Scythia*'s gangplanks, wrapped in thick coats, clutching what they would need for the first few hours of their new lives.

For a few moments Andrew Kayotis may have stood out among them. As a single man, middle-aged, taller than average despite his stoop, it was probably unavoidable. But he did not stand out for long. No one met him. He carried only a suitcase so had no need of a porter. His papers were in order. He showed his passport, walked briskly to the railway station on the Rue Saint-Pierre, and bought a ticket for the first train to Montreal.

"Kayotis" had spent the crossing reading quietly in his cabin, taking walks on the *Scythia*'s promenade deck, and talking very little. The voyage had been a hiatus between two worlds, and two identities. His real name was William Fisher. His future name was Emil Goldfus. His Kayotis papers were a convenience of transition, to be torn up and flushed away as soon as Goldfus was ready to spring to life. His code name was "Arach," and for nine years from the moment he stepped ashore in Quebec he was the most senior Soviet spy in North America.

***

At his trial, Fisher would be called a threat to the free world and to civilization itself. It is more accurate to think of him as the Forrest Gump of Soviet foreign intelligence. Most Americans who had dealings with him decided he was "brilliant," and it was true that he could speak five languages and amuse himself for hours with logarithmic tables and back issues of *Proceedings of the National Academy of Sciences.* But his brilliance never got him far. His luck got him much further. He was a mild, stoic, generous man, far too good natured for his profession, who rode his luck through the terrifying middle decades of the twentieth century straight into the safe haven of the Atlanta Federal Penitentiary.

By the time *Life* magazine published its article on the Bikini blasts, Fisher had been in training for the toughest assignment of his career for nearly a year. It would take him into the heart and soul of the Main Adversary—the United States, that vast and baffling country that somehow produced guns *and* butter (and Rita Hayworth) with no guiding hand at the controls of its economy.

Fisher's main task was to rebuild the Soviet spy network in America. If he succeeded, the flow of information from Los Alamos and the top secret fuel enrichment laboratory at Oak Ridge, Tennessee, would start again. Stalin's scientists would conquer nuclear fission, then leapfrog the West to make a reality of fusion, and the H-bomb as well. Berlin, Washington, and London would quake without a shot being fired. That was the fantasy, and as long as Fisher was safely ensconced at a KGB training facility in the woods outside Moscow, there was no harm in fantasizing.

Fisher's superiors had chosen him for his background and his personality. As far as they could tell he was a man of unswerving loyalty and discipline. He was educated but not overeducated. In the war he had shown respect for tradecraft and courage under fire. He was a genius with radios and able to deflect attention from himself as completely as a mirror.

He was quite unlike the KGB's best-known British recruits, the so-called Cambridge Five, whom he detested. Kim Philby, Donald Maclean, Guy Burgess, John Cairncross, and Anthony Blunt were cosseted products of the English class system. Fisher was a stranger to privilege. He saw himself as a Soviet patriot and the others as traitors to their motherland. They were louche and libidinous. He was ascetic. They were dilettantes. He was a Bolshevik born and bred—yet he was also irresistibly human. "There was something—can I say that?—lovable about him." That was the verdict of the man whom Fisher fooled most comprehensively about his true identity, the New York artist Burton Silverman.

Fisher was rail thin, with the countenance of a weasel and a mental toughness that still amazes those who knew him. He switched identities throughout his working life but never forgot his own. He could hold forth for hours on music theory or mathematics, both of which he taught himself. He was a soulful player of the classical guitar and a passable painter whose work Robert Kennedy would later try to hang in the White House.

He was born in Newcastle upon Tyne in the north of England in 1903 to German parents. He moved with them to Russia at age eighteen. Those bare facts of his biography gave him fluency in the three languages a secret agent of his era needed most. His father gave him his vocation: Heinrich Fisher was already a committed revolutionary when he first met Lenin in the 1890s. Having grown up on an aristocrat's estate in central Russia, he turned to Marxism with the zeal and arrogance of the autodidact. He and Lenin taught and agitated at the Saint Petersburg Technological Institution until Fisher senior was arrested for sedition and exiled to Archangel in the Russian Arctic in 1896. After that, as an ethnic German, he faced deportation and compulsory service in the German army. England offered refuge. Heinrich sailed with his young wife to Newcastle upon Tyne, where they had two sons. The first was named Henry after his father. The second was William, but they called him Willie.

After the 1905 Russian revolution failed, Willie's father turned to gunrunning to help the proletariat he had left behind. (One shipment that was discovered before being dispatched to the Baltic included more than a million rounds of ammunition, including some for the type of Mauser pistol used to assassinate Czar Nicholas.) After the 1917 revolution succeeded, the Fishers returned to Russia to put themselves at its service.

Willie Fisher embraced the great Soviet experiment in utopia building, and it embraced him back. He joined the Communist Youth League, which put him to work as a translator. Then he served two years in the Red Army as a radio operator. He was young enough for his command of languages and experience of a foreign country to be a qualification, not grounds for suspicion. By the age of twenty-four, in the eyes of the ever-expanding Soviet intelligence apparatus, he was ripe for recruitment. He was also married to the illegitimate daughter of a Polish count.

Elena Lebedeva, a ballerina-turned-harpist at the Moscow Conservatory, met Fisher at a party in 1926. She glimpsed in him a loneliness and self-sufficiency at once intriguing and forbidding, which he carried with him all the way to Glienicke Bridge. When he proposed to her she asked him: "But do you love me?"

"How do I know if I love you?" he replied. "Your character is soft and warm. I'm the opposite, but we'll make a good couple. We'll complement each other."

*We'll complement each other.* Such bleak detachment may have helped him withstand the strain of life as a covert agent, but it was born of tragedy. A few weeks after their arrival in Russia, in the summer of 1921, Willie and Henry had been helping to look after a large group of children camping on the banks of a river outside Moscow. One of the children had been dragged under by an unseen current. Henry had dived in and saved the child but drowned immediately afterward. Willie, who had never learned to swim, could only stand and watch. He was inconsolable.

With Elena, he could at least find contentment and security. Through her family's connections he landed his first job with the OGPU, precursor to the KGB. In 1931 they left Moscow with a baby daughter on his first long foreign assignment. Their destination: Norway.

When the Fishers crossed the frontier into Finland in September 1931, they crossed into the netherworld of Soviet "illegals." The term is misleading, as all spies worth the label break the law. But in the language of the Cheka, the original Bolshevik terror apparatus, "illegal" had a special meaning. It recalled the revolutionary underground in which the party's founders had first confronted the czarist secret police; and the code names they had adopted; and the exploits of the first generation of Soviet agents sent abroad to spread the revolution when no other European country would recognize the murderous new regime.

"Lenin" was the code name of one Vladimir Ulyanov. "Stalin" was that of Joseph Dzhugashvili. Fisher's code name, to begin with, was Frank. He did not keep it long, but the intelligence chiefs who ran his career remained fixated by the cult of the illegals until well after they had outlived their usefulness, and they remained convinced that Fisher was ideally suited to the job.

In a sense, he was. Like a nuclear submarine, he proved he could stay hidden almost indefinitely. But hiding took so much of his energy that it is doubtful whether he had much left over to find out anything useful about his enemy. "He was a brilliant and conscientious spy," a retired KGB general who played a central role in securing Fisher's eventual release insists to this day. "It is an obvious fact that he was handling agents about whom the Americans still know nothing." In fact this is not obvious at all. There is no evidence that Fisher recruited any useful agents who have not yet been identified or transmitted any significant intelligence collected by those who have been. This did not stop both sides colluding in the creation of the legend of Willie Fisher—by another name—as the most effective Soviet spy of the cold war.

In Oslo, his work protected him. It was simple and unobtrusive: his job was to build his cover as an importer of electrical appliances and establish a network of radio relay stations to help Moscow communicate with other spies in northern Europe. For three years he busied himself in the attics of Communist sympathizers and unsuspecting clients, hiding and testing radio equipment. He and his young family lived quietly on the Baltic coast, while in Russia the Cheka began to devour its own.

For decades, Stalin's reign of terror was understood as an expression of his own peculiar madness. But his purging of the intelligence apparatus that he relied on to control his empire may have a more rational explanation—that he had been a traitor himself. The claim was first published in the 1990s in a Russian biography of Stalin by Edvard Radzhinsky. Vasili Mitrokhin's treasure trove of documents on Soviet foreign intelligence, smuggled out of Russia as the Soviet Union collapsed, also contained evidence that Stalin may have been a paid informer of the czar's secret police before 1917. If so, the information would go at least some way toward explaining his merciless paranoia toward anyone connected—however tenuously—to the Bolshevik old guard.

As a Chekist whose father had known Lenin, Fisher was lucky not to be woken in the night and summarily executed on his return to Moscow. Instead he was merely fired. A friend of his father's found him a job in an aircraft factory before Hitler changed everything by invading Russia. From the moment the panzers rumbled into Minsk, Soviet national survival took precedence over personal—and national survival would need a functioning intelligence service. In September 1941, Fisher was reinstated as a lieutenant in the Cheka, by then renamed the People's Commissariat for Internal Affairs, or NKVD. "He was lucky," his Russian biographer remarked later. "Russia was inefficient. If it had been Germany, he *would* have been shot."

He had an outstanding war. Adopted as a protégé of Pavel Sudoplatov, the mastermind of Trotsky's murder in Mexico the year before, Fisher edged, Gump-like, onto the main stage of the vast theater of the eastern front. On November 7, 1941, a day still etched in gold in Russia's official history, he found himself in a blizzard in Red Square.

It was the anniversary of the revolution. The Germans had advanced to within a day's march of the Kremlin, but Stalin decreed that the annual Red Army parade should proceed as normal. "My pass to the parade was stamped PROKHOD VSIDY, which meant I was allowed access to the leadership standing in review on top of Lenin's tomb," Sudoplatov recalled. He had been ordered by Lavrenty Beria, Stalin's chief henchman, to report any military developments to him immediately on the rostrum on Lenin's mausoleum. "The situation was critical: the German advance was only thirty miles from Moscow. I brought along with me to Red Square a young captain, William Fisher, chief of the radio communications section of my department.... We stayed in touch with NKVD headquarters and the brigade defending Moscow. It was snowing so heavily that the Germans could not send aircraft to bomb Red Square. However, the order for the troops participating in the parade was very strict: no matter what happens, stay calm and maintain discipline."

As the parade was coming to an end, Captain Fisher received a request from the front for reinforcements. He passed it to Sudoplatov, who passed it to Stalin, who gave perhaps the most cinematic military order of his career. Through driving snow, several battalions marched directly from Red Square to the front, where they covered themselves in glory by deflecting the German advance.

The following year Fisher was involved in what Sudoplatov called "the most successful radio deception game of the war." The game was played with the cooperation of Lieutenant Colonel Heinrich Scherhorn, a German artillery commander trapped by Soviet forces in the forests of Belorussia in the summer of 1944. On August 19, a Soviet double agent code-named Max reported to German intelligence that Scherhorn was surrounded by 2,500 men but still able to fight. In fact he was a prisoner of the Russians and remained one for the rest of the war, while the German high command wasted precious resources resupplying his fictitious force. One supply run involved sixty-seven transport planes, thirteen portable radios, and ten million rubles in cash. Some of the aircraft were allowed to land and return to prolong the hoax. The rest were impounded and their crews taken prisoner.

Fisher was modest to a fault and, later in life, never made the mistake of believing his own publicity. But if his daughter ever asked him what he did in the war, he could reasonably have replied that he helped to win it. That was certainly the view of his bosses in the KGB. His reward was the most prestigious post in Soviet foreign intelligence: America.

* * *

"I would rather perish than betray the secrets entrusted to me.... With every heartbeat, with every day that passes, I swear to serve the Party, the homeland and the Soviet People."

In late October 1948, Willie Fisher swore the illegals' oath at a solemn meeting with his handlers in the Lyubianka, where the NKVD had its headquarters. He was then summoned to the offices of Vyacheslav Molotov, the former Soviet foreign minister. They talked about Fisher's mission and were joined afterward by his family for dinner. It was an astonishing amount of attention to lavish on a mere illegal. Whatever happened to him in America, in Russia he had arrived.

Apart from Stalin himself, no one personified Soviet power and cunning like Molotov. He had dined with Hitler, signed away Poland and the Baltics in the Nazi-Soviet nonaggression pact, girded the Soviet empire for resistance when Hitler invaded, and inspired his very own cocktail, the anti-Soviet petrol bomb. Now he was anointing Willie Fisher as his secret weapon in the new war against America. Old Heinrich Fisher would have burst with pride.

After the dinner Willie returned with his wife and daughter to their dacha and said good-bye. He would not see them again for seven years.

He was driven to the Leningradsky station in a black limousine and seen off by Viktor Abakumov, the founder of SMERSH (in English, Death to Spies, whose Russian acronym Ian Fleming borrowed in his search for a worthy rival for James Bond).* From there Fisher took a train to Warsaw and another to Cuxhaven. Alone and surely lonesome, he boarded the SS *Scythia*. His genuine American passport bore his own picture but the name Andrew Kayotis. Fisher never used his real name again.

The real Kayotis, Lithuanian born and Detroit bred, had conveniently died while visiting relatives in Vilnius the previous year. His papers had been spirited to Moscow. His life story, gleaned from his surviving Lithuanian family, had been absorbed by the tall, spare passenger who ate by himself and read quietly for hours at a time as the *Scythia* set course via Le Havre for the New World.

* * *

On paper, Fisher's workload was crushing. Besides reviving the spy network that had kick-started the Soviet nuclear program, he was tasked with single-handedly softening up the North American continent for the Third World War. "His mission would be to gain access to military installations, warehouses, and stored supplies of ammunition," Sudoplatov wrote, as if none of that should have presented a problem for a competent undercover radio ham. "We badly needed to know how

* Abakumov was second in command only to Lavrenty Beria in the Soviet security apparat and a less-than-cuddly character. When his sister was arrested for profiteering in the war he reputedly told the officer who asked how he would like to handle the case: "Why do you ask me? Don't you know your duty . . . ? Shoot her."

quickly American reinforcements could appear in Europe." Later, Sudoplatov's biographers cast Fisher's role in even grander terms: "He directed preparations to take over the Western Hemisphere in case the rising tensions between the United States and the Soviet Union turned into a new world war."

In practice Fisher had been unleashed on the Western world with few realistic obligations and no serious deadlines. He had ten days in which to make his way by bus through New England to keep a prearranged appointment in New York. There a contact from the Soviet consulate general gave him a thousand dollars in cash and a new identity in the name of Emil Goldfus. As Goldfus he went walkabout.

Willie Fisher was by this time forty-five, happily married, and a deeply committed Communist. He was also more alone than he had ever been, as forcibly reliant on himself as a cosmonaut cut loose from his space station. It is hard to imagine his state of mind as he simultaneously scouted the country for ammunition dumps and fought to reconcile the Soviet caricature of America with his first impressions of the reality—of the richest nation on earth, unscarred by war. He would have had the solo traveler's heightened awareness, the salivary overload of the half-starved Soviet worker released into a place of unimaginable bounty, and the gradually abating paranoia of a spy at large in the land of the free.

It is even harder to know for certain where Fisher went or what he did—though all the clues suggest he headed for the sun. He was drawn first to California. He had orders to find out if the United States was still shipping arms to Chiang Kai-shek and his Chinese nationalists from the port of Long Beach (it was). While in California Fisher also found time to create a brand-new network of "agent informers" recruited mainly from German Jewish émigrés, according to Sudoplatov. Their role in the event of a "Special Period" (a U.S.-Soviet war) would be to join forces with illegals disguised as seasonal workers streaming north from Central America to paralyze the giant defense contractors of the West Coast with a campaign of coordinated sabotage. There never was a Special Period, however, so we may never know how much of Fisher's ambitious agenda was real and how much camouflage for a richly deserved vacation.

On his way back to New York, he probably paused in Santa Fe.

The adobe plaza of New Mexico's favorite tourist destination was the closest a Soviet intelligence officer could get to Los Alamos without attracting too much attention from the FBI. It was fortunate, then, that the KGB already had a safe house there, disguised as a pharmacy. This has been identified by Jerrold Schecter, a former *Time* magazine Moscow bureau chief who smuggled Khrushchev's autobiography out of Russia for publication in the 1960s, as Zook's Drugstore. It no longer exists, but it did in the 1940s. It had a decent lunch counter, and there are reasons to believe it served the purpose Schecter says it did: Santa Fe had been a vital staging point for the NKVD team that murdered Trotsky in a villa outside Mexico City in 1940.

Santa Fe was also the obvious collection point for stolen diagrams from the Manhattan Project, and a former pupil of Fisher's had spent a year there during the war passing secrets from physicists to couriers. Her name was Kitty Harris. The bigamous wife of the head of the Communist Party USA and former lover of the suave British traitor Donald Maclean, Harris had been recruited by Soviet intelligence in the early 1930s. As part of her basic training she had been taught how to use a radio by Willie Fisher.

So many roads led to Santa Fe that he almost certainly dropped by, if only in the spirit of Curious George. And so it was, in all likelihood, that the spearhead of Stalin's foreign intelligence operation, the man Molotov had ordered to wreak havoc across America should the looming clash of ideologies come to war, stepped off a Greyhound bus into the clear light and astringent air of northern New Mexico sometime in the early spring of 1949. He liked to wear a straw hat to cover his balding pate. His tailored Daks trousers conveyed a hint of style and affluence. He dabbed his nose constantly with white linen handkerchiefs and carried a suitcase. If asked, he had lived across the Midwest and worked variously as an accountant, engineer, and photofinisher but was now "semi-retired and self-employed." He lived in New York City.

Forced to live in unfamiliar countries and under layer upon layer of disguise, many illegals went to pieces, or to the other side, or both. Fisher did not. His straightforward devotion to Communism was one reason. His devotion to his family was another: they were the KGB's guarantee that he would not defect. But there may have been a third explanation for his loyalty: a desire to emulate the great illegals in whose footsteps he was following. One of these was Arnold Deutsch, recruiter of the Cambridge Five and indulger of their sexual shenanigans. Deutsch had been rewarded during the war with the promise of the post of senior illegal in New York—in effect, Fisher's job—but he had drowned on the way there when his ship was torpedoed in the mid-Atlantic. Another was Alexander "the Swede" Orlov, code name "Schwed." Orlov had endeared himself to the Kremlin by spiriting the entire gold reserves of the Spanish government to Moscow during the Spanish civil war. He then enraged Stalin by defecting to Chicago and threatening to expose him as a czarist informer should any harm come to the family Orlov had left behind.

If Fisher was in awe of such chutzpah, he did not show it. Around July 11, 1949—his forty-sixth birthday—he returned to New York for another scheduled meeting, this time with a "legal" KGB resident at the Soviet consulate general who refilled his wallet with cash and took him for a walk in Bear Mountain State Park. At one point the resident was about to ask a park ranger the time when Fisher jumped in and did the talking to save his contact from having to reveal his Russian accent.

Two spies, and not a watch between them.

Soon afterward, Fisher was ordered to reactivate the Volunteer network that had handled most of the logistics for the smuggling of nuclear secrets to Russia. This was easier said than done. Most of the network's sources had stopped cooperating. Security at Los Alamos had been tightened since the war, and Fisher was obsessed above all with not getting caught. Even so, he went through the motions. His first move was to contact Lona Cohen, formerly a housekeeper to a wealthy Manhattan family, now married to Morris Cohen and half of a famous KGB double act. Lona and Willie had arranged to meet at the Bronx Zoo, but on the way there she sensed she had a tail. She did; it was Willie, dusting off his tradecraft. She doubled back, changed subway lines, and stepped in and out of train cars as the doors were closing but couldn't shake him. Eventually they sat down next to each other on a bench outside the bird house and introduced themselves.

The Cohens ran the Volunteer network and were veteran couriers themselves. It was Lona, in fact, who had hidden a diagram of the bomb used in the Trinity test of July 1945 in a box of tissues in case she was searched on her way back to New York. Like Fisher, the Cohens would have been much busier in 1949 if Elizabeth Bentley—the Soviet spy who gave her secrets to the FBI in 1945—and J. Edgar Hoover had not between them muzzled many of Moscow's best sources of nuclear intelligence. Yet these sources had not dried up completely.

Soon after the end of the war, Niels Bohr, the Danish genius of atomic structure, had nervously agreed to help Igor Kurchatov achieve a stable nuclear reaction. Klaus Fuchs, the German-born physicist, was also still leaking valuable information, though by this time from the Harwell research laboratory outside London. And yet another Soviet mole, George Koval, who was not unmasked until 2007, provided the critically important recipe for a polonium initiator without which the Los Alamos team had found that a plutonium-based bomb would not achieve a chain reaction. Kurchatov had long since been focused on plutonium—he had found that even with all the uranium in Bulgaria he did not have enough of it—and on August 29, 1949, his plutonium bomb at last went off. Willie Fisher had almost nothing to do with it, but it was still the high point of his espionage career.

The mushroom cloud that rose off the steppe that day ended the American nuclear monopoly and occasioned rare largesse from the Kremlin. On the personal orders of Lavrenty Beria, by then the second-most-powerful man in the Soviet Union, the children of foreign illegals who had been involved in the grand theft of the capitalist bomb were given automatic places at university. For being in roughly the right place at the right time, Fisher and the Cohens were also awarded the Order of the Red Banner, an honor normally reserved for military heroes. But for Fisher in particular the party was over before it had begun. Ted Hall, one of Lona Cohen's best sources at Los Alamos, had moved to Chicago and given up spying: "No more," he told Fisher and Cohen when they tried one last time to talk him out of his decision. "I helped you during the wartime and now it is over." Klaus Fuchs had been identified in the decrypted Venona Soviet intelligence cables and was arrested in London in January 1950. He named his main contact, who in turn identified two idealistic but ineffectual Communist spies, Julius and Ethel Rosenberg. They were tried, convicted, and sentenced to death in 1951. Their appeals would last two years and fail. The Cohens had already fled the country. Fisher tried and failed to recruit a young man Lona Cohen had cared for in her previous life as a housekeeper. He could be grateful that the Rosenbergs did not reveal anything to lead the FBI to him, but otherwise the outlook for his brave new spy network could hardly have been bleaker.

Until, that is, a white thumbtack appeared on a signpost in New York's Central Park in October 1952.

***

Soviet illegals spent years establishing their cover and almost as long practicing secure communications. In the 1950s that did not mean sixty-four-bit digital encryption. It meant pencils and pads of paper (to be destroyed after one use), hollowed-out coins and bolts, rolls and tiny flakes of microfilm, dead drops, and signals for dead drops. Apart from shortwave radios there was not much communication equipment in use by the KGB in the midtwentieth century that would not have been available at the turn of the nineteenth.

The Americans behaved differently. Faced with the new realities of the nuclear age, the CIA went looking for new hardware. It commissioned extraordinary machines that might not be possible to build but would solve big problems if they could be. Roosevelt had done this with the atom bomb. Kennedy would do it with the moon rocket. Was it not the American way?

It was, but it could still take desk jockeys by surprise.

Don Flickinger, later an air force general, was at his desk in the Life Sciences Division of the air force's Aero Research and Development Command in Baltimore one January morning in 1955 when his commanding officer summoned him urgently. Flickinger was told that the secretary of the air force wanted to see him "ASAP." He said he could drive down to Washington anytime in the next day or so. The CO said no: he needed to be there in the next *hour.* A car was waiting.

The drive was quick. On arrival at the Pentagon, Flickinger was taken straight to the secretary and told on strict need-to-know terms that a new high-altitude reconnaissance plane was being built to an extremely tight deadline on the West Coast.

The secretary then asked Flickinger about pressure suits. Could the suits that the air force was using in its rocket planes keep a pilot alive if his cockpit depressurized at seventy thousand feet? They could, Flickinger said, as long as the pilot descended quickly to about ten thousand feet.

"Let us assume that the pilot cannot descend from the specified mission altitude of seventy thousand feet," the secretary said.

"Why not?" Flickinger asked.

"Because underneath is not friendly but strictly forbidden territory," said the secretary.

"Why is it forbidden to the pilot?"

"Because underneath is the Soviet Union."

That put a new complexion on the problem, and the meeting. Flickinger explained that the best suits available at that point were get-me-down suits only. If getting down was not an option, pilot and plane would both be lost. But *that* was the outcome that was not an option, the secretary observed. How long would it take to produce a better suit? Three to five years, Flickinger said, given the necessary funds. The secretary stood up, walked around his desk, and said he didn't have three years. He had ten months.

***

The thumbtack in Central Park was left there by a man who claimed to be a former blacksmith from Lapland. It was true that he had lived in Lapland and worked briefly as a blacksmith, but it would have been more useful for the FBI (and Willie Fisher) to know that he was also a wife beater, an alcoholic, and quite possibly the worst spy in the history of the KGB. It was this man, more than anyone, who made Fisher look good. His name was Reino Hayhanen and he was fresh off the *Queen Mary*.

In 1952 Hayhanen was thirty-two, and his best years were behind him. Why such a dismal underachiever should have been given a central role in the collection of nuclear intelligence and the disruption of what is now called U.S. homeland security remains a mystery. There are explanations, but none suffices. His parents were Soviet citizens but ethnic Finns, so he spoke Finnish and would eventually pass as a Finnish-American. He was a diligent schoolboy who had earned a place at the Leningrad Pedagogical Institute, from which he was sucked into the lower ranks of the NKVD as its higher ranks were decimated in the terrifying purges that became known as the Terror. Perhaps most important, he happened to be known to the new head of the KGB's illegals directorate, Aleksandr Korotkov. A man of naked ambition but no apparent judgment, Korotkov owed his own rise through the bureaucracy to a two-year stint supervising the assassination of Trotskyites in Paris before the war and a willingness to disown his Jewish wife and children during the purges.

Hayhanen could at least claim to have run a few risks in the cause of secrecy. By the time he set sail for New York he had spent two years hammering metal and bribing neighbors in northern Finland to establish his legend as Eugene Maki, the son of returned Finnish-American emigrants. That proved enough to obtain a U.S. passport from the consulate in Helsinki. He had also married an attractive young Finn named Hannah Kurikka (without divorcing his first wife, whom he left in Russia). And he had crossed the Soviet-Finnish border undetected in the trunk of a KGB car not once but three times. He was no coward.

He announced his arrival without incident. As instructed, a week after disembarking the *Queen Mary* he took a walk up the West Side of Manhattan and entered the park at Seventy-ninth Street. There was the Tavern on the Green, exactly where he had been told it would be. There was the bridle path and the white-painted wooden signpost. The thumbtack in his pocket, also white, would be invisible except to someone who was looking for it. He stuck it in and kept walking. No one noticed.

No one at all. For six months, on the twenty-first of each month, Hayhanen took the subway to the Lincoln Road exit of the Prospect Park station in Brooklyn. He would smoke a pipe and wear a blue tie with red stripes. If any Soviet official needed to make contact with the new number two illegal in North America, this was where and when to do it. No one did. The only response to his thumbtack came in a hollowed-out 1948 Jefferson nickel left at a dead drop whose location, like that of the signpost, he had memorized in training. But before Hayhanen had a chance to open the coin, he either spent it or he lost it.

For seven months the hollow nickel rattled around the New York City cash economy, intact. It was found on a hot Friday afternoon the following summer in a stairwell on the Vanderveer Estates in Brooklyn, outside an apartment shared by two lady school teachers, a Mrs. Donnelly and a Mrs. Ash.

James Bozart, then thirteen, fair haired, and freckled, was collecting for the *Brooklyn Eagle,* which he delivered every morning and was paid for every week. "The paper was thirty-five cents for the week, and people gave different types of tips," he remembers. "The nickels were the cheapskates, but Mrs. Ash and Mrs. Donnelly weren't cheapskates. They gave fifty cents—usually two quarters but this time a quarter, two dimes, and a nickel.

"I took the money and turned round. They closed the door. I didn't look at the tip at first—that would be rude. I went downstairs. The light was out and my heel caught on a step, so I tripped and dropped the nickel and it bounced on the edge of one of the steps and broke in half. I'm scrabbling for it in the dark and eventually I find the back of the coin, and inside it is this tiny square of something. I go to the window and hold the square up to the light and I think, *what the hell is that?*"

It was a pertinent question. Only a few days earlier, Ethel and Julius Rosenberg had been electrocuted at the Sing Sing Correctional Facility thirty miles up the Hudson River. Anguished liberals on every continent believed (inaccurately) that the Rosenbergs were innocent of spying for Russia, but Senator Joseph McCarthy considered them guilty as charged. Despite the best efforts of Edward R. Murrow to ridicule him on his CBS television show, McCarthy was still too popular to be disowned even by Eisenhower, the new Republican president. For all anyone knew in the Vanderveer Estates, the Communist conspiracy to destroy America was real and growing in strength with every hollowed-out nickel that happened to break apart in front of you.

Bozart had a school friend, Carolyn Lewind, whose father was an NYPD detective. When the newsboy finished his collection he went round to her house. Detective Lewind wasn't there, so Bozart kept the coin and went home to show it to his mother. She had gone to church for Friday-night bingo, so he showed it to his father. After an inconclusive discussion, he pocketed the coin again and went out to play stickball.

Later that evening Detective Lewind came home to be told by his wife that young Jim Bozart had dropped by with what looked like a secret message on a piece of microfilm. Scenting a national emergency, the detective told his wife she was insane to have let the boy out of the house. "Next thing my father knows, Detective Lewind and his partner are at my house asking where I am," Bozart recalls, "and my father looks at him and says I'm playing stickball."

Emerging from the Bozarts' apartment building, Lewind and his partner seized the tills of two nearby ice cream vans in case either one had received a hollow nickel. Then they interrupted Mrs. Bozart's bingo game and impounded all the money in the church.

"So everybody's pissed at me," Bozart remembers. "Then Lewind and his partner see me playing stickball, and they come running."

* * *

The case of the hollow nickel ended happily for the *Brooklyn Eagle* newsboy. He surrendered the coin but was given a replacement—"so you're not out of anything," as the detectives put it. Four years later he would interrupt his college studies to testify at the celebrated trial of a Russian spy known only as Rudolf Abel. An anonymous admirer rewarded him with a new car, an Oldsmobile 98, which he sold, building a substantial fortune in the entertainment business from the proceeds.

The case did not end badly for Mrs. Ash and Mrs. Donnelly, who were questioned but never suspected of collusion with the enemy. (They assumed they had received the nickel in change either from their local A&P market or the subway ticket office.) But for Fisher and Hayhanen it did not end well at all.

The message in the coin consisted of row upon row of single-digit numbers arranged in groups of five and shrunk to the size of a small cornflake. When eventually decoded, it turned out to be Hayhanen's official welcome to New York. It had been encrypted, transferred to microfilm, and hidden in the coin by Fisher. Unaware that their very first communication had been intercepted and transferred swiftly to the FBI, both men went on doing the only thing they ever definitely did—burrowing deeper and deeper undercover. Fisher was much better at this than his sidekick. Abandoned by the Cohens and no doubt alarmed by the gruesome fate of the Rosenbergs, he set about turning his legend—that of the semiretired photofinisher—into some sort of reality. He slunk across the East River, away from the West Side, where he had rented a one-room apartment, and resurfaced with scarcely a ripple as an artist of no great ambition or talent with a studio in a converted Brooklyn warehouse.

He had little to report to Moscow. In the whole of 1952 and 1953, two critical years in the development in the American hydrogen bomb, the only noteworthy information from the chief Soviet illegal in the

United States to his superiors was a concocted report that he had become a naturalized citizen.

"I could never work out what the hell he was doing there," his friend Kyrill Khenkin said later. There was a real question: which person was now more real—the career KGB officer and former wartime radio expert or the family man forcibly separated from his family, watching the clock go down on his career? And there is a suitably evasive answer: in a city that was quite comfortable with frauds and misfits, Fisher went native.

Burt Silverman first met him in 1954. They were in an ancient, clanking elevator in the Ovington studios building on Fulton Street, where both had space on the fifth floor. They were going up, Silverman reading his mail, Fisher looking at Silverman. "It was the briefest of interactions," Silverman says. "He looked at me in a very direct way and he nodded and he said hello, and he didn't say anything else. And I said hello back. I remembered it as unusual because there were a lot of people in that building who never said hello. He had a certain kind of daring that was unusual."

Silverman had recently left the army after national service and wanted to paint for a living. It irritated him that fifty miles east, on Long Island, a heavy drinker with trademark black jeans and the name Jackson Pollock was cornering the market. He was doing it by splattering paint randomly over huge canvases laid out on the floor of a barn, and this was not Silverman's style. He was politically left leaning but artistically conservative. He wanted to paint things as they were, and he considered Pollock a plaything of shallow Manhattanites who cared only for fashion or a fraud who had beguiled them, which amounted to the same thing. On Pollock, Silverman and Fisher found common ground.

A week or so after their encounter in the elevator, Silverman was sweeping his studio when Fisher knocked quietly on his open door and came in to introduce himself as Emil Goldfus.

"I am retired," he said in what Silverman took to be a mild Scottish accent. He said he had saved enough from running a photographic lab to be able to give up work and paint. He gave himself a tour of the room, admiring Silverman's work and looking, the younger man says, "like a bird." They talked about painting. Silverman lamented the Pollock phenomenon and Fisher said he liked Levitan, the nineteenth-century Russian realist. It was true, and clever, and the start of a quite singular relationship.

Their next meeting was also contrived by Fisher. Late one night Silverman was unwinding in his studio, half naked with a girlfriend whose portrait he had been painting. There was a loud knock at the door, and Fisher appeared asking for a cup of turpentine. Silverman muses later: "I'm not quite sure where the transformation took place between what was a young man's annoyance at an older man coming to borrow turpentine, to the point that it became something very warm and fuzzy.... but it was quite rapid."

Silverman's father had died the previous year, and Burt found in "Emil" a replacement of sorts. Fisher had not seen his own family in six years; he found in Burt and his friends shared interests and a safe haven from suspicion. He would tell made-up stories about previous lives as a Boston accountant and a lumberjack in the Pacific Northwest. He spoke of nights spent playing marching tunes around campfires with Big Bill Haywood of the Industrial Workers of the World. He would invite Burt and his girlfriend to his studio for "jungle coffee" and aimless conversation (and sometimes music; he sought tips on painting but gave them on playing the guitar). Nothing was hidden, and nothing seemed more eccentric than the dozens of boiled white linen handkerchiefs he always had hanging out to dry—not the Hallicrafters shortwave radio standing on its end, apparently for want of a spare part; nor his large collection of bespoke optical equipment, which included an unusual miniature tripod with a slot for a strong magnifying lens; nor even the piles of maps and photographs of Bear Mountain State Park.

Not everyone believed what Emil said about himself. Jules Feiffer, a playwright friend of Silverman's, decided he'd been "on the bum." Another friend, the illustrator Jerry Schwartz, who knew something of the photography business, could not believe that Emil had made money in it. But if there was something not right about his stories, that did not necessarily mean there was something wrong about the man. As Schwartz put it: "People make up stories about who they are and what their life is."

With hindsight, Silverman has come to see Fisher as the lucky winner of a "reverse Fulbright"—a permit to roam and discover America at the Soviet government's expense, with an informal expectation that he would pass on some of what he learned on his return. It is a charming and highly plausible summary of what Fisher was really up to, even though Silverman acknowledges some naïveté in his readiness to take "Emil" at face value. "I can be conned like the next person," he admits. "But sitting in that studio with him endless hours, bullshitting about a whole variety of things, there was something about him that was beyond the con man."

* * *

The courtly artist who so endeared himself to Silverman scared the heck out of Reino Hayhanen.

They did not meet for eighteen months—the timing of such things was left to Moscow—but when they did there was no doubt who was in charge. By early 1954, Hayhanen had been joined in New York by his second wife. They had moved out of the city to a remote lakeside bungalow near Peekskill. A sense of unreality about Hayhanen's first months in America, created by the total absence of communication from his superiors, had eventually lifted when a "legal" *rezident* attached to the Soviet delegation to the United Nations met him at the Prospect Park subway station and recognized him by his pipe.

Those meetings continued through the summer. There is no indication that they achieved anything beyond giving Hayhanen an excuse to drive down from Peekskill in a blue Studebaker bought with money that he was supposed to have used to set up a business as his cover. He picked up the money at dead drops whose locations he had learned in Moscow. Drop One was a hole in a wall in the Bronx. Drop Two was on a footbridge near Ninety-fifth Street in Central Park. Drop Three was under a lamppost in Fort Tryon Park, north of the George Washington Bridge. He would know which one to visit by the number of chalk marks left on a wall in the subway station at Eightieth Street and Central Park West.

Over the winter the money kept coming—five hundred dollars a month in addition to a four-thousand-dollar lump sum meant for his cover. By his own admission he spent most of it on drink. Meanwhile, the meetings stopped. The man from the UN told him that if anyone else needed to reach him they would do so through the drops, then broke off contact. Another six months followed without a single message from his employer. In his rare sober moments, unable to confide even in his lonely and bewildered wife, Hayhanen must have reflected that this was a strange way to prepare for World War III, and an even stranger way to earn a living. Even so, as winter turned to spring and the cherry blossoms lit up Fort Tryon Park, it was more with dread than excitement that he picked up a message to meet a man named only "Mark" at the RKO Keith's Theater in Queens.

The sad shell of RKO Keith's now squats under the final approach to La Guardia. At the time it was a teeming shrine to Hollywood fantasy, and there was plenty that was cinematic about the first U.S. summit of KGB illegals in the H-bomb era.

Mark, whose real name was Willie Fisher, was impatient. Hayhanen's personal file was already full of negative remarks about his personal life, but Fisher hadn't read it and could not understand why Moscow had made him wait so long to meet his assistant. At his instruction they met in the men's restroom under the cinema but moved quickly to a coffee shop three blocks away. He dispensed with passwords. "I know you are the right man," he said. Except that he already knew he was the wrong man for the job.

Hayhanen wore the same striped tie he had worn for his trips to Prospect Park, but it did nothing for him. He smoked the same pipe, but it made him stick out like a bad secret agent at a rendezvous. He ordered in English, but his accent was terrible. Had he set up his cover business? He had not. Fisher told him to get on with it and warned that they would be meeting at least once a week from now on.

In the weeks that followed, Fisher slipped out of his new life as an artist and into his old one as a spy more frequently, giving Hayhanen remedial training in Morse code, photography, and microdot technique and finding to his dismay that his pupil was supremely reluctant to learn. He was baffled as to why Moscow Center would send such a klutz on such a vital assignment (and so was Vasili Mitrokhin, the KGB defector who later saw Hayhanen's file and could only conclude that the KGB decided to keep him in intelligence work "no matter what, regardless of signs that he was in trouble" for fear that he might otherwise betray more useful agents).

Not that Fisher's own tradecraft was flawless. In desperation, he twice took Hayhanen to a storeroom he rented along with his studio on Fulton Street, to give him a radio and then a camera. Despite his befuddled condition Hayhanen was able to remember the address, and it would come in handy.

Senator McCarthy was right, of course. There were reds under the bed; paid-up professional red infiltrators. There were precisely two of them. And then there was one. In June 1955, Fisher slipped a note under Burt Silverman's door saying he would be gone a few months, and disappeared.

***

It was a time when people did just up and vanish, on both sides of the cold war. There were as many reasons as there were secret projects, and Tony Bevacqua was part of such a project. In time it would take him hurtling over Iceland at three and a half times the speed of sound. It would entitle him to quote the version of Psalm 23 favored by the pilots of the 4080th Strategic Reconnaissance Wing of the U.S. Air Force: "Yea though I fly through the valley of the shadow of death I shall fear no evil, for I am at eighty thousand feet... and climbing." It would put him in pressure suits with titanium neck rings and visors with translucent gold leaf sandwiched between layers of toughened glass to fend off the ultraviolet rays hitting his cockpit directly from outer space. In time the project would divulge most of its secrets, but in the early years of the H-bomb era Tony Bevacqua was not yet privy to the best of them.

He was a promising young pilot—promising enough, at twenty-three, to have completed jet fighter training at Luke Air Force Base in Arizona and been assigned to 408th Squadron of the 508th Strategic Fighter Wing at Turner Air Force Base in Georgia. He was in the process of being cleared to drop free-fall nuclear weapons on any target selected for him by the Pentagon. Since there weren't enough atom bombs for everyone to train with, that involved old-fashioned air-to-air gunnery and skip bombing with conventional explosives in swept-wing F-84F Thunderstreaks. "You'd go as low as you wanted to go," Bevacqua remembers. "Fifty feet, even twenty-five."

As a lieutenant he could live off base if he wanted to. The bachelor officers' quarters at Turner were so grim that he and three friends had decided to do just that and share a house. Those friends were Victor

Milam, Wesley Upchurch, and another pilot who was a year older than the rest of them and a year ahead in training; he was already cleared to deliver nukes, which meant he was officially trusted to keep a certain sort of secret.

One morning in January 1956, Bevacqua, Milam, and Upchurch came down to breakfast to find that their friend had gone. There had been no warning. He had left no forwarding address or explanation. He'd simply packed and left. What would have struck them as even stranger, had they known about it, was that on the same day a young man resembling their friend in every detail checked into a Washington hotel under the name of Francis Palmer. It was not a name they'd heard before.

* * *

May 24, 1956, Newark, New Jersey: soon after 8:30 a.m. police answered an emergency call from 806 Bergen Street, a three-story house in a run-down neighborhood half an hour's drive from Manhattan. A man sounding Scandinavian and giving his name as Eugene Maki had suffered a deep cut to the leg and been taken to hospital, where he received three stitches.

The cursory police report did not mention a puddle of blood at the front of the house. It did not mention blood running through the hallway to the back door or blood spattered—Pollock-like—on the interior walls. The police chose to believe the injured man's story that he had cut himself with a knife while packing. His neighbors knew better. They had seen the empty bottles and heard the escalating arguments in a strange European language. The man's wife had had enough. Still unable to speak more than a few words of English and desperately unhappy, Hannah Maki had gone berserk and cut her husband's leg to the bone.

It was not the sort of cover life that Fisher had begged Hayhanen to set up. It was the implosion of a life torn from its roots and denied any real purpose except to hide. The last straw had been the removal of the facade of self-discipline forced on Hayhanen by his chilly and disdainful boss.

Shortly before Fisher's disappearance the previous summer, the two men had driven up to Bear Mountain State Park and buried five thousand dollars in cash beside a secluded stretch of hiking trail. Fisher ordered Hayhanen to return at a later date, dig the money up, and give it to Helen Sobell, the wife of Morton Sobell. (Yet another unmasked Soviet spy, Sobell had been convicted along with the Rosenbergs and sentenced to thirty years in prison, sixteen of which he spent in Alcatraz. He did not confess until 2008, when he was ninety-one.) Hayhanen did dig the money up but didn't give it to Mrs. Sobell. He kept it and used it for the deposit on the damp and depressing premises he leased in the fall of 1955 in Newark, New Jersey.

The idea was to set up a photo-processing shop whose real role would be as hub of a new network of nuclear spies and couriers. The unhappy couple moved down from Peekskill to live above the shop. While preparing the front office, Hayhanen smeared opaque glass wax over the main window. He never cleaned it off. Instead he used the space to store empty vodka bottles, which according to his later sworn testimony he drained at a rate of one a night.

Hayhanen became known on Bergen Street for having money even though he never worked and for beating his beautiful wife unmercifully. "The screams coming from that place during the night were terrible," one neighbor would tell a private investigator sent by a prestigious Brooklyn law office. "People were always calling the police. I called them myself one night, but the cops couldn't get in."

After the knife fight that landed him in hospital, Hayhanen realized he was attracting too much attention. Leaving the Bergen Street premises locked and the wax still on its windows, he took his wife and Studebaker back up the Hudson to Peekskill. The car was once again vital for Hayhanen's routine of checking New York's dead drops for his wages, but it fell apart. Neighbors noted that he returned from one trip to the city minus a rear fender, from another with only one headlight, from a third with the front fender gone. When finally charged with drunk driving and stripped of his license, he was reduced to using taxis. The Hayhanens confined themselves more and more to their bungalow and put on weight.

* * *

There was a perfectly good reason for the dutiful Fisher to abandon Hayhanen to his vices. He had told the credulous Burt Silverman that he was going to California to sell the rights to a device he had invented for producing multiple color prints from a single negative. In fact he was going home on leave. That entailed an impossibly romantic odyssey by rail, road, and Air France Constellation via Mexico City, Paris, and Vienna. It produced poignant pictures for the Fisher family album of the colonel in his own skin and a short-sleeved shirt, relaxing in deck chairs outside Moscow with his wife and friends. And it nearly saved him from what was to come: it is likely that Fisher's superiors considered keeping him in Moscow to teach tradecraft rather than sending him back to what had proved a singularly unproductive stint abroad.

In the end, though, Fisher did return to New York. He phoned Burt Silverman out of the blue one afternoon early in 1956 and said he'd had a good trip to California. To explain the length of his trip—he had been away seven months—he added as an afterthought that he had had a heart attack in Texas. As ever, Silverman suspended disbelief and took weird old Emil at face value. He was concerned about the heart attack but, more than anything, relieved. His friend was back, and for someone who had just cheated death he sounded in remarkably good spirits.

Back in Brooklyn, the artist known as Emil threw himself into painting and the social life of the Ovington studios with a new confidence. It was as if his strange unexplained absence had confirmed his status as a man of many parts who decided for himself which parts could be discussed and which could not. He had immunized himself from gossip and began to test his immunity. One evening, when Silverman joked to a friend on the telephone that he and Emil had been "listening in on Moscow" on the shortwave radio, Fisher snarled at him never to use the phrase again on the phone, even in jest. It was completely out of character but good advice given the times. It was not mentioned again. Another night, sketching a nude model at a life class, Fisher leaned over to a fellow student who thought he knew him well and whispered, "Boy, I'd like to fuck her."

Had he given up spying altogether? It is entirely possible. Stalin had been dead three years. Fisher knew from his long visit home that Russia was already a changed country; less paranoid, less likely to shoot an ineffectual illegal or send his loved ones to the Gulag. And the world knew too. Khrushchev's "secret" speech of February 1956, in which he denounced Stalin's cult of personality, was widely leaked within a month. It allowed an aging Bolshevik like Fisher to hope that the insanity of Stalinism was truly over, but it also laid bare that insanity to

Western sympathizers who had hoped it wasn't real—including those of the American Communist Party. Many of Silverman's friends were party members, but there cannot have been a worse time to try to recruit them as spies.

"It's bad enough when you're out of the loop from the art world point of view," Silverman says, looking back. "But people in the [Ovington] group who were party people were always mildly cynical about the effectiveness of the CP in America to start with, and in their particular party cell it was a joke." Membership had become an excuse "for getting together to have pizza. The revolution was on hold."

That suited Hayhanen. Given his confected existence as an inebriated hillbilly of mysterious private means, the last thing he needed was the scrutiny of zealots. Yet that was what Fisher had in mind for him. On his return from Moscow, Fisher took one look at the pudgy, twitching figure Hayhanen had become and cabled the Center urging that he be ordered home. He was. The KGB's preferred method was to promote Hayhanen to lieutenant colonel and suggest in firm language that he take a holiday, but the message was clear even to its recipient.

Hayhanen took fright. He repeatedly defied Fisher's instructions to buy a ticket to Europe, saying he was being followed by the FBI and feared arrest if he tried to leave the country. Fisher suspected he had cut a deal with the Feds. Before one of their last meetings in Fort Tryon Park he hid in bushes near the rendezvous point before showing himself, fearing a trap. In fact Hayhanen was never followed by the FBI. They had no idea who or where he was until, at last, he sailed for Le Havre and walked into the U.S. embassy in Paris. It was May 1, 1957, and he was wearing his striped tie.

# 3

# THE PILOT

*Nightfall in Turkey, a day's donkey ride from the birthplace of Saint Paul. As the moon rises behind the Taurus Mountains they cast a deepening shadow, and the ancient city of Adana does little to dilute the darkness. The year is 1960. Camel trains still come this way with bales of dyed wool from Kurdistan, and young men are still stoned for thieving. Not long ago a rapist—probably; the American witness was never told—was thrown off a bridge over the Seyhan River with one end of a rope tied round his neck and the other to the balustrade. His body was left hanging there for a day.*

*Shared values and the proximity of the Soviet Armenian border have produced a mutual defense pact between Turkey and the United States. One result, five miles east of Adana, is a smooth, hard stretch of concrete three thousand yards long. It runs northeast to southwest. Along its southerly side, looking at the mountains, stands a tidy row of huts, hangars, and trailers. The whole complex is surrounded by a tall wire fence.*

*In one of the trailers an astronaut sleeps. In fact the astronauts of the Mercury project have not yet slipped the bonds of U.S. airspace, but they have been fitted for their space suits, and this figure looks very like them. He wears heavy black boots and an olive flight suit, bulky yet tight, with half-concealed tubes and lines of crossed lacing down each triceps and leg. The suit is hermetically sealed to a helmet that leaves only its wearer's eyes visible beneath an ovoid faceplate. His mouth and nose are covered by a mask attached to a hose from a canister of pure oxygen, which he has been breathing for two hours.*

*A man enters the trailer, gives the astronaut a signal, and picks up the canister. Keeping close together so the hose stays slack, they step outside.*

*A van is waiting. It drives the pair to a hangar halfway down the concrete runway, in front of which a black-painted aircraft sits so low on its undercarriage that a man standing at its front end can stroke it like a horse's nose. The wings quickly taper to invisibility in the darkness, drooping as they go, laden with fuel.*

*The pilot has eaten a late breakfast of steak and eggs. There are people stationed here who will swear in years to come that steak and eggs were not available in this part of Turkey in 1960, but the balance of evidence suggests that they were, flown in on U.S. Air Force C-47 cargo planes from Wiesbaden, Germany, precisely to ensure that these men in laced pressure suits did not go hungry in the air.*

*Out of the van but still connected to the canister, the pilot takes a final breath and holds it. Disconnected from the hose, he climbs a short flight of metal steps and lowers himself into the black plane's cockpit, where he is immediately reconnected to pure oxygen from the plane's own supply. He starts breathing again while his assistant straps him in. The suit makes even small movements awkward, so the assistant does most of the preflight checks. The canopy closes over the helmet. The single jet that takes up most of the space behind it starts with a low roar, rising quickly to a scream.*

*Turkey in 1960 is a free country, at least in principle. There is nothing to stop anyone from the Soviet embassy three hundred miles away in Ankara making the scenic drive through the mountains to Adana with binoculars or night-vision goggles in the glove box and watching what happens next.*

*The plane does not use the whole runway. It does not even use a tenth of it. As its wings stiffen under their own lift, stabilizers wedged beneath them fall away and the aircraft seems to stand on its tail. In fact it climbs at fifty-five degrees, but this is still so steep that it is two miles high before it clears the perimeter fence and twice the height of Mount McKinley before it makes its first left turn over the southern fringes of Adana. To the pilot, the only view is of stars.*

*The mission planned for this strange black plane with its muted, suited pilot is a seven-thousand-mile tour of Eurasia, ending back here between the mountains and the Mediterranean in a little over twenty-four hours. While it is gone the base personnel will abstain from much of their usual banter, and maybe even from some of their drinking. They will be count-*

*ing down the time until it reappears as a black line high over the eastern horizon. Except that in this case it does not reappear. Fifty years later its wreckage is on permanent display in the Russian Armed Forces Museum in Moscow, next to the Great Hall of Victory, where thousands of schoolchildren each year still contemplate their grandparents' prodigious sacrifices in the defeat of Nazism. The room full of twisted American aluminum is smaller; the lessons there less clear. Both sides claim it as evidence of a victory. Both sides have their reasons. But taken as the remnants of a moment rather than a contest, the crumpled air intakes in room 20 are a monument to hubris and luck—great mounds of it, good and bad, accumulated over years of brinkmanship and blundering in the age of* Dr. Strangelove. *These bits of plane are also a question mark. What if? What if they had stayed in one piece and the aircraft—official manufacturer's designation "Article 360"—had completed its mission and released its pilot as planned to stretch his cramped legs and sink a long martini in the hut by the concrete outside Adana that served as the American officers' club? The question hardly bears thinking about, but it can be answered. If Article 360 had stayed aloft, so would hopes of détente at the great power summit scheduled for mid-May that year in Paris.*

*Paris in the springtime; Eisenhower, Khrushchev, Macmillan, and de Gaulle were all looking forward to it as the last best chance for superpower peace. There were reasons that spring to be quietly optimistic about the course of world affairs, but high over Russia on May 1 that course changed abruptly and irreversibly. One beneficiary was John F. Kennedy, campaigning against Richard Nixon for the presidency of the United States and struggling to persuade voters that he had the requisite international experience. The loss of Article 360, as things turned out, did much to erode the foreign-policy credentials of Nixon as well as Eisenhower and may even have been decisive in an agonizingly tight race. But there were others with reason to be thankful for the disappearance of that peculiar airplane—intelligence professionals enjoying the unprecedented influence conferred on them by the cold war's cult of secrecy; military brass sitting atop armed forces that still consumed a tenth of the nation's gross domestic product seven years after the end of the Korean War; and above all the missile manufacturers—Convair, Douglas, Lockheed, the Martin Company—girding themselves for an open-ended arms race to outproduce the Soviets in the technologies of an exotic new national defense that only Eisenhower seemed ready to resist.*

*It is no surprise that many believed Article 360's loss was no accident on America's part; nor that some still do.*

* * *

Five years earlier, an inspector at the U.S. Postal Service received an unusual request from a postmaster in Los Angeles.

Dozens of heavy parcels every week, some of them from defense contractors, were being sent to a PO box in the name of C & J Engineering in the residential community of Sunland at the foot of the San Gabriel Mountains. C & J Engineering was not listed in any phone book, but the mail drop was emptied regularly by an unmarked van. Would the Post Office inspector be good enough to drop by one day and follow it? The inspector obliged and drove into an ambush. He followed the van south from Sunland toward Burbank, the patchwork of movie studios and subdivisions at the entrance to the San Fernando Valley. Then he turned left into an industrial zone on the east side of Burbank Airport. "Our security people nabbed him just outside the plant and had him signing national security secrecy forms until he pleaded writer's cramp," Ben Rich wrote later.

Rich was at that time a senior Lockheed designer. "The plant" did not officially exist but is better known now as the original Skunk Works, a name adopted by its employees because the smell of a nearby plastics plant recalled the pungent moonshine still that Al Capp named the Skonk Works in his *Li'l Abner* comic strip. It was—if legend even approximates to reality—the throbbing hypothalamus of the American military industrial complex; a mosh pit of young men with slide rules pulling hundred-hour weeks in a permanent fug of sweat and smoke, abducted from their girlfriends and families in the service of a higher cause.

In one beige assembly hall, the Skunk Works was the locus of all that was ingenious, irrepressible, patriotic, and strictly need-to-know in the most warlike years of the cold war. It was the birthplace of stealth as an alternative to mutually assured destruction; of smart bombing as an alternative to carpet bombing; of fantasy as a solution to reality. It was the cradle of radar absorption, of machines that could cruise over Siberia at Mach 3, and of the weird black albatross, part jet, part glider, that for want of any hint of poetic imagination among the engineers who built her came to be known as the U-2. Kubrick had nothing on the Skunk Works, nor did Dan Dare.

The plant's output was legendary. So was its secrecy. Kelly Johnson was the irascible genius responsible for both; the man who would be Q if history were a Bond film. Born in Michigan to Swedish parents, he won his first aircraft design prize at age thirteen. As head of Skunk Works, he enjoyed telling prospective employees that if they signed on there would be gaps in their résumés that they could never fill. He cashed personal checks for over one million dollars from the CIA to help it hide the flow of funds toward the aircraft he was building. He was the originator of a special brand of secrecy, more instinctive than learned, that felt as natural to those in his orbit as rock and roll did to those in Elvis Presley's.

The CIA people who flew U-2s out of Adana were in Johnson's orbit, and so were their air force neighbors who occupied the huts and hangars at each end of the runway. "We were Weather Reconnaissance Squadron Number Two as far as the air force was concerned, and that was fine with them; most of them, anyway," the senior agency man there remembers. Another security officer says that even though the base was busy with navy as well as air force personnel, "nobody asked any questions" about the black planes that rolled in and out of the middle hangar apparently at random. "Somebody told the base commander, 'Just don't ask,' and nobody did."

Trainee U-2 pilots were steeped in Johnson's secrecy from the start. As they grow old they still refuse to say how high they flew. When they were mistaken for UFOs, people covered for them. Soaring over Death Valley and Nevada's Jackass Flats at seventy thousand feet and more, the U-2s' silver underbellies (at first they were not painted black) reflected the setting sun long after it had dipped below the horizon for airliners seven miles below them. People noticed. In the winter of 1955–56 there was a spike in puzzled comments to air traffic controllers from commercial pilots craning upward while crossing the southwestern United States. These reports were forwarded to Wright-Patterson Air Force Base in Ohio, where the nation's UFO intelligence was being collated. A hastily assembled team called Operation Blue Book was given a number in Washington to call when nothing else could explain a silver point sailing across the western sky. In Washington a flight log would be consulted and more often than not the point of light turned out to be explicable. Operation Blue Book would ask no further questions and invent a story.

One place these stories never mentioned was Groom Lake, also known as Watertown, or Area 51. The first two names are legitimate entries in the gazetteer of Kelly Johnson's secret world. The third is not. It has appeared on maps of southern Nevada but has never been used officially by the U.S. military. It identifies the user as a likely believer in jellied aliens and secret swarms of helicopters. Most of all it is a place in the American imagination—though it does exist: a hard, flat lake bed ringed by bone-dry mountains seventy-five miles into the desert from Las Vegas, almost but not quite out of range of a four-wheel drive and a high-powered pair of binoculars. It was chosen by Johnson's chief test pilot as a suitably private proving ground for the U-2.

Willie Fisher should have known about Groom Lake. If he was the master spy they made him out to be, he should have come back from his field trips with its dust in his hatband and images of spy planes stuffed into his hollow nickels. There is no evidence that he ever went near the place or had the slightest inkling of what happened there. To this extent the Johnson brand of secrecy worked wonders. But the truth is that Fisher, the amiable reverse Fulbright, was not much of a challenge. The U-2 was only as secret as it could be for a plane built ten minutes from Hollywood. It was an American secret. Quite quickly, it was an open one.

The U-2's first foreign deployment was to England in 1956. Within days, plane spotters with long lenses had gravitated to the perimeter fence at Royal Air Force Lakenheath in Suffolk. Within a year, London's *Daily Express* was reporting, more or less accurately, that "Lockheed U-2 high altitude aircraft have been flying at 65,000 feet, out of reach of Soviet interceptors, mapping large areas behind the Iron Curtain with revolutionary new aerial cameras." As soon as a U-2 detachment arrived in Germany, so did KGB emissaries in black sedans to watch it. As soon as it transferred to Turkey, listening posts and radar stations in the Caucasus began to track its every foray toward the Soviet border. It first penetrated Soviet airspace on July 4, 1956, and though the *Express* was right that it could not be shot down, it was spotted by radar at once.

This was not spying by any previous definition. Compared with the Soviet fetish for deep cover it was brazen. It was clever, bold, arduous, and dangerous but also dead simple. It was just the sort of spying for someone like Francis Gary Powers.

* * *

When Jessica Powers-Hileman looks back on the way her brother was received on his return to the United States in 1962, she says after what seems like a long pause: "I don't think he was expecting it to be like it was. At least I'm assuming he did not expect it to be like it was. He knew a little about what the good old *New York Times* had been writing about him while he was in prison, but we came from a part of the country where you trusted everybody. We didn't lock our doors. We were poor, but if you needed a bed for the night we'd have you in and make you comfortable. Didn't matter who you were."

The part of the country where the Powers family came from was the extreme southwestern corner of Virginia, a few miles off the Trail of the Lonesome Pine. The forested mounds of the Appalachians rise gradually to the Kentucky state line, and in the folds between them sits the town of Pound, population 1,075 and falling. Pound has a knack for national prominence. For twenty years, until 2001, reporters from the Associated Press would periodically make the scenic drive from Kingsport, Tennessee, to meet diners at the Golden Pine and watch them dance, because the dancing was illegal. (The town's ban on dancing in public places was ruled unconstitutional, but in deference to local churches an ordinance still requires permits.)

Before the dancing ban, there was Gary Powers. And before Gary there was his grandfather, a carpenter, who rode five miles into the hills from the eastern edge of town sometime before the First World War and found a level piece of land where he decided his family would settle.

It did work out that way, but not without a struggle. "Oliver Powers worked his whole life to buy that land," his son-in-law, Jack Goff, remembers. Oliver was Gary's father. He also had to provide for six children, including an only son who he had vowed would never have to work the mines.

Powers senior worked the mines—something he later found he had in common with the first secretary of the Soviet Communist Party.

But in the meantime they nearly killed him. A runaway coal train deep under Harman, Virginia, crushed him against the roof of a tunnel and left him with a permanent limp and fierce hopes for a better life for Gary. "Oliver wanted Gary to be wealthy; that was the main drive with him," said Goff. To that end the older Powers labored obsessively. When the only work was in Harman, he moved the family there, driving coal trains again despite his limp. When mine work slackened, he opened a shoe repair business that has wife could mind when he went back underground. When too few shoes came in, he earned a little extra by carrying mail. When the war brought better-paying work to Michigan, he moved the family to Michigan. When it was over, they came back to Pound.

Jack Goff was Gary Powers's best friend. As if to prove it, he apprenticed himself to Gary's father, married one of Gary's five sisters after the war, and still lives with her on Gary Powers Road, on land Oliver Powers bought.

They met in Harman in a four-room schoolhouse, "then ran around together for twenty years," he says. They played with the same horsehide football after school, hunted rabbit together, and spelunked together through the old bootleggers' caves that burrow under Pine Mountain near the Appalachian watershed. Powers would later call himself a loner on account of growing up the only boy among five sisters. In reality he grew up with Jack, who has a photograph of his friend that is quite unlike the many that exist of Powers as a pilot. He sits on a granite boulder high in the Cumberland Mountains, alone except for Jack Goff and his camera, transparently content.

There were other boys in the valley. Jessica Powers-Hileman tells a story about two of them who persuaded her brother, against her father's wishes, to help them roll a decrepit Model A Ford down the dirt road leading back to Pound. The steering stuck. The car plunged off the road, and Oliver Powers took a maple switch to all six of his children, including young Jessica, even though she had been asleep in bed at the time. "It was the only time I ever got switched, and it was Gary's fault," says Jessica. Yet he was easy to forgive. He was calm, quiet, good-natured, and good-looking. He had smooth skin, jet black hair, and "dreamy eyes," especially in what his first wife called his "wholesome, hamburger-loving stage." His homecomings, from college and then the air force, were big events. This is the first thing his sister says when asked how she remembers him, and the last: "We only had one brother. I can't say exactly how it was. I can't express it, but when he came home we were all happy."

Powers was athletic and proud of it, left guard on his high school football team in Michigan and a contender in the hundred-yard dash at college. He brought his athleticism home. The family kept caged albino squirrels that once greeted his return by escaping up the maple trees from which his father had harvested switches after the business with the errant Ford. So Gary shinned up the trees and recovered all the squirrels. "That was him all over," Jessica recalls. "That was the kind of thing he liked to do."

For a while there was also an alligator on the Powers property. It ended up in the Knoxville Zoo but was even then a useful reminder of Oliver Powers's small eccentricities and stubborn cast of mind.

He wanted very badly for his son to be a doctor. "My dad only got to go to fourth grade, but he wasn't easily fooled." Jessica says. "When he sent Gary to college, he wanted him to have a position that would make him a lot of money. He knew doctors made a lot of money."

Oliver Powers was setting himself up for disappointment. When not climbing mountains and hurling footballs at each other, his son and Jack Goff had been true children of the aviation age. They played "air wardens," collecting and comparing aircraft silhouettes cut from cornflake packets until nothing flew over the Cumberlands that they could not identify from thirty thousand feet. As a fourteen-year-old, Gary had begged his father for a joyride in a Piper Cub at a fair in West Virginia. He never really came down. He went dutifully to medical school after college, but dropped out, joined the air force, and by the spring of 1954, a year before Tony Bevacqua, had checked out on F-84s and been cleared to load and drop a medium-sized nuclear bomb.

He later said to his friend Jack, in a pause during a rabbit hunt: "If anything ever happens to me, just remember I was doing what I thought was best for the most people."

It was as neat an expression of utilitarian altruism as you could expect from a philosopher, never mind a pilot—and there is no doubt that Gary Powers was what the patrons of the Golden Pine would consider a good man. But he was not that simple. He could be moody. He was fiercely jealous of his wife, and in his own quiet way he was as driven as his father.

By the time of his arrival at Turner Air Force Base outside Albany, Georgia, Powers was a twenty-four-year-old fighter jock with a degree, a second lieutenant's silver bar, and everything to live for. But he also had a sense of history passing him by. He had felt awed at Milligan College in Kentucky by fellow freshmen starting their studies after fighting and winning the war in the Pacific. He wanted to enlist and serve in Korea but went to medical school instead to please his father. Korea was still drawing in young men when he attended air gunnery school in Arizona in 1953, but this time he was waylaid by appendicitis. "Again I felt I'd lost my chance to fight, to prove myself," he wrote.

In July 1954 Powers was promoted to first lieutenant and found himself taking home four hundred dollars a month. For someone who had collected lumps of coal from beside the railway tracks in Harman for Popsicle money, it was a princely sum. But it was not a doctor's pay, and he did not have a doctor's prospects. Small wonder that when his name appeared on a list of men required to report to wing headquarters at Turner AFB early one morning in January 1956, he paid attention.

* * *

Powers was about to be drawn into the most audacious espionage extravaganza since the nineteenth-century showdown between the British and Russian empires known as the Great Game. It would make his whole life a secret, then turn it inside out and shake it until there was nothing left in it that wasn't public. It would take him to places no son of a Virginia coal miner had ever been, soaring over the mountain ranges where the British and Russian empires had confronted each other with brass telescopes and Enfield revolvers nearly a century earlier.

At that time the engine of history was Russia's search for natural frontiers. In 1956 it was the Soviet Union's unbending resolve to keep them shut.

Anyone brave enough, even now, to hike north up the Afghan-Pakistan border from the Khyber Pass will notice a striking change in the built environment at about thirty-six degrees north and seventy-two east. As the border swings to the east, Tajikistan comes into view across the Wakhan Corridor. And unlike the unguarded line between Afghanistan and Pakistan, the Tajik frontier is marked with a ten-foot barbed-wire fence. It is a holdover from Soviet times that the current Tajik government values highly. (It even outsources patrol duties to Russian frontier troops who trudge its entire length 365 days a year in fake fur hats against the bitter cold of the Pamirs, with authentic AK-47s slung over their shoulders.) The Tajik fence is only a few hundred miles long, but it is part of an epic feat of rudimentary self-defense that delineates the former Soviet border along six thousand miles of wild terrain from the Caspian to the Pacific.

Between that fence and the North Pole, in 1956, lay 8.6 million square miles of denied territory—nearly three times the area of the lower forty-eight U.S. states. In this vastness a foreigner could travel only under the strictest supervision of the KGB and its subsidiaries, if at all. North of the fence lay forests that took seven days to cross by train and three-thousand-mile rivers debouching under pack ice into the Arctic Ocean. There were whole mountain ranges never sullied by a human foot. There was the great water-filled gash in the earth's crust known as Lake Baikal, the endless land ocean of the steppe, and the terrible frozen emptiness of the taiga. And there were launchpads, test sites, and closed nuclear cities devoted entirely to the design and manufacture of the instruments of Armageddon. This much the CIA knew from cautious reconnaissance flights along the edges of Soviet airspace and a small cadre of defectors and informants. But it was not enough.

In August 1953 an earth-shattering explosion about one hundred miles west of Semipalatinsk in Kazakhstan marked the Soviet Union's arrival in the age of the superbomb—the H-bomb. The Americans had already detonated one. It vaporized Eniwetok atoll near Bikini and produced a mushroom cloud twenty-five miles high, filmed in glorious orange Technicolor for the president. They called it Ivy Mike. The Russians called theirs a layer cake, or *sloika:* it was based on Andrei Sakharov's "first idea," to pile fission and fusion fuel layer on layer in search of the biggest bang in history. The result was not a true hydrogen bomb by some purists' definition, but it was entirely homemade and a respectable thirty times more powerful than the one that killed 140,000 people at Hiroshima.

In 1954 the Soviets reverted to type and copied the American H-bomb design. Yield: 1.6 megatons, or one hundred Hiroshimas. The arms race was picking up speed, and the steppe was starting to betray the cost with giant craters and concentric scorch marks. (Deformed fetuses would come later, collected by doctors in Semipalatinsk and stored secretly in jars.)

Not only the steppe suffered. A thousand miles to the north, off the island of Novaya Zemlya, the Soviet navy had loaded a nuclear warhead onto a torpedo and fired it into a fleet of more than thirty ships crewed by five hundred sheep and goats. The animals died swiftly, and the destroyer closest to the blast sank without trace. In due course word of the new northern test site seeped out, and its skyline of frigid mountains floating on white cloud served as the target of General Jack D. Ripper's 843rd bomb wing, flown into oblivion in *Dr. Strangelove.*

In the film it is President "Dmitri," interrupted in the course of a loud musical diversion, who provides the terrifying unpredictability at the eastern end of the hotline. In reality it was Nikita Khrushchev—showman, warrior, and Soviet premier, constantly trying not to be outflanked by his more hawkish colleagues in the politburo.

In November 1956 Khrushchev hosted a reception in Moscow for the visiting Polish prime minister. Weeks earlier, he had ordered Soviet tanks to crush the Hungarian uprising in Budapest. Western condemnation was still running at full flow, and Western diplomats invited to the reception were being careful not to seem too grateful to their hosts. Emboldened by vodka, Khrushchev struck a pose in the middle of the room, called for silence, and offered those capitalists present an impromptu harangue.

"We are Bolsheviks!" he began. "If you don't like us, don't accept our invitations, and don't invite us to come to see you! Whether you like it or not, history is on our side. We will bury you!" In Russian: *Myi vas pokhoronim!* Those three words—four in translation—were pure bluster; a delusional socioeconomic forecast based on the Marxist adage that the proletariat is the undertaker of the bourgeoisie. But the speaker was one of two men in the world who could launch a nuclear cataclysm. His words were widely misinterpreted to suggest burial under mountains of radioactive rubble. More than any other single threat they seemed to confirm that Khrushchev was out to escalate and win the thermonuclear arms race. But could he?

There was only one way to find out. Aerial photography from unmanned balloons had been tried, but they only took pictures of where the wind sent them, and they often came down in Russia. In 1953 the Royal Air Force (RAF) flew a stripped-down B-57 bomber over a new missile test range near the Volga delta, but it landed in Iran pockmarked with bullet holes and returned few useful photographs. The result was a National Intelligence Estimate in 1954 that had no intelligence on the test range or on missile production or numbers and therefore gave no estimate. No one in the American intelligence community thought the answer was more spies. The only serious suggestion was a new spy plane. As General Philip Strong told his boss, Robert Amory, chief intelligence gatherer at the CIA: "We've just got to get upstairs."

Initially the air force insisted on being in charge. It invited designs for a new reconnaissance plane in 1953 and backed a beautiful but flimsy twin-engined idea from one of Kelly Johnson's rivals. It was called the Bell X-16 and never flew. Then the charismatic inventor and entrepreneur Edwin "Din" Land, millionaire inventor of the Polaroid camera, called on Allen Dulles, head of the CIA, and urged him to take control. In a letter following up their discussion, he pressed home the argument that the time was ripe for a wholesale reinvention of the spying game.

"I am not sure that we have made it clear that we feel there are many reasons why this activity is appropriate for the CIA," he wrote. "We told you that this seems to us the kind of action and technique that is right for the contemporary version of the CIA; a modern and scientific way for an Agency that is always supposed to be looking, to do its looking."

Land headed a top secret panel within a semisecret commission appointed by President Eisenhower to solve the most pressing national security problem of the age—how to prevent a nuclear Pearl Harbor. He was the Thomas Edison of his time: a promiscuous inventor and a natural entrepreneur whose stake in the Polaroid Corporation made him a multibillionaire in twenty-first-century terms and whose immaculate dark eyebrows made him look a little like Cary Grant. He appended to his letter to Dulles a summary of the case for aerial reconnaissance that managed to be both concise and splendidly pompous: "During a period in which Russia has free access to the geography of all our bases and major nuclear facilities, as well as to our entirely military and civilian economy, we have no corresponding knowledge about Russia.... Unfortunately it is the US, the more mature, more civilized, and more responsible country that must bear the burden of not knowing what is happening [there]."

Land believed that the mature, civilized, responsible way of bearing this burden was straight out of *Popular Mechanics:* "a jet-powered glider," "an extraordinary and unorthodox vehicle" that his good friend Kelly Johnson at the Lockheed Corporation had already designed and offered to build in total secrecy to fly over the Soviet Union at seventy thousand feet and photograph in minute detail on each clear-weather mission a strip of Russia two hundred miles wide and 2,500 miles long.

The "Lockheed super glider," Land went on, would fly "well out of reach of present Russian interception and high enough to have a good chance of avoiding detection." But even if it were detected, he averred quite wrongly, it would be "so obviously unarmed and devoid of military usefulness, that it would minimize affront to the Russians."

For an inventor, Land had an impressive grasp of the military-strategic balance. He was also a terrific salesman. The clock was ticking, he said: Russian fighters and surface-to-air missiles were flying ever higher, meaning that "the opportunity for safe overflight may last only a few years....We therefore recommend immediate action through special channels in CIA in procuring the Lockheed glider and in establishing the CIA taskforce. No proposal or program that we have seen in intelligence planning can so quickly bring so much vital information at so little risk and at so little cost."

The letter was sent on November 5, 1954. Two days later a B-29 (combat ceiling 36,000 feet) was shot down over the Sea of Japan while photographing a Soviet base in the Kuril Islands. On November 24, at 8:15 a.m., Eisenhower sat behind his desk in the Oval Office as his most senior military and intelligence planners, including Dulles, his number two at the CIA, and a somewhat grudging General Nathan Twining of the air force, filed in and made the case for the U-2. By 8:30 a.m. they were filing out again. At four that afternoon a call was placed from the Pentagon to Kelly Johnson in his windowless Burbank office. He could go ahead and build his glider.

***

In the love story of Frank and Barbara Powers, both principals would have looked at home on an eight-by-ten-foot movie poster. He was the fighter pilot with the dreamy eyes who blushed deep red when introduced to Barbara at the air force cafeteria where her mother worked the night shift. She was the eighteen-year-old secretary who called in there most evenings on her way home from work. They fell hard for each other despite her reputation for trouble among his friends and fellow fliers. Or maybe because of it.

They were married in the spring of 1955, and the first night of their new life, at least, was happy. "Lordy, but how that handsome Ridge Runner of mine could make love!" Barbara would write. (She always gave him credit for his performance in bed, even when she gave him credit for nothing else.) Disappointment set in early. Nine months after a blissful honeymoon in the Bahamas, her husband came home to tell her he was leaving the air force—the next day. For the time being he was also leaving her. He would be gone for three years but could not say where or why; only that he would still be flying.

Both would later plead their cases in the divorce court of public opinion. In Barbara's account the "bombshell" is a fait accompli. After dropping it her husband even has the gall to accuse her of worrying first about how she will pay the bills. In Frank's version, he is offered "risky but patriotic work" outside the air force but his first reaction is to turn it down for Barbara. He changes his mind only when she points out that they could use the extra money it would bring: "We had recently made payment on a new car; the balance was still due."

It was the perfect rationale for the imperfect spy. Money was always a concern for Powers, as his sister Jessica was reminded when he called on her in Washington soon after starting his new job.

"I was nineteen, working in DC and living there with my sister Janice," she recalls. "He dropped in to see us and the only thing he ever said about his work was: 'I pay more taxes than you make.' And I thought, *hey, you got a good job.* He was not giving anything away. But you sort of got the idea that he was proud of what he was doing, or proud that he was making so much."

Or, most likely, both. Powers was his father's son, driven by a sense of obligation to provide. But in his own unspoken thoughts he was also an all-American hero, a brother to five adoring sisters, a Kentucky college track star, and now master of the seven thousand pounds of thrust that he could blast from the rear end of a Thunderstreak. From such beginnings serious accomplishment was surely possible. He might have been a soft-spoken spelunker on the outside, but that hid a tightly wound coil of potential.

The meeting at Turner AFB wing headquarters was at 8:00 a.m. A handful of other pilots showed up. A major from wing command made a simple announcement. On account of their exceptional pilot ratings and top secret clearance, those present were invited to apply for unspecified non–air force work. No further information was available, but anyone wanting to know more was told where to go and when. Powers wanted to know more. At 1900 hours that evening he knocked self-consciously on the door of cottage 1 at the Radium Springs Motel, not far from Turner. As instructed, he wore civilian clothes and asked for a Mr. William Collins.

Mr. Collins was not alone. He was one of a small group of youngish men in trim civilian clothes who had checked into the motel as if for a convention of clones. There was nothing remarkable about any of them except their sameness and their calm professionalism.

"The rationale for meeting off base was to have an environment where a pilot can feel free to talk if he expresses an interest in separating from his normal air force activity," says one of those who played the Collins role from time to time. Perhaps. But there were two other reasons for the peculiar venue: to keep the meetings secret and to generate a certain excitement. Who the heck was Collins? What did he mean by the chance to do "something important for your country"? Why the backdrop of king-size beds and shower curtains?

He was with the CIA, Collins said at a follow-up meeting the next day, as if that explained it.

In a sense, it did. In 1956 the Central Intelligence Agency was still a genuine mystery to everyone except those who ran it, and to some of them as well. Almost no one could point to it on a map, since its headquarters in Virginia was not yet built. No one knew for sure where its responsibilities started and those of the Pentagon and State Department ended, because it was in the process of stealing territory from both. And no one could equate it with disastrous arrogance or extra-judicial adventurism, because the Bay of Pigs was still a little-known beauty spot on the south coast of Cuba. To the likes of Francis Gary Powers there was just the acronym, and whatever it made him feel felt good.

The agency was building a brand-new plane, Collins said. It would fly higher than anything he had ever flown before. It would penetrate deep into Russia. It would photograph whatever they were building there that Mr. Khrushchev wanted to keep secret, and it needed pilots willing to take it there for $2,500 a month.

"I was amazed," Powers wrote later. "And immensely proud, not only of being chosen to participate in such a venture, but, even more, proud of my country... for having the courage, and guts, to do what it believed essential and right." Those words were written in 1970 with a skeptical public in mind, but they ring true. Forget Korea—*this* was the summons he had been waiting for. This was the call-up that suited his quiet ambition, that would catapult him from the great herd of combat-ready but untested first lieutenants into an elite of specialists. This was real. Its secrecy made it so, because secrecy was currency in the existential standoff with Communism that brought duck-and-cover drills to Minnesota high schools and ever-bigger mushroom clouds to the evening news. Powers would be airborne in a silhouette that Jack Goff wouldn't recognize even if he could see it, squinting up from Big Stone Gap or wherever Jack was working nowadays. And the pay would be five times what Frank was earning at Turner. He was in. He said so there and then at the Radium Springs Motel, even though Bill Collins insisted that he take another night to think it over.

So it was that Francis G. Powers left Turner AFB on orders for temporary duty off base, and Francis G. Palmer checked into the Dupont Plaza Hotel in Washington. He went to his room and waited for a call.

He left behind a wife whose world had been upended. It might have helped their marriage if Powers had been allowed to tell her more about his work, but Bill Collins had forbidden it. He had supplied a PO box number in California for wives who wanted to write letters and a phone number in Virginia for emergencies. Still, for all Barbara knew her husband had been recruited to fly drugs in from the Caribbean. She wasn't happy.

The same was true of many of those left behind, pilots as well as relatives. Soon after Powers's disappearance, flight commander Lieutenant Jerry McIlmoyle reported for duty with the 515th Strategic Fighter Bomber Squadron at Malmstrom AFB in Great Falls, Montana. He had been home on leave. In his absence, three friends had gone. Lieutenants Barry Baker and Jim Barnes and Captain Frank Grace had resigned and vanished without saying anything to anyone.

"We just never heard from them again," McIlmoyle would write. "I thought Frank, Barry and James had been good and close friends. We had all been in Korea together; we partied together, played bridge and poker and camped out together. Christmas rolled around and we received no cards, no phone calls, absolutely nothing from any of them. I really didn't understand why." There were chance encounters in the decades that followed, "but there was no camaraderie, just a handshake and smile, no small talk. I was reminded of the old Pentagon euphemism: those three friends 'evanesced.'"

There was nothing like a disappearing pilot to spark rumors about where he'd gone. When one of them died—it turned out to be Frank Grace—those rumors gathered urgency. McIlmoyle and others were ordered to fly four Thunderstreaks to Texas for the funeral. They learned en route that Grace had hit a telegraph pole while taking off at night from an unlighted airstrip, but they were ordered "not to ask any questions about the crash, where, what, how, when and most especially not about what aircraft he had been flying."

So what *had* he been flying? Human nature demanded an answer. The CIA conspired heroically to withhold it. With no closed cities, no six-thousand-mile fences, no way of muzzling the press, and no standing threat of a no-questions-asked bullet for suspected traitors, this wasn't easy, which is why Powers found himself booked into the Dupont Plaza in someone else's name, sitting on the bed and waiting for the phone to ring. He felt "more than a little foolish." When the call came through, it was Bill Collins again, directing him to another room in the same hotel for a more detailed briefing on the mission and a primer on rudimentary tradecraft. There were several other recruits in the room. Whenever Collins talked, he kept the radio on. When Powers turned it off to hear better—which he did only once—Collins fell silent.

Briefing over, the pilots were invited individually into an adjoining room to take a lie-detector test. Powers went through with this even though he considered it an unpardonable affront to his integrity. He was then dispatched—via Saint Louis, Omaha, and Saint Louis again, to shake off any tails—to New Mexico.

At the Lovelace Clinic in Albuquerque, Colonel Flickinger of the Air Research and Development Command had devised a medical exam to test the sinews and sanity of the toughest pilots in the business. It was in their best interests, of course—Flickinger had done pioneering work in "upper air medicine" to help pilots flying transports over the Himalayas during the war. It just didn't feel like it.

The tests lasted a week. In his memoir Powers called them "incredibly thorough" and left it at that, but he admitted to his friend Jack Goff that after a subsequent checkup he flunked an important exercise and had to fly back to Albuquerque to redo it. It was deceptively simple: he had to sit on a chair in a silent room for two hours, but he had fallen asleep.

Tony Bevacqua rememberes some of the more uncomfortable tests. "We had to put an arm in a bucket of ice until we didn't want it to be there anymore, and they had us hyperventilate on purpose to see if we'd have some kind of fit or seizure. We ended up with our arms rigid across our chests, like a corpse, and then they'd try to force them open again."

There was more. The pilots were spun in centrifuges, sometimes until they blacked out. They had electrodes attached to their scalps for hours at a time and barium inserted "everywhere you could think of." They were even asked for semen samples. Why? It turned out that the U-2 boys were being used as guinea pigs for the Mercury astronauts' physicals, though whether John Glenn's sperm count or motility was ever a factor in his selection remains unknown.

Glenn was compensated for his privations at Lovelace with space travel, enduring fame and a career as a U.S. senator. The U-2 pilots were required to suffer in silence. Only one of Powers's group was eliminated at this stage. The rest were handed sheaves of airline tickets and ordered to report to a manufacturer of ladies' bras and girdles two time zones to the east.

The tickets took them, one at a time, to the David Clark Company of Worcester, Massachusetts. Mr. Clark still made bras. He also made pressure suits. As part of their training, the pilots would be shown why. They would sit in a depressurization chamber at the Wright Field aeromedical laboratory wearing a pressure suit and holding a condom full of water. As the pilot breathed piped oxygen and the suit gradually inflated, the air would be sucked out of the chamber to simulate increasing altitude. At about 55,000 feet the water in the condom would begin to boil. At 70,000 sudden depressurization in a cockpit would kill an unprotected pilot in ten seconds, and sudden depressurization happened in U-2s all the time: the power source for pressurizing the cockpit was the engine, and engine flameouts because of the thin air were practically routine.

Hence Colonel Flickinger's visit to the Pentagon the previous year. The template was Richard III's horseshoe at the Battle of Bosworth in 1485; without a shoe his kingdom was lost. Without a decent pressure suit for the CIA, the cold war was liable to heat up. The stakes were no higher than for Kelly Johnson, but they were still extremely high. Given ten months when he had said he needed at least three years, Flickinger's first call had been to Clark.

As self-effacing as he was stubborn, David G. Clark left school at fifteen with no qualifications but a deep interest in science. He channeled it into two-way stretch fibers and the knitting business. The results included six patents and a thriving factory churning out the kind of supportive women's underwear that was much in demand in Eisenhower's years of plenty. From the war years onward, Clark also built a niche business custom sewing anti-G suits for fighter pilots. But as Flickinger had told the impatient secretary of the air force, the best pressure suit that Clark or anyone had yet produced was of the "get me down" variety; a high flier's life vest, strictly for emergencies.

The new specification was for a suit that could be worn uninflated for twelve hours and for four hours providing full life support. It was to inflate whenever pressure in the cockpit fell below the equivalent of 28,000 feet (roughly the height of Annapurna).

Clark's early suits had been based on a prototype designed by a Dr. James Henry of the University of Southern California. The prototype had been tested by Dr. Henry himself in long sessions in the low-pressure chamber at Wright Field. There was something distinctly Victorian about his masochism, which Clark described with a dry eye for detail: "Several of us watched through the chamber windows while Dr. Henry demonstrated the suit at various simulated altitudes up to 90,000 feet," he wrote.

> *He remained above 65,000 feet for over half an hour. The suit was obviously intended to fit closely and extended well up his neck. The "helmet" was designed to overlap the suit at the neck, but did not quite make it. As Dr. Henry moved about at the higher altitudes, his flesh would frequently pop out about as much as a hen's egg and then reduce again.*

The "helmet" was not a helmet in any modern sense. Rather,

> *it consisted of curved plexiglass with a black rubber inflatable seal at the edges to cover [Dr. Henry's] eyes, nose and mouth.... Closely fitted fabric covered his chin and the back of his head. The top of his head and his ears were not covered. As he moved about his scalp would lift, seemingly as much as an inch. Dr. Henry appeared not to notice these phenomena. The other watchers did not mention it either.*

The U-2 pilots had to be allowed to keep their scalps. For them, Clark used a proprietary elasticated fabric to create an airtight seal between suit and helmet. But Dr. Henry's basic idea of using compressed oxygen to apply direct pressure all over the body via inflatable tubes and bladders survived. When everything else went wrong at seventy thousand feet, the pilots could be reasonably sure of fifteen pounds of pressure per square inch of their bodies, three around their heads, and a steady supply to breathe.

Survival in the stratosphere came at the price of comfort. The only way to ingest anything was via a straw fed through a self-sealing hole at the bottom of the helmet's faceplate. Secretion and excretion were still more awkward. If a pilot had to sit in the sun for more than a few minutes before takeoff, his regulation long johns would be drenched in sweat for the whole flight. If he had to urinate, well, he had to urinate. And so on. As Tony Bevacqua says over eggs Benedict at a diner near his home in California, "Shit happens."

Form followed function. The suits' tubes, or capstans, necessarily ran along the outside of the suit. It was the principle used later by the architects Renzo Piano and Richard Rogers when they garlanded the outside of the Centre Pompidou in Paris with its innards. In both cases the effect was spectacularly modern. Not many people saw the U-2 pilots, but those who did knew they were glimpsing the future.

Just in case the Russians were watching Clark's factory in Worcester for signs of a sudden spike in output of girdles or anything else, his staff were enlisted to the cause of security. They were instructed not to fraternize with visiting pilots or even admit they recognized them if they did. This meant that measuring could be unnerving. As Jerry McIlmoyle remembered it long after finally being admitted to the program, the pressure suit room was reached via the factory's open-plan ground floor, full of women sewing bras and corsets and carefully not making eye contact. A wooden stairway led from there to a basement corridor ending in a green door. Beyond that was the regular flight suit department, and beyond that a black door leading to another room, where he was told to strip to his undershorts and stand on a two-foot-high wooden podium.

"A stoop-shouldered, wizened old man" then entered the room and measured every inch—"and I mean *every* inch"—of his body, using a cup to determine the volume of his genitals.

The session ended with the words "Okay, we're through. Come back in the morning." Clark's people then worked through the night to complete two perfectly fitting pressure suits. A company rep added another sheaf of airline tickets. Rather than head straight back to Malmstrom AFB, McIlmoyle was ordered to spend a weekend in Manhattan at taxpayers' expense, "just like you're a tourist." If the idea was to fool people like Fisher and Hayhanen, it would have worked. From all the available evidence, they could not have been less interested.

* * *

If frequent flier miles existed in 1956, Powers would have racked them up.

Suited and indoctrinated into the ways of the agency, he formally resigned his air force commission and flew to the West Coast to report, as a civilian, to March Air Force Base at the foot of the San Bernardino Mountains. Five other ex–fighter pilots made the same trip: fit young men in patterned shirts with short haircuts and heavy shoulder bags courtesy of the David Clark Company. They climbed into a Douglas C-47 with blacked-out windows and flew northeast to what would become the most famous lake bed in the history of conspiracy theories.

The Watertown strip at Groom Lake had been used before, for emergency landings by trainee pilots in the war. It was rediscovered ten years later by Tony LeVier, Lockheed's chief test pilot. His orders were to take the company Beechcraft and search the wide-open spaces of Nevada for somewhere to test a secret plane.

In fact there was nothing open about Groom Lake, and not only because of the mountains that ringed it. The airspace above was closed to commercial traffic because of the nuclear test site immediately to the west. This would complicate U-2 pilot training because the whole operation had to be evacuated to Phoenix whenever there was a test at Jackass Flats. But for the time being the lake bed looked perfect. On his first reconnaissance LeVier made a low pass and dropped a sixteen-pound shot put ball out of his cockpit window. It bounced. Soon afterward he returned with Johnson and a tall passenger with a high forehead and patrician mien. He was dressed in chinos, tennis shoes, and a checkered blazer, and Johnson referred to him as Mr. B.

"B" was for "Bissell"—Richard Bissell—but it might as well have been for "blue blood." The son of a Connecticut insurance mogul who had grown up in Mark Twain's gingerbread house in Hartford, Bissell was a world-class economist who liked to call himself a man-eating shark when confronted with red tape. This was his first trip to Groom Lake but by no means his first out west on U-2 business. He was the favorite troubleshooter of Allen Dulles, director of Central Intelligence, and he shared his boss's fascination with the idea of covert mischief in a free society. He had been assigned to run the agency's in-house air force the moment Eisenhower had approved the U-2 plan in 1954.

At this stage of his career there was more than a hint of the young Donald Rumsfeld about Bissell. He was brilliant, arrogant, iconoclastic, funny, and successful. He was also inclined to push things a bit too far. Bissell later took the fall, deservedly, for the Bay of Pigs disaster. He had no shortage of critics before that, either, among them a senior U-2 pilot who despaired of his blindness toward mounting morale and security problems four thousand miles away in Turkey. "Bissell refused to accept my advice or anyone else's," Harry Cordes wrote bitterly. "He thought he knew it all." But certain things he did know better than anyone else in government, and one of them was how to get things done. His was the only number Johnson needed to know on the East Coast, and without it the U-2 might never have been built.

No photographs survive of Bissell, Johnson, and LeVier stepping out of their Bonanza in the dry heat of the Nevada spring and chatting quietly about how to build a nonexistent airport. But if such images did exist, they would deserve space in the cold war pantheon.

Seen from the air, Bissell remembered, Groom Lake "was approximately three to four miles in diameter and smooth as a billiard table." As LeVier came down, they saw the outline of the old airstrip ending at the southern edge of the lake. Having done his homework, LeVier landed on the lake bed, not the strip. "Once on the ground, we walked over to the airstrip to see if it was viable," said Bissell. "The closer we got, the deeper we sank into soft, sagebrush-covered soil. Had we attempted to land on it, we most assuredly would have crashed."

Still, Bissell agreed that this was the place. They flew back to Los Angeles (over an atom bomb perched on a scaffold and primed to go off nine hours later), and Bissell returned to Washington. He talked to Dulles, who talked to Eisenhower, who in a single Oval Office meeting agreed to add the lake and its environs to the adjacent test site. Johnson had his secret sandbox. Bissell called it Watertown in a nod to Dulles's birthplace in upstate New York. Johnson called it Paradise Ranch.

In the next three months a contractor who thought he was working for C & J Engineering paved the airstrip, sunk a well alongside it, and put up three hangars, a mess hall, and basic accommodation for two hundred people, all for $800,000. Workers and building materials were flown in from Burbank on air force shuttles.

Most of the buildings were positioned on a fresh slab of paving at the north end of the runway near the lake bed, where there was also room to park incoming aircraft. It was here, in May 1956, at the foot of the barren Belted Mountains, that Powers saw his first U-2. He was polite about it in his memoir: "It was a strange-looking aircraft, unlike any other I had ever seen... a jet, but with the body of a glider. Though a hybrid, it was nevertheless very individual, with a beautiful symmetry all its own."

Jerry McIlmoyle was more enthusiastic: "What did I feel when I first saw the U2? It was total, unbridled excitement.... What was it like to take off and climb above 70,000 feet? It was total euphoria; I was thrilled to the core with absolute and complete focus on what I was doing."

Marty Knutson, whose exploits in the U-2 became the stuff of legend, "almost died of disappointment" when he first saw it. "I looked in the cockpit and saw that the damn thing had a yoke.... The last straw. Either you flew with a stick like a self-respecting fighter jock or you were a crappy bomber driver—a goddam disgrace."

The truth is the U-2 did not appeal to a fighter jock's outer machismo or his inner aesthete. It was not a hot rod. It was not cute or sexy. It would not land on a carrier, at least not in this form, and it would never break the sound barrier. It looked like a child's drawing of a plane, with oversize wings and a generic tail that could have been stuck on as an afterthought. It was also a work in progress.

History has looked favorably on the U-2 because it did what was asked of it. But when first delivered to Groom Lake and rolled out of the clamshell doors of a double-decker Globemaster transport in July 1955, it was a hunch wrapped in a boast covered in a tarpaulin.

Like Burt Rutan, the maverick aircraft designer from Mojave who won the X Prize for private space flight with a rocket plane powered by laughing gas, Kelly Johnson lived on his reputation as well as his wits. He had helped design Lockheed's Electra airliner and F-104 Starfighter, so when he told General Philip Strong it would be a cinch to put "wings like a tent" on a Starfighter's body, the hunch carried weight. When he boasted that he could produce a prototype U-2 in eight months flat and a detachment of operational versions in a year and a half, the East Coast people trusted him. But that trust was not based on flow charts and organograms. It was based on Kelly's experience of driving engineers to their limits under the pressures of a "hot" war, and on his intimidating chutzpah. When the first U-2's disassembled wings and fuselage arrived at Watertown, there was no guarantee that they would fly, let alone for four thousand miles at seventy thousand feet. That miracle was to come. The first was that the prototype existed at all.

Johnson famously produced his first detailed plan of the U-2 *after* winning the contract, not before. It was a twenty-three-page document put together in seven days that served as the blueprint for three dozen designers who would work hundred-hour weeks, in shifts, around the clock, to meet his eight-month deadline. Johnson's team were all male and all white and they all smoked heavily. Since no janitors had security clearance for the Skunk Works, they had to clean their own toilets and empty their own ashtrays at the same time as saving the free world.

Since no women were present in the flesh, pictures of them without too many clothes on went up on the walls.

The design problems were all to do with altitude. Johnson's rule of thumb was that every extra pound of weight would cost a foot of height, bringing the planes that much closer to Soviet surface-to-air missiles. He insisted on using aluminum up to two thirds thinner than usual, and titanium where possible. The tail was attached with three short bolts (an engineering decision that was to have a spectacular impact on the course of human affairs). There was a grand total of two landing wheels, forcing pilots to land the U-2 like a bicycle with an eighty-foot wingspan. To save weight and clear space for cameras, there was no central spar connecting the two wings through the fuselage. The wings were simply bolted on, but they still had to support the weight of six hundred gallons of fuel each. Their length and fragility created a serious danger once in flight. Engineers called it aeroelastic divergence leading to catastrophic failure. Others called it flapping leading to falling off. Hence, in Johnson's diary for June 20, 1955: "A very busy time in that we have only 650 hours to airplane completion point. Having terrific struggle with the wing." But three weeks was a long time in the Skunk Works. "Airplane is essentially completed," Johnson wrote on July 15. "Terrifically long hours. Everybody almost dead."

In the end the only real answer to the midair disintegration problem was to beg the pilots to take it easy and stay above any turbulence. But solving one set of altitude problems created another. The higher the U-2 flew, the thinner the air rushing over its wings and into its engine. That meant an ever-narrower gap between stall speed and "Mach buffet" and an ever-greater chance of the engine packing up. These were occupational hazards the pilots would have to learn to live with.

Powers did just that. He was a natural in the U-2. Unlike Marty Knutson, he never complained about the yoke. He came through his two months at the ranch without a hitch (and with high praise for the food, which, with pilot morale in mind, was "exceptional by any standard"). He wrote later of a "special aloneness" in the cockpit, which seems to have suited his temperament. There were discomforts to be borne in return for membership in the U-2 elite, including long hours in the pressure suit and prebreathing of pure oxygen before each flight to purge the body of nitrogen as a defense against the bends in the event of depressurization. But he took them in stride, marveling instead at the extraordinary views to be had of the American West from thirteen miles up. On one flight, when his drift sight showed the Colorado River slicing through Arizona below him, he could see a six-hundred-mile sweep of the West Coast up ahead, from the Monterey Peninsula to Baja California.

The flight training was thorough. It had to be. The only easy part about flying the U-2 was taking off, which Tony LeVier discovered on his first test took place automatically at seventy knots (he had not intended to leave the ground). The initial climb was spectacular, but if the pilot forgot to ease his angle of attack at 35,000 feet the plane was liable to explode because of the expanding fuel in its wings. At 70,000 feet the giant Pratt & Whitney engine that occupied most of the fuselage had 7 percent of the power it boasted at sea level. That high up, the margin between stalling and speed wobble was no more than five knots, meaning that in a tight turn one wingtip could shudder for one reason and the other for the other. All of which was straightforward compared with landing. The U-2 was supremely reluctant to lose height. It was designed to have a gliding radius of 250 miles in the event of engine failure, and some pilots found they could double that. Close to the ground, especially the hot ground of Groom Lake, it defied Newton. A pilot could be ten feet from landing and yet not land. Even with its engine idling, Mr. Johnson's albatross would skim clear across the lake bed unless actively forced down. Johnson assumed the way to do this was nose first, but his prototype nearly disintegrated when LeVier tried it. LeVier eventually made landing look easy with a more conventional tail-wheel-first approach, but even then it was a delicate business requiring a countdown from a chase car and a stall timed to perfection. For him, as for those who followed, there was no simulator, no copilot, and no ejector seat.

In the end, each pilot had to figure out the U-2 for himself. It could be a hairy business. One afternoon Bissell was in his office in Washington when Groom Lake called to say that a U-2 had reported an engine flameout over Tennessee and was gliding toward an air force base near Albuquerque.

"He believed he could make the base in about half an hour on a long, flat glide," Bissell recalled. "I got on the telephone to the commander of the Albuquerque base and told him that in about 30 to 40 minutes he should expect a special aircraft, a U-2, to land; he was to move it to a remote part of the base as quickly as possible, have a tarpaulin put over it to disguise its shape, and post a guard. I can only imagine his surprise at receiving a call from the CIA, but 45 minutes later the phone rang and he reported that the flight did indeed land... and the pilot was available to speak with me."

When Bissell flew to Groom Lake to inspect the faulty engine, he reached into its tail end and pulled out the remains of a compressor blade that had crystallized and disintegrated in the extreme cold of seventy thousand feet.

Powers was lucky. He had no near misses in training and no doubt that he would be able to glide down and restart his engine if it flamed out over the United States. What nagged at the back of his mind was what to do should it happen over Russia, but it was not a question anyone actually asked—or answered.

Each group that passed through the ranch spent a week at a CIA farm back east, part of which had been converted to resemble a Soviet border installation. The pilots learned how to scramble under a fence and walk across a plowed field without leaving footprints, but there was no discussion of what to do if the border was a thousand miles away. Powers concluded that the exercise was more for psychological than practical purposes. He was surely right. And he would just as surely have been disturbed to know that both Bissell and Dulles had assured Eisenhower it was "a given" that no pilot would survive a crash on Soviet territory.

By the end of his time at Watertown, reports were reaching the CIA of tests on a monstrous Russian rocket engine designed to develop 450 tons of thrust—enough to hurl a thermonuclear warhead five thousand miles through space. A National Security Agency listening post in Iran, in the mountains near Mashhad, had picked up signs of missile tests deep in the Soviet hinterland and farther east than the known test range at Kapustin Yar. It was past time to find out where.

Powers's group was given two weeks' leave, then sent to Turkey. He dropped in on Pound and dodged questions about his work but failed to allay his father's suspicions. When he telephoned from the airport to say a final good-bye, Powers senior said he'd figured out that Frank was working for the FBI. His sister Jessica was less suspicious but had more evidence to work with. Frank had paid her a visit too. "I had a folding canvas cot and we asked him if he'd like to stay," she says. "He said yes, and he took off his shirt and it looked to me as though you could play checkers on his back. I didn't ask—he could have been in a fight. But I guess now it was that suit."

* * *

Powers's departure for foreign parts had a peculiar effect on his friends and family. A large number of them followed him. Jessica would be among them, in circumstances she could scarcely credit and that even now she struggles to believe were real. But before her there was her brother's wife.

Barbara Powers had a good deal in common with her father-in-law, including an instant mutual dislike. Like him, she was hardworking, hotheaded, mainly self-taught, and not easily intimidated. Like him, she made up for what she lacked in formal education with a ferocious impatience with anyone who might be keeping something from her. With Frank's disappearance, that meant Frank, but also the whole damned outfit he was working for. It was not an outfit that particularly wanted to hear from her.

In Richard Bissell's air force, deniability was everything. His aircraft flew without markings. His pilots flew without dog tags. Their underpants had no labels, and the brand names were ground off the zippers on their pressure suits. His Washington headquarters was a decrepit suite of upstairs offices in an old brothel on E Street, and his business, should anyone ask, was meteorology.

The cover story he approved for the first detachment of U-2s and pilots shipped overseas was that they would be gathering high-altitude weather data for the National Advisory Committee for Aeronautics. An unclassified press release announced that by arrangement with the USAF's Air Weather Service the planes would be studying the jet stream, convective clouds, and cosmic ray effects at 55,000 feet. It was the same story for Powers's detachment, Detachment B, which would be based in "Greece." NACA went along with it, and so did most pilots' families.

Not Barbara. Shorn of her husband, she had left Turner Air Force

Base and gone home to Milledgeville, Georgia, to live with her mother. The plan had been to sit tight and bank Frank's implausible earnings for a down payment on a house. It palled quickly. He had been gone all of three months when she dialed the number Frank had left her for emergencies and told a startled agency man that she would be flying to Athens the following day to find her husband.

The agency man tried to put her off, but it was too late. The tickets were bought: Air France via Paris.

"All right, then," he told her. "You are instructed to go to the King George Hotel immediately upon your arrival."

Later that day, Turkish time, Powers climbed out of a U-2 after a training flight, his long johns drenched in sweat and his head spinning with tactical pilotage charts of the Soviet border, to be handed a note by an irritated detachment commander, a Colonel Perry. He couldn't take it in, so Colonel Perry had to spell it out. Barbara was on her way.

There was time, as things turned out. A few hours out of Washington Barbara woke to see two of the Air France Constellation's four engines on fire. She was marooned in Newfoundland for five days.

She was eventually reunited with her husband, as instructed, at the finest hotel in Greece—two bright young things enjoying peerless views of the Acropolis and all the freedoms of the Pax Americana. They enjoyed each other's company as well, until Frank screwed up his face and broke it to her that he was not based in Greece; nor could he say where he'd flown in from.

Barbara was dismayed but not defeated. He'd flown in once. He could do it again. She would stay in Athens.

The agency appears to have sensed quickly that it would be counterproductive to pick a fight with the redoubtable Mrs. Powers. With some discreet nudging she was found work as secretary to an air force judge advocate based in Athens, a Captain Reuben B. Jackson. It was a humane arrangement, and soon a human one. Captain Jackson, whose wife and three children had tired of the expat life and returned home, asked Barbara to perform the role of hostess at his cocktail parties. She obliged; he fell in love.

Barbara later claimed she was entirely unaware of Captain Jackson's feelings for her until he stunned her with a letter saying he was seeking a divorce. Frank wanted to believe her, but friends of his who knew her couldn't. "How d'you tell your buddy?" Tony Bevacqua muses. "She was a lush."

***

Powers the pilot tried to seal off his life from that of Powers the conflicted husband. It wasn't easy. For his first three months in Turkey there was little to do except train, play poker, and wait for a go code from Washington for the type of mission the U-2 had been built to fly. The food was dreadful, he remembered. There was the small matter of the Suez Crisis to monitor—and it certainly added to Eisenhower's irritation with Sir Anthony Eden, the British prime minister, that he was not informed in advance of British troop movements near the Suez Canal when his U-2 pilots could see them quite clearly through their drift sights. But Europe's postimperial delusions were not really the U-2's business. The black planes with the drooping wings at Adana were there to penetrate a newer and more frightening sort of empire.

It was only a matter of time before the order came. On July 4 that year, under budget, on deadline, and on Independence Day, Richard Bissell's hunt for WMD had started with the taut roar of a J-57 engine and a flight plan of epic impertinence. The pilot assigned to fly it was Harvey Stockman of the first NACA Weather Reconnaissance Squadron (Provisional).

Fewer than ten souls on earth knew exactly where Harvey Stockman was headed or why, and not one of these was in the White House. The only people definitely in the loop were Bissell, a small handful of flight planners on E Street, Stockman's detachment commander, and Stockman himself.

The go code was an encrypted one-line cable sent over secure CIA lines to a tightly guarded communications room at Wiesbaden Air Force Base in Germany. It was authorized by Eisenhower, but the precise route and timing were up to Bissell. He launched the mission shortly before midnight on June 3, Washington time. In Germany Stockman's plane was fueled with 1,200 gallons of kerosene, specially modified so as not to freeze solid in the sub-Arctic temperatures of seventy thousand feet.

Stockman took off from Wiesbaden at dawn, fortified as usual with steak and eggs and oxygen. As he brought his nose up to its absurd fifty-five-degree climb-out angle and set course for Poznan, he probably didn't dwell on the sociohistorical significance of the moment. Still, it was considerable. Trussed in Dave Clark's two-way stretch fibers, half hidden by helmet and oxygen mask, encased in a pressurized titanium capsule, and headed for the penthouse viewing platform of the upper troposphere, he embodied American conviction and American hypocrisy; the conviction that no problem could not be surmounted with ingenuity and hard work, and the hypocrisy of the spy whose president traded on his reputation for openness and honesty in his dealings with an otherwise duplicitous world.

Stockman flew northwest over Poland and Minsk before turning left for Leningrad. In his payload bay, a Hycon B camera the size and weight of a substantial stove, loaded with six thousand feet of ultrathin Mylar film on two contra-rotating drums, clicked away at three long-range bomber bases near the city. Then it turned its attention to a series of naval shipyards on the Baltic coast that were being rapidly expanded to build nuclear submarines. As Stockman turned for home, the U.S. ambassador to Moscow was treating Khrushchev to a traditional July 4 barbecue at his official residence. Khrushchev was not informed of the incursion while a guest of the Americans, but he knew soon enough.

Even Dulles did not know that Stockman was headed for Leningrad. When Bissell strolled into the then CIA headquarters building on H Street on the morning of July 5 and told him, Dulles blanched. "The first time is the safest," Bissell reassured him.

It was the attitude of a tightrope walker so confident that he performs without a net. The U-2 was an astonishing piece of aeronautical improvisation that had broken its own altitude records time and again on training flights from Watertown and infuriated the very few air force brass who knew about it but had not been able to get their hands on it. But Bissell's confidence belied reality. He did not know whether Soviet radar would pick it up. What he *did* know was that if Stockman had a flameout over Leningrad there would be hell to pay.

Stockman didn't have a flameout. After eight hours and forty-five minutes in the air, he returned to Wiesbaden and staggered out of his cockpit while technicians transferred the two great rolls of film from his camera to a waiting plane that left at once for Washington.

While Stockman made up for lost time at the officers' club, another pilot tried to sleep. Carmine Vito was up next. At dawn on the fifth he was suited up, strapped in, and dispatched to Moscow. He photographed the Kremlin, the city's air defenses, and a rocket engine test site in a northwestern suburb best known today for its IKEA.

The U-2s kept coming, each one an enormous calculated risk; each one an expression of Bissell's relentless curiosity. On July 9, Marty Knutson, who had been so disgusted by the U-2's yoke, sublimated his objections and flew a historic mission up the Baltic coast and over an air base southeast of Leningrad. He identified it as Engels Airfield. It has since been confused by historians with another Engels air base near Saratov on the Volga. The one Knutson saw remained etched in his mind because of what he saw, peering down through the drift sight that protruded from his instrument panel to give a view of the ground directly beneath him. Glinting in bright sunlight thirteen miles below were thirty long-range Bison bombers drawn up next to the runway.

"Pay dirt" was what Knutson called the pictures he took that day, but it was an alarming sort of pay dirt. The Bison was a malevolent-looking bomber with a range of five thousand miles and room in its belly for twenty-four tons of nuclear ordnance. At a rehearsal for the May Day fly-past over Red Square in 1955, Western journalists and military attachés had looked up in awe as dozens of them had thundered overhead. In practice a mere handful had circled several times over the city, but the ruse was enough to sow fears among security hawks in Washington of a "bomber gap" being neglected by a president who was overly confident of his security credentials.

Senator Stuart Symington, a stainless steel tycoon and Democratic member of the Senate Armed Services Committee, formally accused the administration of "misleading the American people...as to the relative military strength of the United States vis a vis the Communists." As a former secretary of the air force, he was especially vexed by Eisenhower's decision to slow down production of the Big Ugly Fat Fella, as the mighty B-52 American long-range bomber was known to its admirers.

Knutson's pictures seemed to confirm that the Soviets did have Bisons in numbers. But they were the only ones spotted in nine U-2 overflights of European Russia that July. What was more, they were in plain view and were unlikely to have been exposed at one base and hidden at others. The conclusion was inescapable: if this was all the Soviets had, it was less than a third as many as Symington and his friends in the air force claimed. In five days flat the U-2 had demolished the bomber gap.

The film from the returning planes was rushed to Washington and analyzed above a car repair shop near Mount Vernon Square. Then the best prints were taken to the White House, pinned to boards five feet across, and presented to the president.

He was entranced. Dulles later said he and Eisenhower pored over the images on the Oval Office floor "like two kids running a model train." Here was the enemy, as promised, stripped of Khrushchev's posturing, in black and white.

It was not just the military sites that fascinated. As Herb Miller, a senior CIA official, wrote in an excited memo after the first overflight, "We are no longer dependent on an 'estimate' or 'judgment' or 'assessment' of what the situation is. We now have a cross section of a part of the whole of Soviet life for that date—their military systems, their farms, their irrigation systems, their factories, their power systems to feed the factories, their housing for the people who run the factories, their recreation, their railroads and the amount of traffic they carry."

The pictures also revealed that even though Soviet radar was all over the U-2, "fighter aircraft at the five most important bases covered were drawn up in orderly rows as if for formal inspection on parade." Bombers were not dispersed for their own protection. Antiaircraft guns were not pointing skyward for anyone else's. They were at ease, horizontal. "These are but a few examples of the many things which tend to spell out the real intentions, objectives and qualities of the Soviet Union that we must fully understand and appreciate if we are to be successful in negotiating a lasting peace for the world," Miller concluded.

In hard cash terms the images were worth billions, literally: Congress had demanded at least four billion dollars to modernize the air force against the apocalyptic threat talked up by the bomber-gap lobby. Having seen the U-2 pictures, the president allowed less than one billion dollars. Furthermore, they had been brought back without the loss of a plane or pilot. Willie Fisher and his handlers in Moscow had never dreamed of intelligence gathering on such a scale or with such swift and tangible results.

That was the good news. The bad news was that, unlike Fisher, the U-2s' cover had been blown the moment they went to work.

The official protest was hand delivered to the State Department by the Soviet ambassador to Washington on July 10. It was not accurate in every detail, but it was on the right track. It timed Stockman's entry into East German airspace at 8:18 a.m. on the fourth and charted his route over Grodno, Minsk, Vilnius, Kaunas, and Kaliningrad.

Fighters scrambled to intercept the intruder had not come within fifteen thousand feet of its cruising altitude, but the CIA knew from receivers inside the U-2 that Soviet radar had followed it all the way. It was the same with every ensuing flight. At one point on Knutson's foray toward Leningrad he counted fifteen MiGs in his drift sight, climbing toward him and falling away as their control surfaces lost grip in the thin air.

On July 19, Eisenhower summoned Dulles to his office and reminded him that he had been assured the U-2 would be virtually undetectable. More even than golf, Ike liked the idea of a legacy of superpower peace. From the outset the U-2 program had struck him as a potential destroyer as well as creator of that peace. He admitted that if a hostile power tried to fly reconnaissance planes over the United States he would consider it an act of war. Long after it was too late, he wrote in his memoirs: "I was the only principal who consistently expressed a conviction that if ever one of the planes fell in Soviet territory a wave of excitement mounting almost to panic would sweep the world."

The protest note was deeply embarrassing for Khrushchev to have to send, since it implicitly acknowledged he had been powerless to bring the U-2s down. But he would manage that soon enough, as Edwin Land had pointed out as part of his original pitch for the "super glider." ("The opportunity for safe overflight may last only a few years," Land warned, "because Russians will develop radars and interceptors or guided missile defenses for the 70,000 foot region. We therefore recommend immediate action.")

Two years on, Eisenhower told Dulles he was already falling out of love with the U-2. From now on he would personally approve each overflight. There would be no more blanket permissions for Mr. Bissell and no more flights at all unless the benefit clearly outweighed the potential cost. And there the program might have died, but for Khrushchev's tragic tendency to overplay his hand.

On November 5, 1956, as Barbara Powers killed time in Athens and her husband in Adana, Soviet troops crushed the Hungarian revolution, killing twenty thousand civilians and taking fifteen hundred casualties themselves. Khrushchev had agonized for two weeks before deciding that the only alternative to invading was the collapse of the Soviet empire. "We have to act," he told his closest ally. "We have no other course." Two weeks later he overcompensated for his earlier hesitation by issuing his notorious threat to bury capitalism. Toward the end of his rant to Western diplomats, they started walking out, but his words rang in their ears and flashed down cables to their respective capitals. This was the leader who earlier in the year had said he was "quite sure that we shall very soon have a guided missile with a hydrogen-bomb warhead which could hit any point in the world."

There was a wild man in the Kremlin, no doubt about it.

Eisenhower was more concerned than anyone not to provoke him. But he also knew better than most how much of Khrushchev's foreign policy was bluff and how badly the United States needed to know the realities behind it.

Bissell had responded nimbly to the news that the president was unhappy that his secret air force had been detected so quickly. He had sent Detachment B to Turkey. From there, he argued, U-2s would encounter sleepier radar stations and fewer fighter squadrons than the Wiesbaden group. It was another hunch, but Eisenhower was angry with the butcher of Budapest and politically confident, having just been reelected to the White House. He bought it.

Powers and the other seven pilots were sleeping two to a trailer. Their officers' club was a Quonset hut with a single bare bulb. The agency was processing a request for water skis and a power boat, but they had not arrived and the summer had been hot. The pilots' poker games could last three days. Adana felt like Watertown without the food.

On or about November 18, Powers happened to be walking past the base's secure cryptographic unit to which orders from Washington were sent. The detachment commander saw him. "You're it, Powers," he said. Weather permitting, he would be making the first overflight from Turkey. The coal miner's son from Virginia would be the first American to peer beyond European Russia into the empty spaces where some people said the arms race was being won.

There was still no word from the agency on what he should do if shot down. There were only hints. A survival kit stowed under the pilot's seat included a selection of men's and women's gold watches, heavy winter hunting gear, two dozen gold Napoleon francs, a message in more than a dozen languages requesting help and promising to do no harm, and a .22-caliber handgun with silencer, presumably in case the message was not understood.

Powers was also offered an L pill. "L" stood for lethal. It was a glass cyanide capsule to be crushed between the teeth if he wanted to commit suicide, and he was by no means the first American to be given the choice. The B-29 crews who dropped atom bombs on Hiroshima and Nagasaki were given L pills in case they were captured and tortured for information about the weapons in their bomb bays. U.S. agents in the Korean War were also often offered cyanide in case of torture. A CIA manual from that era stated that after crushing the pill the user should inhale through the mouth. The manual continued: "It is expected that there will be no pain, but there may be a feeling of constriction about the chest. Death will follow."

As recently as 2007 it was claimed in an otherwise authoritative study of the early arms race that U-2 pilots "were under instructions not to survive." In fact, the one life-threatening aspect of these flights on which the CIA was crystal clear was that taking the L pill along for the ride—never mind ingesting it—was strictly optional.

Joe Murphy was the CIA security officer at Adana with Powers in 1956 and again in 1958. He says: "There was never an instruction to these guys to take their own lives. They had the capability to do that were they in a torture situation, but there was never an instruction."

For this flight, Powers did not even pack an L pill. On November 20 he took off from Adana, turned east, and crossed into Iran. Then, as his wife and sisters and most of the free world slept, he checked his drift sight, eased his yoke very carefully to the left, and headed north, up the middle of the Caspian, into the unknown.

# 4

# THE INNOCENT

Machu Picchu, high in the Peruvian Andes, attracts both main tribes of Western traveler—the tourist and the wanderer. They mingle warily among its ancient walls. They recognize each other by their sneakers and their boots. They may briefly forget who they are, swept up in the magnificence of the views of the mountains and the Urubamba River, but they almost always come and go as separate species. Only occasionally do they arrive together.

In the summer of 1955, twin twenty-two-year-old brothers from Mansfield, Ohio, flew to Lima and made the spectacular journey to Cuzco and the lost city of the Incas on a trip funded by their father to celebrate their recent graduation. They were sons to be proud of: tall and handsome but also quiet, curious, and unfailingly polite. Each had a sense of humor, one more evident than the other. Both were expensively educated. Their names were Millard and Frederic Pryor.

After a few days in the mountains they parted, Millard for home.

"That's it," he said, "I have a job to do."

"He was going to be assistant to the president of some small company, something in business," Frederic recalls. "My brother was a very hardworking traditional bourgeois who made tons of money."

For his own part Frederic headed south. He had a backpack but no idea what he wanted to do with his life and no inkling that it would lead him surprisingly quickly to somewhere much more unsettled and unsettling than South America. He took a train across the Bolivian altiplano and tumbled out of the highlands in the general direction of Paraguay, where he had a notion he might find utopia.

General Alfredo Stroessner, "El Excelentísimo," was barely a year into his dictatorship, and Asunción was filled with military parades that Pryor wasn't interested in watching. While wandering the city's back streets he saw a sign saying SOCIEDAD DE HERMANOS.

"So I knocked on the door."

A man's head appeared in a second-floor window.

*"Was wollen Sie?"*

The young American had studied some German at college. *"Ich will mit Ihnen arbeiten,"* he said, looking up. I want to work with you. He was let in and given directions and the next day caught a boat up the River Paraguay to Rosario. It was about an eighty-mile overnight chug.

"From Rosario it was another fifty miles to the *sociedad,* mainly through forest," Pryor says. "They told me where to get off the boat and pointed in the right direction, and I was on my own. I started walking at about nine in the morning and got there by about ten a.m. the next morning. Fifty miles isn't far when you've got nothing else to do.

"I got lost twice along the way, the second time quite close to the community, as it turned out. And it was while I was lost the second time that I saw this little blond girl skipping through the woods. I asked her in German if she knew where the Sociedad de Hermanos was, and she looked at me blankly. So I tried Spanish, then French. Eventually she said, 'Do you speak English?'"

The Sociedad de Hermanos was founded as the Bruderhof in a Germany laid waste by the First World War. It was the dream of the Anabaptist preacher Eberhard Arnold to create a Christian brotherhood "which held all property in common, regarded all work as of equal worth, upheld a radical peace testimony with complete non-participation in war . . . practiced simplicity of life, was governed by unanimous consent of the members in each community and based membership on unity of faith in Christ regardless of race, class or nationality."

The Bruderhof was too communistic for the Nazis, who expelled its members from Germany in 1937. It was too German for the British, who allowed its refugee members to establish a commune in the Cotswolds but then threatened them with internment when war broke out.

It was unconditionally welcome—as the Nazis themselves would later be—only in Paraguay.

Fred Pryor had read about Paraguay's peculiar patchwork of utopian enclaves as an undergraduate at Oberlin, Ohio. He majored there in chemistry, but the most important thing he learned was that he didn't want to be a chemist. How much more fascinating, in an otherwise bipolar world of capitalists and Communists, was the idea of anarchists, Mennonites, and ecumenically minded Anabaptists scraping together their visions of paradise in the dark heart of South America? "How could these people live together? Why didn't things fall apart?"

Pretty soon they did, but for a few years in the mid-1950s the Society of Brothers in the Paraguayan forest prospered and grew, welcoming more or less anyone who stumbled on its neat white bungalows.

The blond girl led Pryor there, and he was found work as a cowboy. "They asked if I could ride a horse, which I could," he says. "They asked if I could lasso, which I could. What they didn't ask me was if I could ride a horse and lasso at the same time, and the answer was I couldn't." He was taken off horses and put on house painting. He stayed three months, marveling at the work of the Society's hospital, which treated ten thousand Paraguayan Indians a year without charge and was funded entirely by the sale of wooden toys, and adapting without much difficulty to the realities of communal property and the simple life. These included the sharing of gramophones by strict order of rotation, because the society owned only six of them.

Pryor then hitched a ride back to Asunción with a Mennonite farmer, who gave him something to eat that he would later blame for a bad case of hepatitis. But before the disease took hold he traveled to Buenos Aires, grew a beard, and took ship for England, working his passage aboard the *Ovington Grange* having persuaded the captain that he knew about engines: "Smart-ass that I was, I said I'd studied thermodynamics, which I had." The vessel carried birdseed. As far as he could tell, it carried enough to feed every British bird for the next hundred years.

At Oberlin, Pryor had acquired a reputation as an intellectual clown. One contemporary who went on to serve in several presidential administrations calls him "not serious" as an undergraduate (even though he would become "superserious" as a professor). Others tell stories—untrue, he says—of how he once spent a summer testing toilet seats for the Dow Chemical Company, and of the time he tried to prove that male students' choice of toilet stall in the campus restrooms depended on their mood and level of self-confidence.

Ill with jaundice, Pryor returned to America in the spring of 1956. He still had no firm plans. He knew only that he wanted to recuperate and prove to himself—and possibly to his brother and father—that he could be serious. He was already finding that "college humor does not work on adults" and was anxious to show that even though he seemed to have been given the family's whole portion of wanderlust, he could still get a decent job. He took and passed a civil service exam and spent a few months examining chemical patents at the Federal Trade Commission in Washington. In fact he almost lost the job before reporting for work because of budget cuts but was saved by a blind date with the daughter of a senior official at the Civil Service Commission, who intervened on his behalf.

Patents bored him anyway. In September, still fascinated to know what made one Paraguayan commune hum while another tore itself apart, he went to Yale to start a PhD in economics.

At this point in his peregrinations, Carolyn Cooper, a friend from Oberlin, saw in her old classmate "a certain naïveté... a certain lack of caution, a certain trustfulness." Another college contemporary who remains close to him after many decades describes him as one of those who sensed that a "fundamental purity of heart" will protect them from life's ambushes.

Pryor hated Yale. From the start he found it stifling and overly intense. It turned out that traditional economics bored him almost as much as patents, and having studied almost none of it as an undergraduate he struggled to keep up with the thoroughbreds whose doctorates would catapult them to capitalism's commanding heights. He stuck with it for two and a half years, but when the time came to pick a topic for his thesis, he wanted out. "I just chose a topic that would take me as far away from New Haven, Connecticut, as humanly possible," he says.

He chose Berlin.

* * *

It was not hard to enroll as an American at the Free University of West Berlin at the end of the 1950s. The university had been established by General Lucius Clay, the hero of the Berlin Airlift, on the first day of the blockade of the city in 1948. Like the blockade, the university was an expression of American defiance funded largely by the American taxpayer, for both of which West Berliners were deeply grateful. Tuition was fifty dollars per semester for all comers.

Pryor didn't even phone ahead. "I went to Berlin. I showed up at their admissions office. I was admitted on the spot," he says. It may have helped that he was still attached to Yale and studying for a PhD on Communism, but he abandoned his chosen thesis subject soon after arriving to specialize in Soviet bloc foreign trade. He would soon know more about how the East German and Soviet governments fixed export prices than almost anyone in the world, and it would get him into trouble. But first he had to improve his German. He enrolled in a crash course for foreigners. "I read German all day. I went to classes in German. I made an enormous effort, memorizing ten or twenty words a night, forgetting half of them the next day," he says.

*Time* magazine nosed around the university while he was there and pronounced the eleven-thousand-strong student body "a happy lot, inclined toward U.S. jazz and blue jeans." Yet for all their openness to America and his effort with their language, Pryor's first year in Berlin was lonely. There were no dorms, so he lived alone in a rented room near the city center. Students who didn't know one another well addressed one another with the formal *"Sie."* When he stood up in a lecture theater to argue with a professor whose remarks on Eastern Bloc trade he found especially preposterous, his fellow students rushed to defend the professor and his German let him down on cross-examination.

Still, he kept his chin up. "German is not a difficult language to learn," he decided when the twenty words a night began to stick. As his confidence grew, he started phoning East German academics at the Hochschule für Planökonomie, the brain of the command economy that Khrushchev still believed would conquer the world. He began asking for interviews. The Ministerium für Staatssicherheit or Ministry for State Security—"Stasi" for short—had no rules on this. It had not occurred to the world's most meticulous secret police force that simple curiosity might induce a Westerner to open the phone book and start asking how nonmarket economics worked. People were eager to tell him. (It turned out, for example, that the price East Germany paid for Soviet wheat was not plucked from thin air but based on the world market price at Newport News, Virginia.) Some of the people Pryor met became lifelong friends. In all he conducted thirty-five interviews with the East German economists who served as the high priests of five-year planning, and the interviews became the basis of his thesis.

Getting to East Berlin was easy. "You just hopped on the subway and you were there," he says. "Or the S-Bahn." Or you drove, and the strong dollar made driving eminently possible even for a student. In 1960 Pryor bought a bright red VW Karmann Ghia and switched rooms to a more desirable address in an old apartment house on Viktoria-Luise-Platz. There were nightclubs aplenty in the brave island of freedom that was West Berlin, but Pryor was not the clubbing sort. His preference after a long day transcribing insights into state-sanctioned price fixing was for Brahms or Bach at the Hochschule für Musik, and there was plenty of that too.

As the pages of his thesis started piling up, he put an ad in the student paper for someone to help him type it. It was answered by a fellow student named Eleonora, and they developed a serious mutual interest that went beyond economics, though not as far as marriage. His loneliness was a memory. All in all, he said, "I had a very pleasant life." It was not to last.

*part two*

# SPY CATCHERS

# 5

# STAKEOUT

"I am a lieutenant colonel of the Soviet intelligence service. For the past five years I have been operating in the United States. Now I need your help."

When Reino Hayhanen walked into the American embassy in Paris and started talking in May of 1957, Stalin had been dead four years. The Soviet prison camps had briefly come alive with rumors that the thaw after the dictator's death would bring mass amnesties. But the rumors fizzled and the camps stayed open. There was still plenty of room in the Gulag for a failed spy.

Hayhanen knew it. He had no shortage of reasons to defect. He loathed and feared Willie Fisher, his immediate superior. He resented the system Fisher represented, which hadn't given him a respectable post inside an embassy. But he was also timid; the confidence of the younger KGB staffer who once crossed and recrossed the Soviet-Finnish border in car trunks had been eroded by alcohol and underemployment. Only the knowledge that his trip to Moscow might end in Siberia could have pushed him to take the life-threatening step of betraying the KGB.

He was a weak man in a desperate situation, and he was showing the strain. When he announced himself at the embassy on Avenue Gabriel on the morning of May 4, he appeared drunk. When his demand to see the ambassador was not immediately granted, he became angry.

His puffy face and strangulated accent did not convince. Nor did the smell of his breath or his fake U.S. passport in the name of Eugene Maki. So he produced from his pocket a doctored Finnish five-mark coin. He opened the coin with a pin to reveal a square of microfilm like the one young Jimmy Bozart had found four years earlier on a stairwell in Brooklyn, and the Americans at last began to take him seriously. They let him talk, and he talked for a week: about his training, his legend, his passage to America, and his inebriated, bloodstained life there. Each evening the salient details were cabled to Washington, and most of them checked out. He asked for asylum and was told he might get it if he continued to cooperate. It may be that only then did he begin to see the true cost of the choice he had made. Either that or he was afraid of flying and the prospect drew him to his old friend, the nightly pint of vodka. When he was escorted onto a Constellation to return to the United States on May 11, he tried to kick the windows out.

Hayhanen had said enough in Paris for the news of his defection to be passed up the chain of command almost to the top. Allen Dulles ("the bumbling Dulles," Kim Philby called him) flew up to New York to meet the incoming transatlantic flight and to hand Hayhanen over to the FBI. It must have been a gratifying trip for him: the CIA had uncovered a sinister new Soviet spy ring, but since it was operating on U.S. territory it was the FBI's problem.

Hoover's men went to work. They sequestered Hayhanen in a hotel and grilled him for another seven days. He gave them everything they wanted, starting, on May 12, with his home address in Peekskill. At 12:25 p.m. that day he granted permission for his house to be searched. By 5:00 p.m. Special Agents Edward F. Gamber and John T. Mulhern were at the property revealing to Hannah Maki that her husband was a Soviet spy.

Mrs. Maki was drinking when they arrived and drinking a bit faster when they left, though she was not left alone. From now on she would have to endure the permanent presence of Bureau bodyguards assigned to protect her from the long and presumably murderous arm of Soviet vengeance.

Agents Gamber and Mulhern wanted names, not just addresses. Without them there would be no "ring." Here, too, Hayhanen did his best. His first Soviet contact in New York had been called "Mikhail," he said. Mikhail was middle-aged, of medium build, with a long nose and dark hair. Presented with photographs of every Soviet official matching that description who had been legally resident in the United States between 1952 and 1954, Hayhanen picked out his old handler, Mikhail Svirin. But just when the ring seemed about to expand, it contracted again. Svirin was long gone. He had indeed met Hayhanen once or twice at the Prospect Park subway station but had been back in Moscow for two years.

The Feds kept digging. Who came after Svirin? There must have been someone.

There was. His name was "Mark," Hayhanen said. That was the only name he could offer because it was the only one Moscow or Fisher had given him. But he was much more helpful as to Fisher's whereabouts. He knew about the studio and the rented storage space on Fulton Street in Brooklyn because of the time an exasperated Fisher had taken him there to give him a shortwave radio and then a camera. Hayhanen, in turn, took Gamber and Mulhern. On or about May 16, the FBI moved into rooms in the Hotel Touraine across the street from the Ovington Studios. Equipped with coffee money and ten-fifty binoculars, they settled down to wait.

The official FBI account of the arrest of Rudolf Abel—even now—depicts it as the climax of a triumphant four-year struggle to decode the message found by Jimmy Bozart in his hollow nickel. It was nothing of the sort. The message was indeed decoded but would not have been without Hayhanen's help; he provided his personal code word, "snegopad" (or snowfall), which unlocked the cipher and revealed nineteen lines of anticlimactic housekeeping from Moscow, congratulating him on his safe arrival in New York and reassuring him that "the package was delivered to your wife personally." It ended: "Greetings from the comrades. Number 1. 3rd of December." A positive identification of the typewriter used for the encrypted version helped to convict "Abel" but had nothing to do with his arrest.

The truth is that Willie Fisher, Soviet superspy, was caught because he was handed to U.S. officials on a plate and chose to sit there rather than slip away.

* * *

On the morning of April 26, 1957, a Friday, Fisher was busy. He checked out of a cheap hotel on Broadway where he had been staying that week under the name of Martin Collins, paid two months' advance rent on his Brooklyn studio, and told his friends on Fulton Street that he was heading south on doctor's orders for a long vacation. He blamed his sinuses. Then he returned to Manhattan to catch the Silver Meteor from Penn Station to Florida.

What was he up to? His original assignments hardly explain the trip. Preparation for the Third World War had slipped a long way down the Soviet agenda since Khrushchev's arrival in the Kremlin. And no one seriously expected a sudden breakthrough by the slow-moving Agent Mark—as Fisher was referred to by his employers—in the recruitment of a new network of nuclear informers.

It is conceivable that he was hoping to make contact with the Cuban revolutionary underground, which would seize power in Havana two years later. Or this could have been a real holiday. One of Fisher's main reasons for returning to New York after his long leave despite worsening bronchial disorders (thanks to his smoking habit) was to sort out the Hayhanen mess. That seemed to have been accomplished. The miserable Finn was at last out of his hair, two days into the Atlantic on the French liner the *Liberté.* He would pick up fresh travel papers in Paris to take him to Moscow via Czechoslovakia, and he would get whatever he deserved.

Fisher may simply have asked himself, *what now?* One thing he could do was paint, and he did pack his brushes for the journey south.

If his own time in America was coming to an end, this would make the perfect final chapter. He had started with a long trip to California, gazing out at the Pacific while counting suspected military shipments from Long Beach to nationalist China. He would finish by gazing out at the Atlantic.

He certainly made time for the views. Checking into the Plaza Hotel at Daytona Beach on April 28, he set up his easel and at some point over the next three weeks painted a large seascape that he liked enough to bring back with him to New York. That is all he ever admitted doing in Florida, and it may indeed be all he did, apart from sit and sniff. But his life to that point—his steady conscientiousness—says there is something wrong with this account; something too indolent even for the semiretired raconteur known to Burt Silverman and his friends as Emil Goldfus. And as it happens there is an alternative explanation for his long vacation. Liberated by Hayhanen's departure and energized by world events, Fisher may actually have done some spying.

The previous December a gigantic missile, seven stories tall, had been lowered into a horizontal position in a purpose-built San Diego hangar and wrapped in a white shroud. It was then loaded onto a truck and hauled 2,500 miles east. Fisher would have known this—not from his own sleuthing but from reading *Time* magazine. He devoured the press. Given how much it revealed and how little else he had to do, consuming media was a big part of his job. As Matthew Brzezinski has written in a study of the Soviet space program inspired by his time as Moscow correspondent for the *Wall Street Journal,* "For the Soviets, it was mind-boggling how much information the Americans naively left lying around for the KGB to scoop up."

*Time*'s April 1 cover story devoted eight pages to the looming triumph of ballistic missiles over bombers as the best delivery mechanism for a nuclear holocaust. The critical breakthrough had been achieved five years earlier with the fusion bomb: the blast radius of a thermonuclear warhead was so much larger than that of an old-fashioned atom bomb that missiles no longer had to be especially accurate to destroy their targets. Suddenly the weight, size, and complexity of ICBM (intercontinental ballistic missile) guidance systems looked manageable. Fuel systems were still leaking liquid oxygen and nose cones burning up on atmospheric reentry, but these were modest challenges by comparison. Once they were overcome, nowhere on earth would be more than twenty minutes from doomsday.

The *Time* story identified the missile under the shroud as the first Atlas ICBM. Its destination was the Air Force Missile Test Center at Cape Canaveral. "One day soon," the piece noted helpfully, "perhaps late in April, perhaps early in May, the Bird will make its first flight. From a sickle-shaped launching pad near a sunny vacation shore the Bird will be fired, minus its warhead, on an 1,800-mile test shot southeastward across tropic islands and into an empty sea."

Fisher also read the *New York Times.* Though ideologically bound to disdain its values, he bought it every day and demanded a subscription from his lawyer when he later found himself in an Atlanta prison. He is not likely to have missed a five-thousand-word feature by Richard Witkin on April 7, starting on page one and continuing across eight columns inside under the headline "Missiles Program Dwarfs First Atom Bomb Project—U.S. to Spend More Than 4 Billion in Developing 5 Ballistic Weapons."

The *Times* gave useful progress reports on the Atlas and the Titan, the other American ICBM, still a year from its first test. It gave detailed descriptions of the Thor and Jupiter intermediate-range missiles, which were further advanced: one of them (the Thor) had actually lifted off. On its first test launch in January, it reached an altitude of six inches before slumping back onto its launchpad and exploding. Finally, the paper mentioned the Polaris ship-borne missile, plagued by the difficulty of launching from choppy seas.

On the face of it the article was reassuring to a Russian reader. Wherever the Soviets' missile program had gotten to—and only a handful of people on the planet knew—the Americans' was not far advanced. No wonder four billion dollars had been earmarked to push it along.

But any reassurance was strictly superficial. These missiles were also space rockets. The race to produce one that could put a satellite in orbit had been all but declared in the form of challenges the superpowers had set themselves for the International Geophysical Year, a peculiar initiative based on International Polar Years of decades past, but with realpolitik lurking much closer beneath a veneer of scientific cooperation. The IGY was not actually a year—it ran from July 1957 to December 1958—and it had little to do with geophysics. It acquired a significance out of all proportion to its original aims because it provided a convenient civilian excuse to build forests of ICBM prototypes and test them to destruction. Both superpowers vowed to launch "scientific" satellites during the IGY—Russia to study solar radiation, America the atmosphere. When James Hagerty, the White House press secretary, made the announcement on Eisenhower's behalf, neither man knew how it was to be achieved—only that the National Security Council had decided that "the stake of prestige that is involved makes this a race that we cannot afford to lose."

Two years on there was still no proven launch vehicle in the American arsenal. The Russians were further along with their colossal R7, but this did not stop their chief designer, the maniacal Sergey Korolyov, from worrying himself sick that the Americans would suddenly leapfrog him into space.

Korolyov's lover—an interpreter at his design bureau—kept him supplied with translations of every published news item on the American space program. Its litany of setbacks did not convince him. His adversary, after all, was Wernher von Braun, the German rocket whiz spirited to the United States after the war, whose V-2 had been the starting point for Korolyov's lunge toward space. If von Braun could hit London with a guided missile from across the English Channel in 1944, he could surely put a basketball in space in 1957.

In fact Korolyov's suspicions were well founded. Von Braun's Redstone missile could almost certainly have won the satellite race if adapted for the purpose. But the Redstone was an army weapon. Von Braun was on the army's payroll, and Eisenhower was determined to keep the space race as far as possible a scientific affair. That way, if and when a U-2 was shot down, satellites could quite innocently take over the vitally important business of snooping on the Soviet Union.

In 1956 *National Geographic* had confidently predicted that the first man-made satellite would be launched aboard a Vanguard rocket built by the Glenn Martin Company. The *New York Times* was sticking with that story. If accurate, Korolyov still had time. The first Vanguard test was not due until December. But why the shroud over the Atlas when so much about the American missile program was so open? Was "the Bird" about to lay an egg in orbit, winning the space race in the process? It was a vastly more urgent question for Moscow than whatever Castro and his friends were up to, and it is hard to imagine the subject did not come up in the encrypted cables received by Willie Fisher's shortwave radio.

On the separate but still vexing subject of Soviet security, the *Times* noted that the pace of production of the Thor intermediate-range ballistic missile (IRBM) (range 1,500 miles, designed specifically to hit Russian targets from Britain) was picking up. "Getting the Thor to the firing range at Cape Canaveral is simpler than transporting the ICBMs," the obliging Witkin wrote. "The intermediate range weapon can be accommodated in an Air Force C-125 Globemaster."

It was a good thing Fisher had packed his brushes. There would be plenty for a painter to look out for.

On April 19 a Thor took off from the Cape and flew for thirty-five seconds in the wrong direction before being destroyed from the ground.

In case Fisher was not already packing, his morning read on April 21 announced construction of "a huge platform able to subject intermediate range ballistic missiles to the same motions they would encounter in launching on heavy seas." It ran under a boys' own artist's impression of a Thor atop a terrifying four-legged machine in a hardened silo ten times the height of a man. Location: Cape Canaveral.

On the twenty-fourth the Associated Press reported that a Lockheed X-17 missile launched from the Cape had attained a top speed of 9,240 miles per hour on its return to earth. The flight ended in a splash, but Fisher would have known its significance: to test their tolerance to intense heat, the air force was experimenting with missile nose cones at speeds close to those achieved by ICBMs on reentry.

No self-respecting Soviet spy could read all this and stay in Brooklyn strumming his guitar. The Cape would not be formally unveiled as America's gateway to space until December, but missile-themed motels were already springing up nearby. Restaurants were holding beach parties timed so customers could toast the bright glow of rocket engines hurtling into the night. It would not be hard for a man in a straw hat to blend in.

Two days after the X-17 flight, yet another rocket shook the bungalows along Cocoa Beach, this time in the presence of Defense Secretary Charles E. Wilson. And Willie Fisher headed for the sun.

If he wanted to meet Cubans he would have stayed on the Silver Meteor all the way to Miami. Instead he stepped off the train 250 miles north of there, a short bus ride from the natural grandstand that the Space Coast's beaches provided for the greatest technological show on earth. In a sense, he would have company. The day before Fisher's departure from New York, Senator Styles Bridges, Republican from New Hampshire and a member of the Armed Services Committee, told an American Legion luncheon that "about a dozen" Soviet submarines were thought to be lingering in the shallow waters between Cape Canaveral and the Bahamas. "The story is not substantiated," Styles admitted, "but we do know that the Russians spare no effort to learn what we are doing."

***

Fisher's KGB file has never been opened to scholars. The theory that in April 1957 he bestirred himself to go and squint into the sun at space rockets is based on what he read, where he went, and when. It explains an otherwise baffling trip—though no more baffling than what happened to him next.

Burt Silverman has probably gotten as close to the truth about Fisher's capture as anyone. "Throughout the course of the time that I knew him, there was a sense about him that was genuine," he says. "Even in his exposure there was something kind of like, 'Oh, I fucked up.'"

Allen Dulles took Fisher and people like him much more seriously, not least because his agency depended on spies being taken seriously. "I have the impression that the Soviet intelligence officer represents the species homo Sovieticus in its unalloyed and most successful form," he wrote in *The Craft of Intelligence,* a work of occasional insight and considerable pomposity. "It is as if the Soviet intelligence officer were a kind of final and extreme product of the Soviet system.... He is blindly and unquestioningly dedicated to the cause, at least at the outset. He has been fully indoctrinated in the political and philosophical beliefs of Communism." He is constantly subject to a rigid discipline, Dulles continued (forgetting about Hayhanen). "On the one hand he belongs to an elite and has privilege and power of a very special kind.... On the other hand, neither rank nor seniority nor past achievement will protect him if he makes a mistake."

Dulles never knew how ineffectual Fisher really was. He once said: "I wish we had three or four like him in Moscow." The FBI was similarly in awe of him just from Hayhanen's description. It was not expecting mistakes. By the time Fisher finally returned from Florida and switched on the light in his studio, thirty agents were on his case. One of them, Neil Heiner, was across the street on the twelfth floor of the Hotel Touraine, wide awake.

Heiner timed Fisher's arrival at 10:45 p.m. He watched him for more than an hour. "One light was turned on in the studio," he testified. "I could see a male figure moving around in the room. From time to time it would pass in back of this light." Heiner described the man as middle-aged and bald headed. "He had a fringe of gray hair around the edges. He was wearing glasses." At a minute to midnight he put on a dark straw hat with a bright white band and switched off the light. Heiner got on the radio to say so. At 12:02 a man in the same hat exited 252

Fulton Street and turned right. Agent Joe MacDonald was waiting in shadows in a small park opposite. He followed, up Clinton Street and down into the Borough Hall subway station.

It was a Thursday night, technically Friday. There was a small crowd at one end of the platform heading back into Manhattan. Fisher and MacDonald joined it, but as the train pulled in Fisher moved away and stepped into the second-to-last car. MacDonald watched him from the last car. They both got out at City Hall and walked up to street level, where Fisher caught a bus north on Broadway to Twenty-seventh Street. MacDonald followed in a taxi, but when Fisher got off the bus and started walking, MacDonald lost him.

That was the FBI's first good look at Fisher. It should have been their last. Three weeks had passed since Hayhanen's defection. Even allowing for the very real possibility of his falling down drunk or succumbing to the temptations of the Place Pigalle, he should long since have reached Berlin, crossed to the Soviet sector, and reported to the KGB's European headquarters in Lichtenberg. When he failed to show, an alarm did sound. According to KGB documents seen by Vasili Mitrokhin, the KGB defector, Moscow assumed the worst and recalled Fisher in late May or early June. Mitrokhin claimed Fisher simply disobeyed his orders, but escape was complicated. If there was a danger that he had been compromised as "Mark," there was a danger that his other covers had been blown as well. He could not risk leaving the country as Martin Collins, Emil Goldfus, or even that long-forgotten Lithuanian Andrew Kayotis. The Center—the KGB's Moscow headquarters—staggered into action. With the help of the Canadian Communist Party and the KGB's Ottawa resident, it set about procuring two new passports for Fisher in the names of Robert Callan and Vasili Dzogol. But the process would take time. Fisher would have to wait.

There are other theories. According to one, Fisher allowed himself to be caught to test the loyalty of the notorious Alexander Orlov, the grand thief of Spain's gold reserves and blackmailer of Stalin. Having defected in 1938, Orlov was by now living in Michigan, the only person in the United States who knew Fisher's true identity. If Fisher was arrested and his picture appeared in newspapers, Orlov would see it and have the chance to reveal all. If he took that chance, his treachery would be complete. If not, the Center would know that deep in his soul he had kept the faith. So goes the theory. It is exquisitely convoluted and presupposes a KGB high command obsessed with personalities and the past, and to that extent is plausible. But it also assumes Moscow was willing to sacrifice Fisher for a largely pointless piece of closure, and it ignores the evidence that he was in fact recalled.

Another theory holds that Fisher dithered in New York because of money—not his, but money stashed in his names in safe-deposit boxes and savings accounts across the city, earmarked to pay off KGB informers. But there is no evidence that he had any informers, nor that he made much effort to distribute the money. It has been suggested that among the lucky intended beneficiaries were Morris Cohen and Kim Philby. Both were Soviet spies who spent time on the East Coast, but both had been gone more than five years—Cohen to London, Philby via London to Beirut.

There is no doubt that Fisher knew he had to flee. On May 21, three days after his return from Florida, he visited the office of a Dr. Samuel Groopman in his hotel (the Latham, on Twenty-eighth and Fifth) for a smallpox vaccination. If he was planning to stay in New York he would not have needed one—the last known case of smallpox in the United States was in 1949. Fisher was ready to go, presumably via somewhere where smallpox was endemic. He was just waiting for his passport.

The FBI was waiting too. Having lost him somewhere between Broadway and Fifth Avenue, it had no choice.

The stakeout remained at the Hotel Touraine in Brooklyn: studio 505 in the Ovington building across the street was still the only address the bureau had for "Mark." On May 28 agents saw a man resembling him in the park where Agent MacDonald had hidden ten days earlier. The man looked nervous, the agents said. He got up from time to time and walked around as if looking for someone, and left on foot at 6:50 p.m., unfollowed.

For two more weeks, Fisher waited. While the CIA flew spy planes into Russia at seventy thousand feet, the KGB tried to get a passport to a hotel in Manhattan. It never came.

Fisher's eighth-floor room at the Latham cost twenty-eight dollars a week. It had a west-facing bathroom window out of which he had hung an extended antenna for his shortwave radio. He had one-time pads, or cipher keys, for decoding incoming messages from Moscow and an impressive supply of hollowed-out bolts and pencils for sending his replies via dead drops. But eventually he ran out of something or decided that his rented premises across the East River needed tidying up or just got sick of sitting in his room. Even though he almost certainly knew that he had been followed from Brooklyn after his last visit and that the studio would still be under surveillance, he went back there.

"The Agents' long hours of patience were rewarded on the night of June 13, 1957," the FBI's account states. Agent Heiner was once again the man in the Touraine. MacDonald had either pulled another shift or been taken off the case. The entrance to 252 Fulton Street was being watched by Agent Ronald Carlson, not from the park but from a post office building next to it that also housed the courtroom in which Fisher would be tried.

The light in the studio went on at 10:00 p.m. and off at 11:52. Wearing the same hat that MacDonald had followed, and a light sport coat, Fisher appeared on Fulton Street a few minutes before midnight and headed for the subway. Carlson followed. This time Fisher made it easy. He stayed on the subway to the Twenty-eighth Street station and led Carlson straight to the hotel.

The FBI set up a second stakeout and continued waiting. Fisher gave them no trouble. He stayed at the Latham except for occasional walks in the straw hat. It was Hayhanen who was causing problems. He wanted asylum, not infamy, but his protectors were insisting that he testify against the man they now were calling Collins (the name Fisher had given the hotel). Hayhanen refused. They moved him from Manhattan back to Peekskill and his bewildered wife, but still he refused.

Even with Hayhanen's cooperation there was no guarantee of an espionage conviction against Fisher. Without it there was no hope of one. A piece of microfilm found in the Peekskill cottage had led the FBI to the only other potential witness in the case, a former motor sergeant at the U.S. embassy in Moscow named Roy Rhodes. Rhodes was the real deal: a traitor of the most villainous kind who had sold out his country after stumbling into a honey trap and waking up with an attractive young lady from the KGB. Cash payments had followed in one direction; manila envelopes stuffed with secret information about the movements of junior embassy staff in the other. The court record would confirm all this in shameful detail. The trouble from a prosecutor's point of view was that there was nothing to link Rhodes to Fisher, except Hayhanen.

The U.S. Attorney's office in Washington sent two lawyers up to talk some sense into the drunken Hayhanen. They spent all of June 18 and 19 with him and got nowhere; he was frightened for his mother and siblings, as he had been for himself in Paris. U.S. Attorney William F. Tompkins decided there was only one way to proceed. They had brought in Al Capone as a tax evader. They would bring in Martin Collins as an illegal alien.

It was a legalistic trick, but it seemed justified. These were not gentle times. Collins or Goldfus or whoever he was would remain innocent until proven guilty since that was the American way, but in the meantime it was the task of Tompkins and the FBI, despite the lack of any concrete evidence, to take very seriously the idea that this stooping, birdlike figure with the hat band was stealing America's thermonuclear secrets and sabotaging her rockets. Lord knew, someone seemed to be. Atmospheric sampling by U-2s over Alaska and the Aleutians showed that the Soviets were letting off bigger and bigger H-bombs at the rate of nearly one a week. And everyone knew how badly things were going down at the Cape. Less than a week after Fisher's return from Daytona Beach, the next Thor test ended almost before it had begun in yet another launchpad fireball, "lighting up the [predawn] countryside like day and sending a thunderous roar along the beaches." And the mighty Atlas, trucked from San Diego, with its hundred tons of fuel and its 360,000 pounds of thrust? It blasted off on June 11 and blew up at five thousand feet. "The whole show lasted no more than a minute," someone told one of the dozens of reporters who raced to the scene.

Late on June 20, five men met in the offices of the Immigration and Naturalization Service on New York's Columbus Avenue. Three were local. Two had flown up from Washington. After midnight they made their way to the downtown FBI field office and spent two hours rehearsing the operation planned for later that morning.

It was a sweltering night at the end of a weeklong heat wave. There was no relief from the ocean because what breeze there was came from inland, and no air-conditioning for Fisher at the Latham. It was not that sort of hotel. He slept with nothing on—if he slept at all. The stakeout had closed in on him. It was now more like a siege: eight FBI men on the eighth floor taking turns watching the corridor and listening from room 841, immediately next door to Fisher's.

Shortly before seven in the morning the INS men arrived at the hotel. Their instructions were to wait in room 841 until asked for. The FBI would open proceedings.

At 7:00 a.m. Agent Ed Gamber knocked on the door of room 839 and asked for Mr. Collins. Fisher woke and answered as he was. He was not even wearing his false teeth. He made no attempt to resist or run. After answering a few basic questions about himself (as Martin Collins), he fell silent. Gamber watched him sitting naked on a double bed that nearly filled the room and noticed his Adam's apple rising and falling involuntarily in his throat.

# 6

# AMERICAN JUSTICE

In his treatise on "homo Sovieticus," Allen Dulles wrote: "Since the ingrained Soviet approach to the problems of life and politics is conspiratorial, it is no surprise that this approach finds its ultimate fulfillment in intelligence work. When such a man does finally see the light, as has happened, his disillusionment is overwhelming."

Fisher's moment to be overwhelmed came that morning on that bed. *Nine years.* He had spent nine years in this country, pushing his own identity to the very back of his mind and impersonating the unreal people created for him by Moscow Center so perfectly that no one had even heard him whisper his wife's name in his sleep. His wife, a harpist in a children's orchestra in Moscow, had grown used to the life of a single mother. His daughter, a teenager when he left her, had grown up and married. He had followed orders. He had traveled the length and breadth of the Main Adversary trying to revive the spy networks of the war years. He had failed, but this was hardly his fault and he had not been blamed. His tradecraft had been masterly—not a single dead drop discovered or cable intercepted on his watch—and his cover was as deep and unquestioned as any in the history of the illegals. He was a war hero, a devoted Communist, and a colonel in the KGB. He had been inducted, like Stalin and Zhukov before him, into the Order of the Red Banner. And then he had been sent Reino Hayhanen, who had imploded and betrayed him. For want of a fake passport he had been left to wait for this moment in a cheap New York hotel room, where his only options were to keep the faith and pay the price or to implode himself.

"Colonel, we have received information concerning your involvement in espionage," Agent Gamber said.

Fisher kept the faith. Gamber's use of "colonel" confirmed that his information came from Hayhanen, since no one else outside Russia knew Fisher's rank. But he was not about to join the wretched Vik—Hayhanen—in that special circle of hell reserved for traitors. He would admit nothing, reveal nothing, volunteer nothing. That was the Chekist way, and Fisher understood it perfectly.

He would be arrested if he did not cooperate, Gamber said. Fisher, now in underpants, just sat there. It looked passive but it was the biggest, most inspired decision of his life. From that moment the legend of the master spy began to grow; he had found his calling as a stonewall.

It was not, in fact, a difficult decision. Part of Fisher's reasoning was that this whole embarrassing mess might be part of a plan to turn the otherwise inexplicable Hayhanen into a double agent. Despite everything, he still trusted his employers: when his lawyer suggested later that Russia had written him off, he snapped back that he did not believe it and resented the idea. Being written off and being sacrificed for the cause were very different things.

But there was also Fisher's family and his self-respect. "Cooperation" with the FBI was the one way to guarantee he never saw his wife and daughter again. If he kept his counsel there was always the chance, however slight, of being traded in years to come for someone the Americans wanted back. If he kept his counsel, furthermore, no one need know that he had almost nothing to reveal. And what they didn't know they could only imagine.

After twenty-three minutes of staring at Willie Fisher and his Adam's apple and getting nothing out of him, Agent Gamber and another agent conferred sotto voce in the corner. They asked the INS men to come in and make the arrest, and it was done. The Kremlin's most secret weapon had been detained under section 242 of the Immigration and Nationality Act. From where Fisher sat things looked so bad that they could only get better, and that is exactly how they turned out.

He outwitted the INS men almost as soon as they had arrested him, or so he claimed years later in an interview with *Moskovskyi Komsomolets* newspaper in Moscow. Remembering he had left a potentially incriminating sheet of paper from a onetime code pad on a table under the window, he asked if he could tidy up some paints and other artist's materials above it on the windowsill. They said he could, so he calmly wiped his palette clean with the sheet of paper, then flushed it down the lavatory. With it went his last message from Moscow.

He was told to dress and pay his bill and then was taken to the INS office to be booked, photographed, and questioned some more. He looked pissed off but rakish in his mug shot, like an angry reporter.

For seven hours, as the heat wave finally broke outside, he was given reasons and opportunities to cooperate. For seven hours he turned them down, which meant his status did not change. Improvised categories of detainee, such as "enemy combatant," were for the future. Fisher was a suspected illegal alien and subject to well-established procedures. As night fell, he was driven across the Hudson and put on a waiting DC-3 that took off with only him and two INS officers aboard and headed south by southwest.

Fisher wanted to know where he was being taken, but no one would tell him, so he worked it out. He kept an eye on the stars and made estimates of his time and speed in the air. When the plane stopped to refuel at 11:00 p.m. he said, "We're in Alabama," and he was right. They flew on across the Gulf of Mexico to Brownsville, Texas, then drove in darkness to McAllen, ten miles from the Rio Grande.

On leaving New York, Fisher disappeared from all official records for five days. Was this rendition? His lawyer tried to make something of it at his trial, but the judge was unimpressed. Fisher was hit in the face once while being questioned in McAllen but was never blindfolded, drugged, or tortured. That, too, was for the future. The truth was that the INS was going by the book: McAllen was the site of the Federal Alien Detention Facility, and Fisher was held there for six weeks.

In that time his hopes rose briefly when he realized that most of his fellow inmates were being deported to Mexico. To Mexico! The last refuge of Trotsky was the first choice of escape route for any Soviet spy in trouble in America. If Fisher could only get out of solitary he could practically swim there.

He reached McAllen on a Saturday and was questioned in relays over the weekend by the INS men who had flown out with him, and by Gamber and Special Agent Paul Blasco of the FBI, who followed. He gave them nothing. But then, on Monday morning, he was handed a leaflet setting out the rights of an illegal alien, which included a prompt deportation hearing. Fisher changed tactics; he told a story.

"I decided to state that my real name was Rudolf Ivanovich Abel," he wrote in an affidavit, "that I was a Russian citizen; that I had found a large sum of American money in a ruined blockhouse in Russia; that I then bought in Denmark a forged American passport and with this passport I entered the United States from Canada in 1948."

Two days later he had his hearing and retold his story. No one believed it. The name stuck but nothing else did, because by this time the FBI had found in Fisher's New York hotel room four thousand dollars in twenties wrapped in brown paper; a hollow ebony block containing a 250-page Russian codebook; a hollow pencil full of encrypted messages on microfilm; and the key to a safe-deposit box crammed with another fifteen thousand dollars in cash. They had also taken two slips of paper that Fisher had tried to hide up his jacket sleeve before being led away. On each were directions to meetings in Mexico City, the first of which would have been outside a screening of a film called *Balmora* at a cinema on Avenida Oberón and would have started with a script:

> I: Is this an interesting picture?
> L: Yes. Do you wish to see it, Mr. Brandt?
> (L smokes a pipe and has a red book in left hand.)

The blockhouse story might explain the money, but not the directions or the microfilm. Fisher was denied deportation. For another month Blasco and Gamber tried to turn him. They offered better food and hard liquor for his cooperation, then a hotel room, air-conditioning, and a ten-thousand-dollar-a-year government job. Nothing worked. The master spy was courteous and patient but as forthcoming as a sphinx. "You had to admire him," Gamber said.

No one much admired Hayhanen—even when he changed his mind. Sometime in the first week of August he agreed to testify against his boss. In Washington, Assistant U.S. Attorney William Tompkins turned on a dime and had his high-priority alleged illegal alien turned into an even higher-priority alleged spy. On August 7 Fisher was flown back to New York to answer the indictment. This time the press was there to meet him, and the man calling himself Rudolf Abel looked straight into their cameras.

* * *

Burt Silverman—artist, illustrator, ex–National Serviceman, and left-leaning Brooklyn liberal—was going to Rome. He was going elsewhere in Europe too, but Rome would be the start and finish of a grand tour in the old style for the old reasons, because the Old World begat the New and still had something to impart to the inquiring soul.

The trip would also be, among other things, a honeymoon. On March 27 Silverman had married Helen Worthman, the longtime girlfriend with whom "Emil" had found him half naked on a divan in Silverman's studio three years earlier when asking for a cup of turpentine. Emil had been among the guests at a cocktail party at the Hotel Bolivar on Central Park West before the ceremony and had been the last to leave. It was a Jewish wedding. The men were required to wear yarmulkes and the groom said afterward that Fisher looked "like a Hassidic buck on feast day."

Since then he had been away a lot. There had been the extended sinus cure in Florida. Then he had scarcely shown his face at the Ovington building before disappearing again. During the second absence Silverman and several of his friends were visited by agents of the FBI. Dave Levine, another painter, received a letter from Emil dated July 24, asking him to "help me in the disposal of whatever remains of mine in 252 Fulton Street." The letter was shot through with vintage Emil mystery making, but it left little doubt that he was in trouble. "I have no specific desires except that you go through my paintings and preserve those you think worth keeping until—if ever—I may be able to get them again." There was no explanation for the return address—a firm of lawyers in McAllen, Texas.

As for Silverman, the Bureau caught up with him one sweltering July evening as he returned home from a day's work in Manhattan at the *New York Post*. There were two agents, as ever. They gave him the choice of talking in his studio or their car. He chose the car and found himself in the middle of the backseat with no quick exit, answering questions about Goldfus and a mysterious coconspirator ("Did you ever see a fat man who fell asleep while he was talking?") and asking some of his own. He got no satisfactory answers. The agents would only say it was a matter of "the highest national security." Silverman's first thought was that the FBI was using Emil to get to someone else. The McCarthy madness had peaked, but several of his friends were members of the Communist Party—if only for the pizza—and the House Un-American Activities Committee was still in vigorous session. It did not enter his mind that Emil might himself be the national security concern. In the business of covering his tracks, faint as they were, Fisher was that good.

Silverman had not traveled abroad since leaving the army. To go to Rome, he and Helen needed passports, which is why he was in Manhattan again on August 8, passing a newsstand and realizing in a flash that something strange and disorientating had happened.

"I saw his face on the front page of the *New York Times*," he says. "I recognized it instantly. I'd drawn him and painted him many times, hours and hours. His features were so very striking and clear-cut. I didn't buy the paper—didn't even read the headline. I said, 'Why is Emil in the news?'"

Silverman telephoned his wife, who went out and bought a copy. And there was Emil for their scrapbook, torn from their amusing private world of painting and pontificating and rendered in grainy black and white under the headline "Russian Colonel Is Indicted Here as Top Spy in U.S." He wore a dark jacket, a white shirt buttoned to the neck with no tie, and his familiar heavy spectacles. His eyes behind them were anxious, the eyebrows curling up toward the center of his forehead.

Mildred Murphy of the *New York Times* disagreed with Silverman about Fisher's appearance. She called him (paragraph one, line one) "An ordinary looking little man," whose ordinariness was the more extraordinary for his indictment "as the most important Soviet spy ever caught in the United States."

She did not question his identity or provenance: "He is Rudolf Ivanovich Abel, a 55-year-old, Moscow-born citizen of the Soviet Union." She did qualify as an assertion William Tompkins's lie that "Abel" had been under investigation for a year, but she quoted him without comment on what Abel was supposed to represent—"as professional and intricate an operation as we have ever worked on." The master spy legend was now received wisdom, the starting point for whatever was to follow.

Silverman rode the subway home in a daze that in a sense has yet to lift. Here was an answer to the Emil question, but it was other people's answer; an answer announced by people who didn't even know him. "The disconnect between public and private was wrenching," he says, half a lifetime later. "In fact, I still view this as a story somebody made up about my life, a chapter which is totally untrue."

* * *

The made-up stories were, of course, all Fisher's. His latest—the one he told his interrogators about having found a stash of money in a blockhouse in Russia—was intended partly as a signal to Moscow that even though he had been caught, he was revealing nothing. It had also given the Soviet embassy in Washington a chance to recognize him as an errant Soviet citizen and request his deportation. That chance had not been taken. His fate as an illegal was to be disowned when things went wrong, and when they did, he was.

He needed a change in his luck, or at least a decent lawyer. The wheels of American justice turned to find him one.

The call came through to Jim Donovan at his summer cottage in the Adirondacks two weeks after the indictment. It was placed by a colleague but instigated by the Brooklyn Bar Association, whose job it was to ensure that everyone indicted in the borough had an adequate defense. The association was used to finding lawyers for the Mafia, less used to finding them for spies. But the chairman of its selection committee was a neighbor of Donovan's on Prospect Park West and knew his background. The choice seemed obvious.

James Britt Donovan was an oaken pillar of Brooklyn society and the New York legal establishment. Tall and heavyset, he had the face of a man who boxed in college but had the sense to leave it there. His first degree was from Fordham University, where his classmates voted him "best all-round man." When he graduated he wanted to work in newspapers, so he asked his father, a wealthy Irish-American surgeon, to buy him one. His father agreed on condition that he acquire a law degree first, so Harvard Law School followed. Donovan's dream of moguldom was wrecked by the war, in which he served as general counsel for the Office of Strategic Services (OSS), precursor to the CIA. In 1946 he assisted in the prosecution of Göring and Hess at Nuremberg, showing the court harrowing footage of the liberated concentration camps. As a result he had much in common with the man he was being asked to represent. They had both been spies on the right side in the fight against Fascism. And then they had both gravitated to Brooklyn, "Abel" apparently to sabotage capitalism, Donovan to uphold it. (He prospered mightily in private practice and had spent most of 1957 defending a life insurance company against claims by the Polish government.)

He could have turned the Abel case down. His wife and four children doubtless wished he had, and the golf pro at his club near Lake Placid believed he should have.

"Why in hell would anyone want to defend that no-good bum?" the pro demanded as his client tried simultaneously to ponder the request and work on his swing. Donovan reminded him that under the U.S. Constitution "every man, however despised, is entitled to counsel and a fair trial."

Donovan enjoyed belonging. There was the golf club, the Montauk Club with its self-consciously palatial premises in Brooklyn's Park Slope, the Brooklyn Museum (he was a governor), the New York City Art Commission (he was a member), and the Rembrandt Club, "one of Brooklyn's oldest societies," whose all-male membership met monthly in one another's homes for cultural lectures followed by a champagne supper. It was black tie, he noted, "and most enjoyable in a reserved way."

The all-round man from Fordham and Harvard comported himself at times as if afflicted by a ramrod in a painful place, but appearances could be deceptive. He was a workaholic whose idea of a good breakfast after working through the night was black coffee, ice water, and a cigarette. He was a fearless negotiator who later freed nearly ten thousand Cubans and Americans from Havana, clearing up the mess left there by the Bay of Pigs adventure. For all his loyalty to Brooklyn, his experience in Europe during and after the war had made of him a true citizen of the world. He was not blind to Fisher's merits because of ideology. In fact, he became a devoted admirer, ignoring the torrent of abuse that came with defending what one senior judge called the least popular legal cause since that of Captain Preston in the Boston Massacre of 1770. Donovan had a high opinion of himself, but he had an even higher opinion of the law. As he told the prosecution in a pretrial conference: "We want all other countries to recognize that there is no higher justice than that found in American courts."

After his round of golf, Donovan drove to the village of Lake Placid and borrowed a local lawyer's library. Reading through the espionage statutes he found that since the Rosenberg case, spying on behalf of a foreign power had become a capital offense even in peacetime. Abel might have hoped for deportation, but he was looking at the electric chair.

Donovan had supper with his wife, then caught a night train to New York. "I sat alone in the club car, nursing a Scotch," he wrote in his journal. "Before the train reached Utica, about one o'clock in the morning, I decided to undertake the defense of Colonel Abel."

* * *

For the FBI it was no great honor to have unknowingly hosted a KGB colonel for nine years. Nor did it help, from a public relations point of view, that without Hayhanen he would never have been caught.

The Bureau set about looking busy. Evidence was minutely inspected, leads chased down, potential witnesses located and interviewed. The contents of Fisher's room at the Hotel Latham and his studio and storeroom were laid out on twenty-five large trestle tables in the FBI field office in Manhattan. They included a hollow-handled shaving brush, a complete set of cipher tables on edible silver foil, a lathe, three pairs of reading glasses, an Aladdin's cave of specialist photographic equipment, a small library including *The Ribald Reader* and a volume on thermonuclear weapons, dozens of Sucrets throat lozenge boxes, and a half-empty box of Sheik brand condoms. (It is a mystery whom, if anyone, Fisher was having sex with. When walking with one of Burt Silverman's friends he was once startled to be greeted by a woman whom he pretended not to know, but he was never seen inviting anyone up to his studio or propositioning the models who occasionally took their clothes off for life classes in the Ovington building, much as he might have liked to. He may of course have paid for the services of professionals elsewhere, but none came forward when he was unmasked. Or he may have been as monastic as he seemed and used the condoms to keep cash dry in Hayhanen's dead drops.)

Agents tracked down everyone whom Hayhanen identified and many whom he didn't. They went to Colorado and Atlantic City. They quizzed the superintendent of the Ovington building and Mrs. Donnelly and Mrs. Ash of the Vanderveer Estates, who had once passed a hollow nickel to an unsuspecting newsboy. And they put a tail on the newsboy.

In the four years the hollow nickel had lain undeciphered, James Bozart had grown up. By the summer of 1957 he was still a freckled redhead, but he was seventeen and going places. Having graduated high school in Brooklyn, he had won a place at the Rensselaer Polytechnic Institute in Troy, New York, to study engineering. He would come home on weekends, returning on the Monday milk train to Albany, from where he caught a bus to Troy. The train left Grand Central at one in the morning and arrived at six, and he often had a carriage to himself.

One Friday soon after starting at Rensselaer he came home to find two reporters from the *Daily News* waiting to ask him about the hollow nickel and a Russian spy. He told them what he could about the coin; couldn't help them with the spy. The next Monday morning he woke up pulling into Albany to find that he had company—another night owl dozing in a corner seat and hoping not to miss his stop. They both got off at Albany; both took the bus to Troy.

"I didn't think anything of it," Bozart says. "But this happened twice, and the second time the train was delayed and I missed the bus. Class was at nine thirty. I was distressed. So the guy from the train comes up and asks if everything's OK. 'I'm here to make sure nothing happens to you,' he says. He shows his badge, calls Albany Police Department, and I go to class in a police car."

The next Friday the same man was on the train back to New York, and the following morning he was in a car outside the Bozarts' front door on Avenue D in Brooklyn. With an FBI tail *and* a place at the third-best engineering school in the country, it was hard to see how life could get much better. Bozart met up with friends to go to Lynbrook on Long Island and told them about the Fed with the badge. "'Let's lose him,' we said, and we lost him down on the waterfront. But he was waiting when I got home."

Assistant U.S. Attorney William Tompkins had decided that Jimmy Bozart was a vital witness in the biggest case of his career and didn't want to lose him playing cat and mouse on the Long Island Railroad. Bozart was subpoenaed and ordered not to leave the city while waiting his turn in the witness box. "I sat and waited for a month," Bozart recalls. "The court arranged a tutorial at Brooklyn Polytechnic, where I ended up staying." His place at Rensselaer went to someone else.

* * *

Burt and Helen Silverman sailed for Europe on August 12. Considering Burt's closeness to the top-ranking Soviet spy in North America, he had not been too seriously disturbed. He took a call from a *New York Times* reporter wanting to confirm that "Abel" had attended their wedding, and the FBI paid him a second visit, this time to pick up a Remington portable typewriter that he had borrowed from their suspect. Otherwise, nothing.

The newlyweds were anxious not to have their Grand Tour interrupted. It would last three and a half months, they told the Bureau. They had a rough idea where they were going but not many hotel reservations. "OK," said the agent who picked up the Remington. "Have a good trip."

They had been gone six weeks when someone stuck a needle in a tire on their rental car. It made for a less-than-triumphal entry into Rome: they realized they had a flat as they were driving past the Forum. As Burt tried to bolt on a spare wheel, Helen's shoulder bag was snatched from the passenger seat by a thief on a Vespa, and with it went both their passports and their money. Had they dodged the needle their tour might have continued more or less as planned, and the trial of Rudolf Abel might have turned out very differently. Instead, the Silvermans were forced to turn to officialdom for help.

"We had to go to the consulate to get new passports and a loan of money and everything else," Burt remembers. "We were feeling kind of shitty."

Two days later a visitor from the consulate asked for them at their hotel. Burt got ready to be impressed by the State Department's speed at reissuing lost passports. "And this guy comes in and says, no, I'm a special attaché from the U.S. Justice Department and I've been trying to find you for three weeks."

It must have been a congenial three weeks. The long arm of the U.S. Attorney's Office had followed the Silvermans east along the Côte d'Azur from Nice to Monaco and thence to Venice, Florence, and now Rome, where its representative had spent four days scouring hotels without thinking to check the register at the American Express office. Had he done so he would have located the by-now-unhappy couple instantly, since they were hoping to meet up with friends and, as an irritated Helen pointed out, had put "a huge star by our names."

The attaché gave a vague warning that Burt might be required at the unfolding Abel trial and left. He phoned back at two o'clock the next Saturday morning. Passport or no passport, Silverman was booked on the next day's plane to New York to await the court's instructions.

"Suppose I don't go?" Silverman said.

"We'll get a warrant. We'll arrest you."

The honeymoon was over.

* * *

As the Silvermans lay fretting in their bedroom in Rome, the world was changing around them at eighteen thousand miles an hour. Earlier that night, a Soviet R7 rocket shortened to reduce weight and maximize velocity had wrapped itself in curtains of white flame as it left the secret launchpad deep in Kazakhstan, from where the chief designer, Sergey Korolyov, had vowed to win the race to orbit at whatever cost.

The R7 was a fat and brutal thing, a giant cone of liquid oxygen and kerosene feeding five main rocket engines and twelve more directional thrusters. At blastoff, temperamental turbo pumps rammed fuel into the engines at a rate of nearly half a ton per second *per engine.* With the liquid oxygen cooled to below –183 degrees Celsius, pumps and fuel lines could freeze solid in an instant if not purged first with pressurized nitrogen. For a machine designed above all to be functional, there was an awful lot about it that could go wrong.

Eight seconds into its flight, still only one thousand feet above the steppe, the rocket's telemetry reported a fault in one of its four forty-two-ton boosters. For nearly two minutes Korolyov and his exhausted team watched the readouts and the night sky in silence. Four of their last six test launches had ended in disaster, and the misfiring booster could destroy the rocket at any moment.

It didn't. The first downrange tracking stations, clusters of parabolic dishes pointing skyward from beside the old imperial road to Samarqand, reported climb rates and acceleration that were within Korolyov's margins of error. At 315.3 seconds, 250 miles above Siberia, the rocket's nose cone opened and a polished aluminum sphere popped out.

By the time the Silvermans took their unwelcome call from the Justice Department's special attaché, *Sputnik* was on its sixth orbit of planet Earth. Korolyov had waited one full orbit before telephoning Khrushchev and another before informing the rest of the Politburo. But by 2:00 a.m. Rome time—8:00 p.m. in Washington—the Soviet triumph was public and official and its implications were coursing like adrenaline through every newsroom in the world. The official Soviet news service broadcast details of the satellite's wild, dancelike trajectory, which lurched from just 150 miles up to more than 500. Television networks plotted *Sputnik*'s course across the Northern Hemisphere, and viewers in their millions ran outside to scan the western horizon for a fast-moving silver dot.

Eisenhower feigned unconcern. He did not convene a meeting to discuss *Sputnik* until three days after its launch, and he waited yet another day before taking questions on it from the press. He acknowledged that the Russians had achieved "a very powerful thrust in their rocketry" but insisted that from a security point of view the satellite "does not raise my apprehensions."

The trouble was, it raised everybody else's. Lyndon B. Johnson said that when he looked up he saw a sky that suddenly "seemed almost alien." He demanded an all-out drive to build a rocket with a million pounds of thrust. Senator Stuart Symington seized on *Sputnik* to launch the argument that the Soviets had opened up a missile gap far scarier than any bomber gap before it. Symington was not above grandstanding, but he understood perfectly that *Sputnik* was, as NASA's administrator put it half a century later, "an almost unimaginable embarrassment for the United States."

Everyone who read the papers knew that behind the Missouri senator's scaremongering lay one brute fact: the rocket that launched *Sputnik* was essentially a missile. In fact, the stage-two booster that nestled at the core of the R7 and carried its payload chased *Sputnik* through space for several weeks. It did not beep, but it was there, the original mother ship, ninety-six feet long and traveling ninety seconds behind its progeny at twenty-three times the speed of sound. (For anyone who doubted this, the British astrophysicist Sir Bernard Lovell performed a trick. With a team of assistants from Manchester University he worked nonstop for forty-eight hours to turn the 250-foot Jodrell Bank radio telescope—then the world's largest—into a radar scanner. He pointed it at the heavens and captured the carrier rocket's echo as a long line on a cathode-ray tube as it hurtled over the English Lake District.)

By way of damage control Eisenhower claimed that if he had allowed Wernher von Braun to put a satellite in one of the U.S. Army's Redstone missiles the United States could have won the race to space. This was probably true. But it was a big "if," and anyway the coulda-shoulda style of argument somehow didn't suit the former supreme commander of the Allied forces in World War II. Ike also considered revealing that, unlike the Soviet Union, the United States could spy on its adversary with impunity from high-altitude reconnaissance planes. He rejected the idea.

The fact was that even the U-2s had failed to alert Washington to Korolyov's masterstroke. One of them had flown over the Tyuratam launch site during a period of intense preparations in late August, but *Sputnik*'s launch still came as a complete surprise.

* * *

Once the FBI had established Fisher's status as an alleged spy rather than an illegal immigrant, they moved him back to Brooklyn. It was there that he first met James Donovan. He looked his lawyer in the eye and said: "I guess they caught me with my pants down." That was how much of the American public felt at the start of Fisher's trial, and *Sputnik* was a big part of the reason. With satellites beeping down on them and KGB colonels living quietly among them, prospective jurors in the trial could be forgiven for recasting Big Brother in their minds. He was suddenly much more than a distant oppressor and manic builder of H-bombs. He was an infiltrator, closer to the enemy within who still obsessed Joseph McCarthy. And now he was on trial. It was not a trial that U.S. Attorney William F. Tompkins felt he could afford to lose.

It took place in October 1957, four months after Fisher's arrest, and lasted eleven days. Tompkins boasted to Donovan beforehand that it was an open-and-shut case, but he had never prosecuted an alleged spy before, and his key witnesses were liabilities.

Hayhanen was a wreck. He was overweight and barely coherent despite countless hours of coaching by the prosecution. He was so terrified of testifying that he did so in disguise, but even the disguise was somehow pathetic. He wore dark glasses and dyed his white hair and eyebrows and a specially grown mustache jet black. The papers called him plump. Donovan, who was allowed to visit him in Peekskill before the trial, said he bore a remarkable resemblance to Egypt's ousted King Farouk. He was, as Donovan reminded the jury, a bigamist, a drunkard, a professional liar, a traitor to his country, and "the most bumbling, self-defeating, inefficient spy that any country ever sent on any conceivable mission."

Roy A. Rhodes was scarcely more impressive. He was a former motor sergeant from the U.S. embassy in Moscow who admitted under cross-examination that by the end of his time there he was drunk every day. He had been traced with the help of an address on microfilm found in the Peekskill house, but said he had never known or met Hayhanen, "Abel," or any other Russian connected to the case.

If there were any other alleged members of the Rudolf Abel spy network, the prosecution failed to find them. In the end it did not matter. Tompkins had a jury willing to believe everything his improbable star witness said and a defendant who never said a word. He also had Bozart and Silverman. On the second Monday of the trial James Bozart was summoned to retell his story and identify the hollow nickel. The message it contained to Hayhanen was read into the record. Earlier that day, Silverman had taken the stand.

"I looked over to the defense table where he was seated and we exchanged a look," he says. "He nodded to me, and it was as if something in that nod said, 'It's OK. I understand why you're here.' It was not expository or emotional in any way. But it was that look. He nodded, 'It's OK.'"

Then Silverman identified the Remington as Fisher's typewriter. He was as vague as he could be, but an evidentiary link was made to the encrypted message and Hayhanen. If you believed Hayhanen was a spy, it was hard not to believe that "Abel" was one too.

Before the trial Donovan had disarmed reporters with an informal press conference in his duplex condominium on Prospect Park, serving drinks and answering questions until past midnight. In court he dressed his client like a banker ("but in the small loan department") and tried to reinvent him as the very opposite of the scoundrels testifying for the prosecution—a man "serving his country on an extraordinarily dangerous mission," who was also "a devoted husband, a loving father. In short, an outstanding type of family man such as we have in the United States."

It didn't work. What it did do was bolster the legend of the master spy, a legend that was already thriving thanks to two months of feverish press coverage and the twenty-five tables of spy gear submitted as evidence by the prosecution. With William Tompkins's summing up it thrived some more.

Tompkins was a good foil for Donovan. He had thick black hair where Donovan's was thinning and white. He was pugnacious where Donovan was urbane. He had made his name prosecuting racketeers in New Jersey, while Donovan had made his money defending the racket of the insurance industry.

Tompkins knew there was a risk some jurors would refuse to see a serious conspiracy in a hollow nickel, and he decided to confront it. "These items have been referred to as toys," he said. "I don't believe anybody would call these toys for amusement. They are not toys for amusement. Ladies and gentlemen, they are tools for destruction, destruction of our country.... Tools for destruction, believe me!"

And the man who used them? Why, he had shown "the cunning of a professional... a master spy... a real pro.... He knows the rules of the game and is entitled to no sympathy."

Having failed to prove that Fisher had actually stolen or transmitted a single secret of any kind in his nine years at large in the United States, Tompkins went on: "I simply say this—this is a serious offense. This is an offense directed at our very existence, and through us at the free world and civilization itself.... The Government is entitled to protect itself when they find people conspiring to commit an offense. We are not helpless. We don't have to wait for a corpse before we look for a criminal."

*An offense directed at our very existence... We are not helpless.* With these words ringing in their ears the jury retired for three and a half hours and returned on the sultry afternoon of October 25 to find Fisher guilty on all counts. He had spent the trial doodling on notepads, leaning over for amused asides with his defense team, and sometimes, as far as Donovan could tell, daydreaming "in a world of his own." When the verdicts were read out, he did not react. Three weeks later, when the judge spared his life but sentenced him to thirty years in federal prison, he understood that he might never see his wife and daughter again. Still he didn't flinch. This was his moment, after all; the moment when all the threads of a revolutionary life came together at a single point and revealed him as a true, triumphant specimen of *Homo sovieticus*. He had accomplished nothing useful since the war, but no one in the free world knew that. What mattered was that he was here, a socialist-realist polymath, still utterly mysterious to the U.S. District Court in the Eastern District of New York, betrayed and convicted but unbroken and quite possibly omniscient. He was the iron will incarnate, the threat made flesh, a sort of human Sputnik.

Outside the courtroom the jury foreman said this had been "the most important spy case ever." Tompkins said a severe blow had been struck at Soviet espionage. But the spy himself seemed to be riding high. As the court rose, he dropped his mask of impassivity and was "unusually affable" with reporters as he was led away. Donovan found him in a holding cell in the basement, smoking a cigarette and making plans for his appeal.

Everyone admired him—Dulles, Gamber, and even Tompkins said so. For his own part Donovan called him extraordinary and brilliant, possessed of a "consuming intellectual thirst."

As prisoner 80016-A in the Atlanta Federal Penitentiary, Fisher kept busy. He learned silk-screening and played chess with a fellow convicted spy, Morton Sobell (the one whose wife Hayhanen had stiffed of five thousand dollars, which he kept for himself). He wrote logarithmic tables for the fun of it and taught French to a cellmate, Vincent "Jimmy" Squillante, a former New York garbage king and godson of a Gambino family capo.

But busy was not the same as content. He probably missed Russia. He definitely missed his family. He wanted to go home.

Neither Fisher nor his lawyer ever quite lost hope that they would find a way to ensure he didn't die in jail. Both knew there was at least the theoretical possibility of a spy swap sometime in the future. Donovan mentioned it in his written argument against the death penalty, submitted to the trial judge in Brooklyn before sentencing. Fisher mentioned it in February 1958, when he heard that Donovan was going to visit Dulles on his behalf. But there was a problem: he was now officially a master spy. A fair swap would need two of them, and as Fisher himself noted sometime later, there was no one quite like him in jail in Russia. That would not change. There was no one quite like Fisher in jail in Russia at any point in the cold war. What did change was the arrival outside Moscow of an equivalent: a celebrity spy of a very different sort.

The other strategy for freeing Fisher, besides human barter, was to appeal his conviction. Everything about the original trial—from the unanimity of the verdict to what Donovan called the satisfaction of the American public at the sentence—suggested it could not be done. But the trial had been quick. Donovan had barely cleared his throat, let alone shown the world what he could do in a corner. And from the very start he had seen a weakness in the prosecution's case that lodged in his mind and offended his sense of what was right.

It was a technicality, but a technicality that went to the heart of the Constitution. Fisher had been arrested and charged by immigration officers, but only after the FBI had entered his room, searched it, taken evidence, and questioned him without any sort of warrant. The strategy had been to force an entry and try to intimidate Fisher into cooperating. It had failed and in the process had violated the Fourth Amendment's protections against unreasonable search and seizure. Donovan argued that this made the search illegal and anything it turned up inadmissible in court. When he made this case at trial and at Fisher's first appeal, it was swiftly rejected. He then appealed to the Supreme Court of the United States, which took it much more seriously.

On February 25, 1959, in full morning dress, Donovan asked all nine Supreme Court justices a question: "What is our national defense, in an age of intercontinental missiles, hydrogen bombs and man-made satellites?... Will it be our stockpile of atomic bombs? Our development of poison gas or lethal rays? Or will it be that with quiet courage we have maintained a firm belief in the truths of freedom that led our ancestors to migrate to this land?"

The chief justice thanked him profusely for his "self-sacrificing" labors and a month later admitted the court could not make up its mind. It wanted the case reargued. This time Donovan put up in style at the Hay-Adams Hotel and allowed himself a glance at the morning papers before walking to the Court. Abel was once again the talk of the nation. His case was providing what the *Washington Post and Times-Herald* called "a rare spectacle of the protection afforded a defendant, whatever his crime, by the American Bill of Rights."

Camp X-Ray and its shuffling orange jumpsuits were still two generations into the future. But a time traveler would have been interested to note that in all Fisher's appeals there was never any doubt that the Constitution's protections applied to him as an alien.

Back in front of the Court, Donovan drew inspiration from the revolution. He had managed to convince himself that Fisher's arrest under false pretenses recalled the harassment of secessionist Americans by the British in the 1770s. When that harassment was denounced in open court, as President John Adams had said, "American independence was there and then born."

From American independence to the right of a weary Soviet spy to keep his door shut? It was a stretch, but clearly an invigorating one. Donovan felt good about his arguments that day. He shared a bottle of whiskey with friends on the train back to Boston and told Fisher in a letter that the Court "finds it extremely difficult to refute our legal arguments."

For four more months the justices cogitated. On March 28, 1960, they split five-four to uphold the conviction. Fisher heard the result on the radio in Atlanta and immediately telephoned Donovan to ask if the closeness of the vote meant he could appeal again. It didn't. It meant he was stuck in jail for another twenty-seven years unless his strange career had any strangeness left in it.

A month later, Frank Powers was blown out of the sky.

# 7

# FALLING FROM A LONG WAY UP

*"There are no* accidents *and no fatal flaws in the machines; there are only pilots with the wrong stuff."*

Tom Wolfe, *The Right Stuff*

"It was a beautiful, clear day," Nikolai says. "I got up as usual at seven o'clock and went outside. The sky was clear, no clouds at all. I was preparing to report for duty when the siren sounded."

Nikolai Batukhtin still lives a short drive from the missile base where he was stationed in the spring of 1960. From the nearest highway and even the approach road the base is obscured by dense woods; nothing in it rises above treetop height.

The winter of 1960 had been brutal, "the worst cold ever." As a lieutenant Batukhtin had been assigned a *domik*—a wood cabin with a stove—but the enlisted men had been in tents since February. On this clear day the snow had finally melted. There was warmth in the sun and a slack day in prospect for everyone, since it was May 1, May Day, the Day of Spring and Labor and of jubilant comradeship for socialists everywhere. It would be written later that a young Boris Yeltsin was among the marchers under the party banner in nearby Sverdlovsk.

The brand-new rockets were at ease, nearly horizontal on their launchers. There were six in all, one per launcher, positioned in a neat hexagon and connected to one another by tracks cut through the trees that made a Star of David pattern when seen from above. Each stood in a clearing of its own that opened onto a larger central clearing with a control cabin on wheels in the middle. The cabin and the launchers were the color of the forest, dark green and still shiny from the factories where they had been rushed into production on the personal orders of the general secretary. The rockets were gray. Batukhtin was not an excitable soul, but the Dvina—for that was its code name—made him proud. They said that in tests at Sary Shagan it had exceeded expectations, and the expectation was for a missile that could hit an intruder traveling at one thousand miles an hour at eighty thousand feet. Its sharklike fins and long, slim body had a deadly beauty. Comrade Designer Pavel Grushin had surpassed himself.

Fresh from the factory, none of the rockets in Batukhtin's battery had been fired yet, even in training, and even though there was nothing more patriotic than the defense of the motherland, they were not likely to be fired on May Day.

"The siren sounded soon after eight o'clock," he remembers. "It seemed like a normal training alarm, but that made no difference. The same actions were required of us. We had six minutes to run to our stations and check our equipment. That was the time limit set by our government. They believed that any more than six minutes would allow the intruder to escape.

"We checked our equipment, then we waited. Nothing happened. We sat there in the cabin and no one said anything. There was no message from our commander, so we sat there in complete silence for nearly an hour. Then Chelyabinsk gave us the coordinates and we switched on our target acquisition radar. At nine o'clock our commander announced there was an enemy aircraft in the sky."

* * *

Thirteen miles up is a hard place to imagine. If you could drive there, it would be the end point of a straight thirteen-mile drive away from planet Earth. Thirteen miles is five Matterhorns, or forty-four Sears Towers, and there is almost nothing when you get there; so little atmosphere to absorb and deflect the sun's rays that they will feel hot through a pressure suit even though the outside temperature may be as low as –160 degrees Celsius; so little pressure that the human body requires as much protection as in a perfect vacuum. The view is a different matter. The very few people who have seen it say that looking upward they saw a ring of the purest blue deepening nearly to black, while the view down is both humbling and mysterious. It is vast—four hundred miles in every direction—but at the same time reveals the planet in its true, curved, intimate state.

From thirteen miles up even giant cumulonimbus are a whole Everest below and look like cotton candy. The only big clouds this high up are H-bomb clouds. This is above the weather, above the jet stream, above almost all wind noise, since wind is air. It is still a quick free fall back to Earth—about six minutes, since the first forty thousand feet will be very quick indeed—and still a long way below outer space. But thirteen miles up is implacably hostile to life all the same. It is 29,000 feet above the point where human bodily fluids start boiling of their own accord.

To go there gently in a balloon is one thing, and even this proved so fraught with surprises that it killed a series of brave pioneers who tried it in the first half of the twentieth century. To go there in a pressurized cockpit with 450 knots of forward motion is quite another, since if the cockpit breaks up or the canopy pops open the cockpit-sized gas bubble that it contained will be gone in no time, its molecules violently and instantly pulled away from one another and redistributed around the stratosphere too thinly to measure, while the pilot, if conscious, will experience a loss of heat and pressure more sudden than any earthbound machine can simulate. Moreover, whatever happens next will happen fast. He could go into a spin, or lose his head to hypoxia or a passing aileron, or just lose his head. Or he could get lucky and survive those first few seconds and have a moment to begin to think.

From the moment he approved its construction, President Eisenhower was haunted by the idea of a U-2 going down in Russia. He forecast very specifically that if it happened in the midst of superpower negotiations the plane "could be put on display in Moscow and ruin my effectiveness." The plane's champions were adamant that even if it did happen he could deny all knowledge because the pilot would not survive to talk. He would almost certainly die in any midair explosion, they said. If by chance he survived that, he would not be expected to survive the fall. If by some miracle he survived *that,* they intimated, he would, with luck, have the decency to kill himself or go quietly to the execution the enemy would presumably insist on, in the tradition of the American revolutionary hero Nathan Hale, hanged for spying against the British in 1776.

They were wrong on all counts. Not one but two pilots showed it was possible to survive a midair U-2 catastrophe. On a training flight in 1956 Bob Ericson's oxygen supply ran low because of a leak, leaving him hypoxic and groggy as he sailed over Arizona on his way back to Groom Lake. His judgment impaired, he forgot that the U-2 liked to be flown slightly nose up to control its speed. He put it into a shallow dive, picked up too much speed, and regained full consciousness when the machine spontaneously disintegrated around him at 28,000 feet. He did not need to eject since there was nothing left to eject from, and his parachute opened automatically at 15,000 feet.

On another training flight, this time over Texas, Colonel Jack Nole punched out at 53,000 feet and lived. It was in September 1957, a banner month for U-2s over Russia and a hot one in Texas, though not at 53,000 feet, where during routing flight checks Nole's flaps either froze or stuck fully extended as if for landing. This put him into a near-vertical dive as if off the first hill of a monstrous roller coaster but with no good end in view. He reported that he had lost his tail and was ordered to abandon ship, which he was already trying to do, though in truth what followed was not the type of punching out that had earned the process grudging affection among fighter jocks. All they had to do was make one big decision and give one big pull on a cinch ring between their legs. Nole had to unscrew his oxygen tube and his radio wire with stiff, fat gloves fully inflated to prevent the skin and blood vessels on the backs of his hands from distending like blown bubble gum. Then he had to shimmy out of his harness with his torso clamped in a pressure-suit bear hug and pop the canopy by hand. It would have been awkward at ground level. At fifty thousand feet and falling it was that old air force pilot's temptress—the lethal invitation to panic.

Nole declined the invitation. He wrestled free of the plane and for a few seconds fell next to it, faceplate frosting up in the sudden Siberian cold, limbs stiff despite the onrush of thickening air, thinking. He had a choice to make concerning his parachute. Pulling the rip cord would start oxygen flowing to his helmet from an emergency supply in his seat pack. But assuming it deployed correctly, it would also take about one hundred miles per hour off his downward velocity, and he was still so high that he might freeze solid on such a leisurely descent. (Who knew? No one had bailed out from this high before.) The alternative was to keep free-falling, but with nothing to breathe. He pulled the chute.

Nole did not freeze, but he did swing violently and throw up. His escape, like Ericson's, tended to indicate that death was not in fact a "given" in the event of a U-2 disintegration. More particularly it showed that falling from such a long way up did at least give the self-possessed pilot time for a rational review of his options, and it confirmed that David Clark's pressure suits did what was claimed of them—at least at fifty thousand feet.

But fifty thousand feet was not seventy thousand feet. Would the suit hold up in a true worst-case scenario? The air force was anxious to know. It did not send a U-2 all the way up to its operational ceiling for the express purpose of falling apart, but it did send up a series of balloons—the magnificent gossamer helium bubbles code-named Excelsior I, II, and III that took Captain Joe Kittinger to the edge of space.

Kittinger had much in common with Gary Powers. He wrestled with alligators as a teenager and raced speedboats in Florida as a young man. In the air force he showed the requisite nervelessness when climbing into the flying bricks that passed for fighter planes in the early cold war, but he also showed a very human vulnerability at moments of great stress.

In Excelsior I, in November 1959, he soared to 75,000 feet over New Mexico, then jumped. He blacked out while free-falling in a spin but came to on the ground. The next month he did it again from 74,000 feet and remained conscious all the way down. In August 1960 he set a record that still stands by parachuting from 102,000 feet—twenty miles; four Everests—in so many layers of protective clothing that he looked like a teddy bear. On the way up he nearly lost his cool when the sight of a thick layer of cloud below, separating him from his support team, brought him "face to face with a stark and maddening loneliness." But he was soon the picture of nonchalance again. He told *Time* magazine that for the first part of his fall he was on his back looking up at a starry sky (it was 7:00 a.m.) with "a sensation of lying still while the balloon raced away from me." In fact he was accelerating to 614 miles per hour, five times terminal velocity in the lower atmosphere.

On each flight Kittinger's descent was supposed to be controlled by an ingenious sequence of parachutes: drogue, pilot, main canopy, reserve pilot, reserve main canopy. On the first flight four of the five had become fouled around his neck and body and one another. On the third the right glove of his pressure suit failed and his hand expanded to twice its normal size. But the key piece of data from all three flights for anyone interested in the likely fate of a pilot forced into an extremely high-altitude bailout was that his main pressure suit, the tensile preserver of his brain and vital organs, worked flawlessly each time. And each time, at Kittinger's insistence, it was David Clark's standard issue. Eisenhower's "given"—the dead, mute U-2 pilot—was being meticulously resurrected by well-intentioned people under his command who reasonably assumed that their main task was to keep pilots alive.

As for the suicide scenario, no one had thought it through. No one had actually talked about suicide with the president either, because so many euphemisms were available—euphemisms echoed by Eisenhower in his memoirs: "I was assured that the young pilots undertaking these missions were doing so with their eyes wide open," he wrote, "motivated by a high degree of patriotism, a swashbuckling bravado and certain material inducements."

Patriotism was the key word, of course—priceless, immeasurable, sufficient justification for almost anything. But quite apart from the fact that, as Joe Murphy pointed out, there was "never an instruction" that pilots take their own lives, it was never clear in what circumstances a pilot might choose to do so out of patriotism. He might take the L pill as an alternative to torture, but that was different. Did those who invoked Nathan Hale in fact expect a stricken U-2 pilot to take the pill before hitting the ground? While still in the cockpit, perhaps, but after setting the timer on the two-pound explosive charge behind his seat to ensure that no camera or film fell into enemy hands? Or after ejecting, on that long fall to Earth, when the serenity of the heavens and the crisp, thin air of the upper troposphere would combine to reveal the right choice for the good American, who would then reach with gloved hand into the tight outer pocket of his pressure suit, retrieve the pill, and somehow pop it and breathe his last, undistracted by screaming survival instincts or questions about what might actually happen were he to land alive? Not then? Perhaps not. Certainly, standing orders for American officers during the Second World War and since required them to try to escape if captured. Suicide would preclude that. It would also waste the pilots' training at the agency farm in Maryland with the simulated Soviet border. Perhaps the pill was to be kept handy against the dread moment of capture during an escape attempt, when torture and execution were surely to follow in short order. But what if, in fact, he was captured and not tortured, like Hale himself? In that event the pilot might gradually allow himself to hope he might survive. At what point during the emergence of that hope was he expected to put it aside and put his country first? At what point was he finally and irrevocably to reject the possibility that he might be able to withhold from his captors any information that they could use against his country and at the same time stay alive? At what point was he to reject that possibility and kill himself? There was a lot to think about if you were invited to take a mental stroll down the road marked "worst-case scenarios," but the U-2 pilots never were. Nor did those who gave their orders trouble to take the stroll on their behalf.

* * *

When Gary Powers took off in November 1956 on the first overflight of Soviet territory from Turkey, he did not know about Ericson's trouble over Arizona or Nole's over Texas or Kittinger's balloon jumps; they hadn't happened yet. But he did know about what *had* happened. He was flying-safety officer for lonely Detachment B, and even though the agency had not yet supplied it with water skis or speed boat, it supplied Powers with U-2 accident reports from wherever they happened, whenever they happened, in the hope that the detachment might learn from others' mistakes.

So Powers knew better than most U-2 pilots what could go wrong. He knew, for instance, that his good friend Marty Knutson had stalled and spun at twenty thousand feet in training over Groom Lake and had not bailed out only because his canopy had jammed shut. (Knutson managed to recover from the spin.) He knew that a pilot who had followed him to the ranch had died there trying to shake one of the U-2's detachable stabilisers off his wingtip after it failed to drop away automatically. (The Lockheed people decided that too much fuel must have rushed to one wingtip in a tight turn, making the plane impossible to balance.) He knew about Frank Grace's death, also at the ranch, and unlike Grace's friends from Malmstrom who flew to Texas for the funeral, he was allowed to know how it had happened. (Grace climbed too steeply on takeoff after dark and stalled fifty feet off the ground.

His left wingtip dipped and snagged the lake bed, throwing the plane into a cartwheel that ended when it hit a pylon.) And he knew about Howard Carey. Powers and Carey had trained together at Watertown, but Carey had been sent to Germany instead of Turkey. He was returning from an overflight of Eastern Europe when a Canadian-manned early-warning station in France picked him up high over central Poland. The Canadians took him to be an intruder and scrambled four of their own CF-86 Sabre Jets to intercept him. Carey was easy prey: relieved to be back in Western airspace, he descended quickly toward Wiesbaden. Two of the Sabre Jets took up positions on his wingtips and a third behind him. The visitor was unmarked and unrecognizable and did not respond when invited to identify himself. Flight Lieutenant John McElroy armed his guns but never fired them; the U-2 had already fallen apart in the turbulence created by the Sabre Jets.

Other explanations have been offered for Carey's death, but this is the fullest and most plausible. Richard Bissell, the U-2's most ardent fan in Washington, would never have said he found it reassuring, but he did cite it in 1960 as evidence that the U-2 would "pretty much break up in a mishap."

To know the U-2's weaknesses so intimately would have exposed an imaginative pilot to paralyzing fear. No one ever accused Powers of being too imaginative. When he saw his first MiG contrails, peering into his drift sight while sailing over Baku on the morning of November 20, 1957, he trusted that the MiGs wouldn't be able to reach him and flew on. (He counted fifty-six Soviet fighters in the sky below him that day.) When his electrics malfunctioned over Yerevan he calmly rerouted himself home via Mount Ararat, cutting out a detour to Tbilisi. This time he reached Adana in one piece and had his long martini.

* * *

In Turkey they drank gin martinis, never mind the Rat Pack and its predilection for vodka. Turkey wasn't Vegas. The PX at Adana sold fine British Beefeaters flown in from Wiesbaden and not much else in the liquor department, and the U-2 boys developed a certain loyalty to it.

They had plenty of time. That first flight by Powers was the only true overflight of Soviet territory by Detachment B in its first nine months at Adana. Had American taxpayers known, they might have vented their indignation over the U-2 pilots' thirty thousand dollars in annual pay much earlier than they did—and it was true that Powers's fifteen dollars per operational mile flown over that nine-month period was a handsome rate by any standards. Even so, it is hard with hindsight to argue that it was not deserved.

Of the era's three military-trained airborne elites, the most famous—the *Mercury* astronauts—risked their lives and undertook genuinely historic missions but did not actually fly. As Tom Wolfe put it, they sat on top of an enormous roman candle and waited for someone to light the fuse. The fighter jocks did all their own flying, but never into the bear's lair; unlike Slim Pickens in *Dr. Strangelove,* they never went toe to toe with the Russkies. Only the U-2 pilots did both. They did not ask to be killing time on the concrete outside Adana, and they didn't much like it. Three of them were sent home for want of anything to do, and the stay-behinds started saying that the place existed because the world needed an enema. Month after month the decrypted orders from project HQ to the wireless hut read "as you are," or words to that effect. During the Suez crisis in 1956 there was plenty of operational flying over the Middle East, but after that most U-2 flights from Adana were test flights over Turkey or "ferret runs" along the northern edge of the Black Sea to test the Soviets' reactions. Even these were rare because the U-2 did not seem to have been built to last and no one wanted to wear it out. "No one thought the operation would last long," Joe Murphy says. The truth was, no one knew, but Richard Bissell was darned if he was going to let it fizzle out, which was one reason why Jim Cherbonneaux found himself ripping frantically at the main front zipper of his pressure suit on the scorching afternoon of August 22, 1957.

Cherbonneaux was one of those ordered to stay behind. He had trained with Powers, deployed with Powers to Turkey, and then suddenly packed up and moved again with most of the detachment to a borrowed hangar outside Lahore in Pakistan. By the time his black plane dropped quietly through the haze that afternoon, flaps fully extended and compressors idling in the hot, humid air, Cherbonneaux was beyond desperate. He had been airborne for nine hours and acutely aware of his bladder for an hour and a half. He would have soaked his long johns if he could, but when he tried he felt only agonizing spasms. As the aircraft rolled to a stop in an out-of-the-way corner of the airfield, two technicians pulled alongside with a step ladder to open the canopy and help the pilot out. But he was practically out already, scrambling from the cockpit as if on fire. He had three layers to get through—outer suit, pressure suit, and those long johns. Moments later, he told Ben Rich, "not heeding privacy, I set a new world record on that tarmac."

It was a release in more ways than one. After nine months of inactivity and sagging morale, Detachment B had proved its worth in one spectacular flight. Spooked by the Russian protest note of July 1956, and by Soviet radar's ability to track U-2s over the Caucasus, Eisenhower had suspended overflights in November that year. He allowed them to restart the following summer with three flights in one day, because the Skunk Works had radically shrunk the U-2's radar profile with a heavy coat of iron ferrite paint; because Pakistan had allowed the use of the Lahore base in return for a substantial increase in U.S. aid; because Soviet radar defenses seemed to be at their weakest in central Asia; and because central Asia seemed to be hiding the development of a truly terrifying superweapon.

The day before Cherbonneaux relieved himself at Lahore, Sergey Korolyov's outsize R7 missile at last made a successful five-thousand-mile test flight from Tyuratam to the volcano-strewn Kamchatka Peninsula in the Pacific. This much the CIA knew because its partners in the National Security Agency could eavesdrop on Soviet military communications, which still used old-fashioned radio relays to reach across the country's eight time zones. But what sort of warhead could the R7 carry? Where were the warheads being tested and with what success? Was the successful R7 test a fluke or a taste of things to come? Was another test imminent? These were questions only the U-2 could answer.

At ground level, Cherbonneaux's route would have been a backpacker's dream. It took him straight over K2, the second-highest mountain on earth, then northwest over the cotton fields and tobacco plantations of Uzbekistan's lush Fergana Valley and deep into northern Kazakhstan. Above Karaganda (at that time still an important node of the Gulag archipelago) his flight plan required a sharp right turn and a straight run east with his cameras on. He did not know why; it was a route compiled by intelligence analysts in Washington. He found out what they were interested in three hours into the mission, high over the eastern steppe, near where it begins to merge with the grasslands of Mongolia. Where Genghis Khan's horde had fanned out seven centuries earlier in search of settlements to seize and raze, Cherbonneaux saw in his drift sight a familiar pattern of craters and faded blotches. Each blotch was linked to the others by a web of dirt roads, but whatever had made the craters had wiped the desert clean around them. The pattern was familiar from the Nevada nuclear test site. Cherbonneaux selected maximum magnification on the drift sight and stared down it, heart pounding, at a large object on top of a makeshift tower. He had found the Semipalatinsk test site, or polygon, and a weapon apparently primed to blow. But when? Who knew? This was not the kind of scenario they put you through at the Lovelace Clinic. If it had been, he might have failed on account of the propensity of his pulse to surge at moments of acute anxiety. He came as close as a U-2 pilot ever did to panicking, yelling into his faceplate for the Russians to hold their fire.

The bomb on the tower went off the following month, but a separate half-megaton airburst detonated over the site five hours after Cherbonneaux passed through, more or less as he was peeing on the tarmac at Lahore.

A week later another Detachment B pilot found Tyuratam, holy of holies of the Soviet space-industrial complex, one hundred miles east of the Aral Sea. In one sense the razor-sharp pictures taken that day by E. K. Jones confirmed the CIA's worst fears. They revealed a huge launch complex, far bigger than anything at Cape Canaveral, as if the Russians had decided to win the space race before it had begun by planting a cosmonaut on Mars.*

The launchpad was not in fact a pad. It was a steel grid fifty meters square, held in place by sixteen concrete bridge trusses over the fat end of a huge pit shaped like a chemistry flask. Fuel and equipment trains had direct access to the grid along a spur from the main line to Moscow. This gateway to the cosmos was big and deadly serious, but what the U-2 confirmed was that there was only one. The Russians might

* One of the engineers who built the site, initially unaware what it was for, claims to have found out by asking Sergei Korolev if he could stop excavations early because they were causing flooding. The Chief Designer ordered him to keep on digging, inadvertently revealing his great secret by explaining that he needed a flame pit at least half as deep as his rocket was tall. "Will we fly to Mars as well?" the astonished engineer asked. "Of course, and farther than that," Korolev replied.

be going to Mars from Tyuratam, but they were not about to use it to launch a preemptive salvo of ICBMs. That knowledge would underpin Eisenhower's resistance to the missile lobby for the next three years.

* * *

There were no more protest notes from the Soviet embassy in Washington. Had the ferrite paint succeeded in hiding the U-2 from Soviet radar? Hardly. The paint was so heavy that it had forced Cherbonneaux to sneak into Soviet airspace over the Pamirs far below the plane's normal ceiling, at 58,000 feet. He had simply caught the Soviet radar net napping, but at least one of the other flights from Lahore that day was spotted, and a MiG was scrambled from an Andijon air defense squadron in the Fergana Valley to confirm it was an intruder. When the squadron's commander told Moscow that Soviet central Asia was being overflown by unidentified flying objects, the head of all Soviet air defense fighter regiments, a Colonel-General Yevgeni Savitsky, flew out to interview the MiG's pilot. Savitsky decided the pilot was seeing things and had him reassigned.

The Soviet air defense forces were divided into radar and fighter regiments and rocketeers, and the rocketeers were probably the most attuned to the U-2 menace, because Khrushchev had personally insisted that they shoot it down. To this end a promising guided missile designed by Pavel Grushin for the defense of Leningrad, the S-75, was rushed into mass production for the defense of the whole motherland.

Like Sergey Korolyov (who served eight years in the Gulag), Grushin was a student of the hard school of rocketry. It was a field assigned the highest priority by Stalin and Beria, who gave the KGB direct control of hundreds of scientists and engineers working alongside their captured German counterparts in forced-labor conditions throughout the postwar period.

Grushin's S-75 was the grandfather of all modern Soviet surface-to-air missiles. Variants would distinguish themselves from Cuba and Vietnam to Syria and Iraq over the next four decades, but the S-75 took its first bow in November 1957. General Yuri Votintsev, the great-grandson of a Don Cossack warrior chieftain, was deputed to guide it onto the stage at the head of a ground-shaking display of sixty-two missiles in all.

"On 7 November at 0800 hours the column took up its assigned place on Manezhnaya Square [north of Red Square]," he recalled. "All the windows in the Metropol Hotel building were open, and long-barrelled lenses of movie and still cameras were sticking out of the windows. The column of missiles brought up the rear of the parade. When we reached Red Square, everything around us froze for an instant. Then ovations began in the grandstands. After passing over the square, the column stretched out along the embankment, and the soldiers began to cover the missiles quickly.... The first rows of spectators from the square had already appeared. People formed a solid ring around the column, crawled on the vehicles and hugged the soldiers and officers."

* * *

The men of Detachment B flew back to Turkey and were joined there by their wives. The idea was to make life in Adana more tolerable for the pilots. The result was an outpost of the American empire that was unique in the cold war.

The speedboat had at last arrived. Waterskiing happened on a reservoir near the base. For those who preferred bathing or sunbathing on hot, quiet days—and there were plenty—the beaches near Mersin were secluded and spectacular. One faced the ruins of a crusader castle two hundred yards out to sea, stranded there by a sea level that seemed to have risen a few feet since the twelfth century. The pilots called it the castle by the sea and formed an attachment to it, as they might have to the sands of Cocoa Beach or Mission Bay if their flying careers had turned out only slightly differently. They would drive there in big imported Buicks with whitewall tires, and they would horse around in bright Bermuda-length swimming shorts under the supervision of the ranking agency man of the moment, who tended to be paler and skinnier than they.

Mersin was a short drive from Adana. It was not hard to be back for the daily 6:00 p.m. to 8:00 p.m. cocktail hour. With the wives in town, dinner would usually follow at one or another of their homes, prepared by the hostess in turn or occasionally thrown together as a pot luck.

Accommodation was now mainly off base and rented rather than in the two-person Belgian bachelor trailers that had greeted the pilots in 1956. It was basic compared with married quarters on most U.S. bases around the world and downright primitive compared with diplomatic lodgings, which may have seemed unfair considering that no embassy on earth had as much power to affect the course of world affairs as this little community of weather-recon pilots. But there were compensations that would have been worth writing home about if letters did not have to get past the Agency's censors. Compensations like more free time than you could fill and a dedicated C-47 Gooney Bird on standby to help fill it. Lunch and shopping in West Germany? Home via Rome and Naples? These things the agency could arrange.

Barbara Powers was the trailblazer.

After she had been a stenographer for Judge Advocate Captain Reuben Jackson for six months, the Communists staged a coup in Athens. Women were being raped on the streets—so Barbara was told—and Americans were no longer welcome in the cradle of democracy. She was transferred to Wheelus Air Force Base outside Tripoli. Twenty-nine years later a phalanx of swing-wing bombers from Lakenheath in England would rend the night above Tripoli with high explosives to teach Colonel Gadhafi a lesson about sponsoring terrorism, but in the age of Eisenhower—still only fifteen years after the Allied victory in North Africa—the American military was still an honored guest in Libya.

By day Barbara took dictation from another judge advocate. She spent her nights on the base in a bunk bed, tormented by flies that the locals refused to exterminate because they fertilized the date palms.

Gary would fly in when he could in a T-33 Thunderbird, about once a month. He didn't always phone ahead. One day he found Barbara locked in her room saying she'd be ready in a moment, sounding frightened. By her account he forced his way in and, seeing her holding a purse, rifled through it to find a letter in which Captain Jackson declared his love for her and told her he was getting a divorce. He was begging her to do the same.

Gary never wrote about the episode, though he did admit his marriage was in trouble. Barbara remembered the military police dragging him away and his turning the tables by filing a formal complaint against Jackson (who died soon afterward in an air crash).

On another visit, enraged by another fellow officer who wanted to steal his wife, Powers hurled the man over the bar in the Wheelus Officers' Club. This time Barbara was quietly impressed.

The heart-stopping news that she would be able to live with her husband at his mysterious place of work came through in the late fall of 1957, as *Sputnik* was circling the Earth and Burt and Helen Silverman were finishing their European tour after being rudely interrupted by the trial of Rudolf Abel. Barbara was not stupid. She could read a map and had begun to suspect that Gary's base was in Turkey. The idea of living there enthralled her—yet the reality, she wrote, began with Gary removing a pile of excrement from the front room of their new home.

Everyone associated with Richard Bissell's air force was expected to show a high degree of self-reliance as well as discretion, and Barbara and Gary Powers could certainly look after themselves. Gary bought himself a shotgun for hunting (duck, goose, quail, boar). He also bought a gray Mercedes 220SE convertible with red leather seats and a retired German police dog called Eck von Heinerberg. Barbara bought rugs for their home. They started taking drives into the Anatolian hinterland with the wind in their hair and a gun and a dog in their red backseat. It was a life that a reporter could have made to seem extremely glamorous if a reporter had been allowed within a hundred miles of Adana. But it was a life lived in an agency bubble, freedom being a complex thing. Its defenders could not always practice what they preached.

Soon after their arrival the wives were at last given a look at the aircraft in which their husbands were paid so much to study the weather. "She's a real doll," Gary told Barbara in advance. "She gets four miles to the gallon and travels ten times the speed of a truck. Now that ain't bad!" Barbara was less than awestruck. She told him she thought it looked "like a giant black crow." But the plane did not loom as large in their life together as it did in history. He almost never talked about it with her and did not seem to fly it often, either.

In September 1958 all the detachment's pilots disappeared from Turkey for two months. The wives were not told where and would have been unlikely to guess northern Norway. The point of the decampment was to photograph a swath of Russia not far below the Arctic Circle where the Soviets were rumored to be building ICBM silos close enough to the United States to hit it with a straight shot over the North Pole. The pilots ate sumptuously and took pictures of one another in sharp suits with sharp, dark mountains in the background. But they took none of the alleged new missile site; the cloud cover was unrelenting.

Back at Adana the communications hut stayed quiet. For months on end no go codes came from Washington; none for the kind of missions that the pilots might want to tell their grandchildren about, at any rate. A new type of trailer came instead. Barbara called it the superhouse trailer (also known as a double-wide). It was fifty-five feet long and had three bedrooms, and there was one for each married officer. Drawn up in two neat rows, the superhouse trailers brought everyone back inside the base. No one had to drive anywhere at night and Detachment B's partying took on a new intensity.

"Enjoying liquor, I did my share," Powers admitted.

"There was a lot of drinking," says Joe Murphy, by this time on his second Turkish tour, "but I never thought it was out of control."

Major (later General) Harry Cordes, an air force U-2 pilot who didn't think much of Bissell's people management, said later: "I saw the potential for international incidents with automobiles and wives [and] tried to caution [Bissell] about the danger of project compromise."

The new trailers were a response to such warnings, and they did cut the risk of a U-2 pilot spending time in a Turkish jail for drunk driving. But they did not stop one officer—"a handsome man built like a football player"—from throwing too much of his strength into a dance with the beautiful Barbara one rowdy night in the spring of 1960. She fell and broke her leg and was told to say it had been a waterskiing accident if anybody asked.

Barbara complained that Gary wasn't bothered about her leg. But like Cordes, he *was* bothered about project compromise. "How much did the Russians actually know about our outfit?" he mused later. "Talking it over with the intelligence officer we concluded that they probably knew a great deal. It was an unusual unit, set off by itself, flying an easily identified aircraft. Spying was an ancient profession in Turkey. If Russian intelligence was as good as our intelligence repeatedly told us it was, it seemed likely they not only knew how many planes we had but how many pilots, plus our names."

They would know his name soon enough.

* * *

What were the wives doing there? Why double the number of people who had seen the "giant black crow" close up? Why treble (at least) the amount of gossip about the Adana party set that wasn't even part of the air force? The answer went back to Cape Canaveral and a chilly December morning in 1957.

This time Willie Fisher could not be present. He was detained at the West Street federal prison in New York pending his appeal. But the next stage in America's journey to the stars would not go unwitnessed. Several hundred reporters and photographers were crammed onto a dune on Cocoa Beach. The networks had cleared time for live broadcasts. The object of their attention was a tall, thin Vanguard rocket on launchpad 18A that contained the free world's first satellite. It was meant to have blasted off two days earlier. The weather had been dreadful. A liquid oxygen valve had frozen shut and the countdown had been scrubbed. But the sixth was calm. The hour had come. *Sputnik* would be avenged.

The Associated Press put out an advance story for use by subscribers in the event of a successful launch. It began:

> THE RADIO-SIGNALING BABY MOON CIRCLING THE EARTH IS THE U.S.'s REPLY TO RUSSIA THAT IT TOO CAN STAKE A CLAIM TO THE SPACE FRONTIER.

The Vanguard was a Citroën among rockets: clever but fragile. It was also a navy machine, and few in the army would have hesitated to call it effete. As a concept it was hugely ambitious, with all-new guidance and propulsion systems, solar cells to provide some of its electrical power, and printed circuits to shrink its innards. Its engines generated barely one fortieth of the thrust of Korolyov's R7—27,000 pounds to 1.1 million, which may strike the Hummer generation as downright un-American. But if the package worked it could, with a little spin, more than compensate for the humiliation of *Sputnik* by dint of its sheer sophistication.

Would it work? Now there was a question. The previous Vanguard launch had been aborted five times because of technical hitches. This one was untested on the most fundamental level: its second- and third-stage boosters had never been fired in a real flight before. Wernher von Braun, who had nothing to do with its development but knew a thing or two about rockets, said it didn't stand a chance. An engineer at the launchpad told a *Time* reporter: "We'll be pleased if it does go into orbit. We will not be despondent if it does not." The *Pittsburgh Sun-Telegraph* was more optimistic. "MOON—MINUTES TO GO," its morning headline screamed, referring to the minimoon, the size of a grapefruit, that the president's press secretary had promised would be placed in orbit.

At 11:44 the last hose connecting the rocket to its support crane fell away and the first flames spurted from its engines. By 11:45 it was all over. As the official countdown tape put it: ". . . two . . . one . . . zero . . . fire . . . first ignition . . . EXPLOSION!"

The fireball was as fat and ugly as the rocket was slender and beautiful, but it still failed to spare the Vanguard's blushes. Before smoke and flame enveloped the whole launch complex, television viewers saw the rocket simply stop in midair a few feet off the ground and fall back as if deciding orbit wasn't worth the effort. As it did so, the nose cone fell off like an ill-fitting witch's hat.

With a little tolerance for excuses, it was all completely understandable. Project Vanguard had been meticulously denied military funding and von Braun's expertise in order to keep space exploration civilian and honor the spirit of the International Geophysical Year. It was overseen by an astronomer, not a general. There was no strategic imperative to succeed, no relentless pressure from government, no threat of exile to a labor camp in the event of failure, and no privacy in which to make the inevitable early mistakes that dogged any new rocket program. According to acting Defense Secretary Donald Quarles, the explosion was merely "an incident in the perfection of the Vanguard satellite system."

But America was in no mood for excuses. For two months Democrats and the media had withheld final judgment on the technological Pearl Harbor that was *Sputnik* on the basis that the Pentagon (or whoever was running the U.S. missile program—it wasn't at all clear) had a right of reply. In those two months the Soviets had put up a second satellite, this time with a dog in it. Khrushchev had boasted that he could put up twenty more "tomorrow" and was churning out missiles "like sausages." Eisenhower's poll ratings had plunged twenty-two points. Now this. Flopnik. The president's numbers sank another eight points. There were calls for him to go, and he seriously considered doing so. In the post-*Sputnik* stress he had suffered a minor stroke. In the post-

Vanguard recriminations there was a salutary national backlash against consumerist excess, which seemed to have been achieved at the expense of national security. But there was also a wholesale reevaluation of the Soviet threat—technologically supreme and now being wielded from the moral high ground, since the *Sputniks* were IGY experiments, not warheads. For the first time in his career Eisenhower doubted whether he was equal to the fight.

One thing he did not doubt was that Khrushchev, yet again, was bluffing. The U-2 flights of August 1957 had yielded an intelligence bonanza, most of it reassuring. Detailed analysis of the Tyuratam launch facility suggested that while the R7 was a mighty space rocket it was a highly impractical missile that took days to fuel and was impossible to hide. Overflights of the closed nuclear cities along the Trans-Siberian railway revealed intensive fuel enrichment activity but not the mass production of thermonuclear warheads, which was a much more challenging proposition.

For the time being the world could live with Mr. Khrushchev's sausages. If you were privy to the dazzling fruits of the U-2's twenty-twenty overhead vision, this much was clear. But if you weren't, it wasn't, and almost no one was. Senators Symington and Johnson were not, which is why they felt so free to flagellate themselves and the administration with the looming so-called missile gap. Joe Alsop was not, which is why he started using the lethal "F" word—flaccid—with such confidence in his influential columns in 1958. Even the authors of the Gaither Report, a supposedly authoritative survey of U.S. defense capabilities commissioned by Eisenhower and published in late 1957, knew nothing about the U-2 when their findings were leaked to the *Washington Post*. The report called for a crash missile-building program, a nationwide network of nuclear bomb shelters, and a thirteen-billion-dollar boost to the annual defense budget. It concluded that the country was in "the gravest danger in its history."

These were the six words of the report that the *Post* chose to quote most prominently when it obtained a copy. It was a great scoop, and it elevated the missile gap to the status of received wisdom when in fact it was little more than a paranoid delusion. Such was the political context of the Vanguard mess—though you did not have to be delusional to infer from the wreckage at Cape Canaveral that the U.S. missile program was at least in trouble.

Sooner or later, Eisenhower had to make a decision about the U-2. Would he reveal to the world what it had revealed to him and his inner circle, or would he hang tough, absorb the accusations of complacency, and keep the plane secret so that it could go on doing its extraordinary work? He did neither. In the end he kept the U-2 secret and, for much of 1958 and 1959, he grounded it.

When Richard Bissell asked permission for more overflights soon after Sputnik, Eisenhower said no. When Secretary of State John Foster Dulles and General Nathan Twining, chairman of the Joint Chiefs of Staff—a formidable pair of petitioners if ever there was one—asked again in January 1958, the answer was the same. Ike didn't like violating Soviet airspace for anything. He cherished his reputation as a straight shooter and knew that would be the least of the casualties if a U-2 was lost over Russia. More particularly, he believed that soaring Soviet confidence made an overreaction to U-2 incursions more likely, not less. That could mean nuclear war, and his priority as president was to keep a nuclear peace.

For decades afterward, Bissell allowed it to be understood that U-2s had continued flying over Russia throughout 1958 and 1959. In fact there was a total of three overflights in those two years. Of these just one involved an American pilot over central Russia. (Of the other two, one was flown by a British pilot and the other photographed parts of the Soviet Far East, starting and finishing in Japan.)

Ailing, wary of Khrushchev, and almost as wary of his own defense chiefs, Eisenhower had come to regard the U-2 as more trouble than it was worth. Time and again his experts trooped into the Oval Office with mission profiles, target lists, and urgent intelligence priorities. Time and again he told them the time wasn't right. It seemed to many a policy of timidity. In reality it was a policy of epic restraint.

Eisenhower even suggested handing the whole program over to the air force, which would effectively have ended overflights of Soviet territory, since they would no longer be civilian or deniable. Bissell had already relinquished the selection and training of new U-2 pilots to the air force. The new recruits were being checked out at a remote Texas air force base, not the ranch, and were used mainly for border flights and atmospheric sampling. Now Bissell dug in his heels. He implored the president's close aide, General Andrew Goodpaster, to be allowed to keep the overflight operation active, small, autonomous, and secret.

His got his way, but to keep the program as he wanted it he would need to keep his original contract pilots—the old-timers from Watertown and the Dupont Plaza and easily forgotten places like the Radium Springs Motel. And he would need to keep them happy, which was not easy with so little flying to be done. They were civilians, after all, and they could quit. As his first contract came to an end, Gary Powers had a mind to do just that, and he was not the only one. He wrote later: "Several other married pilots had decided that an eighteen-month separation from their families was more than enough. Having little choice, the agency capitulated." It sent the wives.

***

At project HQ, Bissell and his U-2 diehards thought hard about how to get the plane back over Russia where it belonged. They tried everything.

A top secret CIA memo from early 1959, declassified in 2003, tells part of the story. Headed "U2 Vulnerability Tests," the memo states:

> *Vulnerability of the U2 was tested against the F-102 and F-104 fighters at Eglin AFB in December 1958. The tests were conducted under optimum controlled ground and air environment for the attacking pilot (ie. outstanding pilots, isolated air space, ideal weather, pre-selected intercept point etc.). The F-104 cannot cruise at altitudes over 60,000 feet, but it possesses a capability to convert speed to altitude and attain co-altitude of the U2 for a period of less than 30 seconds.*

It was a confession. With the rock-solid pretext of defending the nation and wraparound secrecy provided by the CIA, the fighter jocks had finally had a crack at the dragon lady up in the stratosphere where they thought they belonged. And how had they done this, given their sixty-thousand-foot ceiling? By "converting speed to altitude," kinetic energy to potential energy. By lighting their afterburners and keeping them lit until they flamed out while performing that idiot maneuver most guaranteed to mock their control surfaces and put them into a flat spin—the zoom climb.

The zoom climb is the fighter pilot's answer to the ski jump, with the difference that the placid-looking Finn in the chinless helmet and the spongy jumpsuit will never rise higher than his narrow bench at the top of the 120-meter tower, because once he eases his bottom off the bench he has only gravity to power him. Gravity will take him to eighty miles an hour in a few seconds and make him look as if he is flying if he times his muscular explosion just right at the lip of the jump, but in fact he is falling all the time.

The fighter pilot performing the zoom climb uses gravity but also kerosene. He starts his run at, say, an Everest and a half, in a shallow dive, punching through the sound barrier and continuing to accelerate to the maximum speed he can sustain without risking the disintegration of his airplane when he pulls his nose up. Then he pulls his nose up.

With the "outstanding pilots" and "ideal weather" available at Eglin AFB in the Florida panhandle, the machines chosen to go up against the U-2 at the end of 1958 could stand on their tails even at ground level immediately after takeoff. The point of the zoom climb was to do this when already flying as fast and almost as high as they were designed to fly, to push their proverbial envelopes and then tear them open with enough "isolated air space" below to fix whatever problems might ensue. Somewhere around sixty thousand feet the engines on an F-102 or an F-104 Starfighter would tend to give out for want of fuel or air or both, but this did not mean the aircraft suddenly fell out of the sky. At this point it went ballistic, like a bullet or a missile, and if the pilot had chosen exactly the right angle of attack he had a few seconds of weightless calm, coming over the top of his climb, in which to locate any hostile ultrahigh-altitude reconnaissance planes with his airborne radar, engage them with his air-to-air missiles, and shoot them down. (If all went well, he would restart his engine while gliding back to earth.)

For pilots who were not satisfied with the punch in the lower back delivered by a Pratt & Whitney J-57 or a General Electric J79 at full power, there was an even more visceral thrill to be had from flying rocket planes. Two years before the Eglin tests, Iven Kincheloe, a Korean War ace with a chin like an anvil and an unbeaten record of four MiGs downed in six days, had zoomed to an astonishing 126,000 feet over Edwards Air Force Base in California in a Bell X-2 that owed nothing to the atmosphere and everything to the liquid oxygen in its tanks. Chuck Yeager, the king of all test pilots, later strapped a rocket bottle onto a Starfighter and zoomed it up to 104,000 feet, where even he lost control, and nearly his life. (He fell 97,000 feet in the spinning plane before bailing out at 7,000 feet and landing with half his head covered in burning rocket fuel from his own ejector seat.)

The Eglin boys did not have rocket bottles and did not give the U-2 much to worry about.

"The F-104 radar malfunctioned at high altitudes," the vulnerability test memo said. "The pilot of this fighter could not visually acquire the target in sufficient time to solve the fire control problem." The F-102 did better but would only have been able to shoot the U-2 down with better air-to-air missiles than it had or, the agency believed, than the Soviets had. Conclusion: "Successful intercept of the U2 by the Soviet defensive fighters for the next few months is unlikely."

A quarter of a century later, Flight Lieutenant Mike Hale of the RAF claimed to have drawn level with a U-2 at cruising altitude after a zoom climb in an English Electric Lightning—but that was a quarter of a century later.

* * *

In late 1958 a new detachment commander arrived in Adana. His name was Colonel Stan Beerli, and until America was dragged into World War II he had fancied a career as a professional skier. It would have been a natural fit. His parents were Swiss and he grew up in Oregon City, at the foot of Mount Hood and its tremendous snows.

As the storms started rolling in off the Pacific to mark the start of winter in December 1941, Beerli was twenty-one years old and had a job lined up. He was going to Sun Valley, the resort that Averell Harriman had built from scratch and sprinkled with celebrities in Idaho's Sawtooth Mountains. Beerli was going to teach the stars to ski and do a bit of racing on the side, but then the Japanese attacked Pearl Harbor. He joined the U.S. Army Air Forces, trained as a bombardier and navigator, and flew thirty-eight sorties over Italy in B-17s of the second bomb group of the fifth wing of the 15th Air Force. After the war he witnessed the early nuclear tests in Bikini, also from a B-17, and trained as a fighter pilot. He joined the CIA in 1956.

Beerli was too thoughtful and too skinny to be a jock. He had lost most of his hair in his thirties and felt quite comfortable in the dark hat that went so well with the dark suit that Agency people tended to wear, rain or shine, on duty or off. But he did not forget his air force training and did not hold with the view that the U-2, which he flew a fair amount himself, was tough to land. "That is bullshit," he says back within sight of Mount Hood in his eighty-ninth year. "That is such a bunch of horse."

On Beerli's watch at Adana there were no chase cars. If you were a U-2 pilot you landed the damn thing yourself, like any other plane.

Beerli's number two, in charge of security for Detachment B, was a younger, heavier man, well liked by the pilots' wives for organizing their shopping trips to Germany. His name was John Perengosky.

In the early summer of 1959, Beerli and Perengosky left the detachment to run itself for a few days and flew to Tehran. They checked into one of the city's better hotels and made contact with the Agency station chief, who provided them with a twin-engine C-47 with inconspicuous markings and plenty of fuel. The following day they went looking for an airfield.

"The Shah of course was still in power, and there were no questions asked about what we were doing," Beerli says. "It was a simple thing, to look and see what they had available that could possibly be used. But we were looking specifically for a base that was remote."

They found one seven hundred miles southeast of Tehran, in bone-dry Baluchistan, where there was no evidence of anything having landed since the war and no trace of human habitation for a long day's camel ride in every direction. The Afghan border was close by. There were no hangars, no tower, no wells, no trees—just an airstrip and a radio hiding in a horseshoe of brown mountains. Beerli and Perengosky landed their C-47 to make sure the strip would still take the weight of an airplane, then took off again. The nearest town of any size was called Zahedan, and the name stuck.

A month later the quiet of the desert was broken again by the sound of an approaching aircraft. This time it was a C-130 Hercules that would have been a familiar sight on any NATO base and could have been engaged in any humdrum NATO chore. It landed at around midday. Twelve men got out, most of them civilians. They rolled a dozen or so oil drums down the plane's loading ramp, then waited. Around 3:00 p.m. the black line that they recognized as an approaching U-2 appeared over the mountains northeast of the airstrip, already in the final seconds of its long descent from seventy thousand feet. It landed in a hurry—no questions from the cockpit, no go-arounds to get the lay of the land. Out of it climbed an exhausted but exhilarated Marty Knutson.

For the first time in nearly two years a U-2 had photographed Tyuratam. Ike had been persuaded to grant permission for the flight because of a sudden increase in ICBM activity at the Cosmodrome, and because Dulles and Bissell had told him about Stan Beerli's clever new system for getting in and out of Russia unobserved.

The Agency called it Quickmove. Pakistan was still the only country with no qualms about U-2 overflights originating from its bases, but as Beerli says, "You knew darn well that if the Russians knew which bases we were using they'd have people there." The point of Quickmove was "to give them as little time as possible to intercept us or to know that we were doing something." That meant packing all the support people and equipment a U-2 needed into boring C-130s that would not attract attention. It meant flying at night whenever possible, and it meant no more round-trip overflights from and to Pakistan.

The Quickmove procedure would require one Hercules to fly from Adana to Peshawar in northern Pakistan with fuel, oxygen, and a pilot for the main mission. It would also carry specialists from Lockheed and the David Clark Company to take care of the U-2 and the pressure suit. Another Hercules would fly the next day to Zahedan with more fuel and another U-2 pilot for the final leg back to Adana.

"It was the complete package," Beerli says, "but with the minimum number of people to do the job of getting an airplane ready in a hurry."

A few people would see the C-130s; almost no one would see the U-2.

"It was set up so that we'd arrive in Peshawar late in the afternoon when most people would be off the base. We went to a hangar and stayed in the hangar. Didn't come out. That first time Knutson flew the mission, but Powers flew the plane in from Adana. He brought it in at midnight. He landed, we got it refueled, got Marty into it and launched it before the people came to work in Peshawar."

As Knutson headed into Kazakhstan, Powers caught a ride home in the first Hercules, and NSA eavesdroppers in northern Iran strained to pick up any Soviet air-defense chatter about a high-altitude intruder. As Beerli remembers it, they picked up almost nothing.

"Somebody would report that they saw a speck or a blip on their screen, but there was no coherent response, no warning, no complaints from the Russians. It was almost as if it never happened."

Knutson took off that day with 1,300 gallons of fuel in his wings. He landed at Zahedan with 20—enough for ten more minutes after nine hours in the air. Someone handed him a cold beer and asked if he'd mind sending a Morse code message to Adana to let them know he'd landed; no one in the Quickmove team knew Morse. Knutson obliged.

"I'm sitting there in the blazing sun, still in my pressure suit, sipping a beer in one hand and with the other tapping out the dots and dashes," he recalled later. (He also claimed to have been told to abort his landing and bail out if he saw smoke rising from the runway, because that would be a signal that the airstrip's security had been compromised by bandits. The claim irked Beerli. "If there had been any indication that there was opposition we never would have landed there," he said.)

A third pilot from Detachment B, who'd been prebreathing oxygen in the second Hercules, spirited the refueled U-2 back to Turkey. Knutson was helped out of his suit. The empty oil drums were rolled back up the loading ramp, and as the sun went down on Zahedan the second Hercules took off, leaving the strip to the wind and the camels.

The last plane was back in Turkey fifty-four hours after the first had left, and still nothing from the Russians.

* * *

The intelligence take from Knutson's flight was summarized in a top secret double-spaced typed document with the word "talent" printed vertically in huge capitals on its cover page. Next to that in conventional twelve-point type readers were warned that the contents affected the national defense of the United States and were covered by the country's espionage laws. So America had talent, even then. It happened to be the code word for U-2 photography.

It was "completely unexpected" that there was still only one launch facility at Tyuratam, the summary said. Given the number of launches recently detected, and Khrushchev's claim to be in serial production of ICBMs, that meant two things. First, the Russians were clearly speeding up their turnaround times between rocket launches at Tyuratam, but second, Tyuratam was obviously still only a proving ground. The

Soviets' main operational deployment of ICBMs—which must exist, or there would be no missile gap—had to be elsewhere. Not for the first time, the Agency had analysts poring over their maps of central Russia, looking for railways going nowhere. Not for the first time, they settled on the northern Urals, where a spur off the main line from Moscow to the labor camps of Vorkuta cut eastward into the mountains fifty miles north of the Arctic Circle. That had to be it.

"Conduct additional high priority overflights as soon and as often as possible," the summary concluded. Specifically, "we recommend the early coverage of rail lines in the POLYARNYY URAL area as the most likely prototype operational deployment facility for Soviet ICBMs".

The U-2 had proved itself again. It was answering some of the biggest questions that the United States faced in its existential shadowboxing match with Communism, and asking more. Surely Ike understood that now. Surely the hunt for WMD could kick into high gear at last.

But Eisenhower had other things on his mind: he had to get ready for a visit by Comrade Khrushchev. The leader of world Communism and most powerful dictator on the planet was coming to America. He was coming, moreover, with a plan to stop the cold war in its tracks.*

Like so much about the superpower relations in the prehotline era, the invitation was an accident. For nine months international diplomacy had been in turmoil over an ultimatum from Khrushchev for Western troops to leave Berlin, but any curb on West Berlin's freedom was something Eisenhower could not begin to contemplate.

Since the start of the crisis, Khrushchev had been dropping hints that he wanted to visit America and that if he were invited and listened to with sufficient respect the unfortunate Berlin affair would go away. At last, on July 8, Ike took the hint, or seemed to. He told his secre-

* For decades afterward this was not the fashionable view, nor one supported by evidence available in the West. Khrushchev was a shoe-banging cold warrior crazy enough to risk World War III by putting nuclear missiles in Cuba, and anyone who credited him with more peaceable intentions—including Eisenhower—was soft in the head. But post–cold war research has largely demolished this stereotype. In particular the writings of Khrushchev's son, Sergei, and Kremlin papers seen by Aleksandr Fursenko, the father of Vladimir Putin's education minister in Mr. Putin's second presidential term, reveal a Khrushchev even more anxious to call off the arms race than Eisenhower himself.

tary of state that an invitation might be "a device to break the stalemate." State Department staffers started writing drafts, supposedly on the understanding that any invitation was to be conditional on Soviet cooperation over Berlin. Specifically, the two sides needed to make enough progress to warrant a full-blown Great Power summit the following spring.

An invitation was issued without preconditions by Robert Murphy, under secretary of state for political affairs, to Frol Kozlov, a senior politburo member, who happened to be in New York to open a Soviet exhibition.

Khrushchev received it at his dacha in a spirit of triumphant vindication, and accepted. He would come to Camp David, wherever that was—no one in the Kremlin knew. Since the president had been kind enough to offer to make the arrangements, he would also tour the country.

Eisenhower heard the news on July 22 and was furious. His plan had worked perfectly—for Khrushchev. Ike summoned Murphy, who said he knew nothing about the conditions he was supposed to have attached to the invitation and resigned later that year.

The prospect of hosting Khrushchev depressed Eisenhower immensely. As far as he could tell, his Soviet counterpart was a half-educated maverick with a wild temper, a medicine-ball stomach, a growing nuclear arsenal, and what one aide called a "super-colossal inferiority complex." Nor was there any evidence that he played golf. But if Eisenhower had known what daring plans were forming in Khrushchev's restless mind, he might have been more optimistic.

Even before the Soviet premier set foot on U.S. soil, he knew he was losing the cold war. He bragged compulsively about his nuclear firepower, but the truth was he did not have a single operational ICBM. When Richard Nixon visited Russia that summer and asked to see some of Khrushchev's fabled missiles, he was turned down because, as Sergei Khrushchev wrote, "nothing of the kind was as yet in existence." When Tyuratam fell silent for months at a time in 1958 and 1959, American eavesdroppers assumed it was because the R7 had passed all its tests. In fact its designers were still struggling to build a nose cone that could protect a warhead from the searing heat of atmospheric reentry. Meanwhile, Khrushchev knew that the main adversary's Strategic Air Command had enough free-fall bombs and long-range bombers to wipe out every important Soviet target at a few hours' notice. He also knew America was outproducing the Soviet Union in fridges, ovens, cars, tractors, and even corn and outbuilding it in roads and houses.

Khrushchev knew he had to change the rules. After listening to a presentation in the spring of 1959 on how Siberia could be overlaid with a network of R7 launch sites at a cost of half a billion rubles per site, he told his son: "If we're forced into doing this, we'll all lose our pants."

Capitulation was not an option. No admission of weakness was possible, either; his rivals in the politburo had tried to oust him in 1957 and would pounce again. His solution, which he could not share with them, was the wholesale demilitarization of the cold war.

Khrushchev would travel to America with an unserious speech on total disarmament in his pocket but serious ideas on how to start disarmament in the back of his mind. He would raise them with the president if and when the time seemed right. And then—who knew?—he might even lift his ultimatum on Berlin. One thing Khrushchev did know was that to have any chance of making progress he would have to negotiate from strength.

He picked up the phone and called his favorite rocketeer.

* * *

Saturday, September 12, was a glorious late-summer day in northern England. Village cricket was still very much in season, and Bernard Lovell had a game to play. He was serious about cricket. He would later serve as chairman of the Lancashire County side and never missed playing for Lower Withington if he could help it. He was also serious about astronomy, and that Saturday morning he walked as usual across the fields from his home to his office beneath the giant Jodrell Bank radio telescope that would later bear his name. After a pleasant hour or two immersed in the data that poured constantly from the telescope as it listened to the faint whispers of deep space, he gathered up his papers and prepared to leave.

The phone rang. It was not a good connection, nor a voice he recognized, but the accent was distinctly Russian. The voice at the other end belonged to a scientist attached to the Lunik 2 Soviet moon-rocket program, or so its owner claimed. Would Mr. Lovell be so kind as to verify trajectory and impact?

Lovell was cordial but vague. He had grown used to crank calls since his success in tracking the *Sputnik* carrier rocket had thrust him and his telescope into the limelight two years earlier. He hung up and headed for his cricket match, which lasted all afternoon. As the light faded and stumps were drawn, he remembered the peculiar call and returned to his office to find the telex machine pumping out "streams of coordinates from Moscow." He understood at once what they were supposed to indicate and trained his telescope on the moon.

By this time the Russians had their own radar arrays capable of tracking probes in orbit and beyond, but they knew Washington might choose not to believe a Soviet announcement that one of their rockets had won the latest installment in the space race. It was a problem of mutual mistrust that both sides had considered overcoming by sending a nuclear weapon to explode on the moon so that no one could doubt their "success." Sergey Korolyov had decided to enlist Lovell instead.

Embedded in the nose of an adapted R7 stage-three booster, Lunik II hurtled precisely on course across 240,000 miles of nothing and slammed into the Mare Serenitatis at 7:30 in the morning London time, on Monday, September 14. Lovell tracked it all the way. When asked, he confirmed that the rocket had performed as Moscow claimed. It so happened that two more R7s, complete with warheads, were at that moment being prepared at last for installation near the village of Plesetsk in northern Russia.

The next day, Khrushchev landed at Andrews Air Force Base in the world's largest airplane—the very Tupolev that had carried Frol Kozlov back from New York two months earlier. On his first visit to the Oval Office, he presented Eisenhower with a replica of the Lunik probe. "It seemed a strange gift," the president reflected later. It was, but not half as strange as the journey of mutual discovery on which the two of them were about to embark.

Khrushchev's parade through America was a two-week fever dream of colliding prejudice and rough, remarkable enlightenment. He got stuck in a lift in the Waldorf-Astoria (a "capitalistic malfunction") and royally insulted by a bumptious mayor of Los Angeles. He met Shirley MacLaine and Marilyn Monroe and lost his temper when turned down for a visit to Disneyland out of fear for his security. He dropped in on an old friend in Iowa, the corn guru Roswell Garst, and roared with laughter when Garst started throwing silage at the press horde covering his every step. There were no visits to General Curtis LeMay's nuclear bomber bases, but there were several carefully contrived drives through American suburbia and its relentless proof of prosperity. Khrushchev didn't like these parts of his itinerary, but he could not deny the evidence of his own eyes. Toward the end he breakfasted on steak and eggs in Camp David's Aspen Lodge and backed down on Berlin. There had been no mention of U-2s and no progress on disarmament, but that could wait. Eisenhower had given him the respect he craved and had spoken sincerely of his desire for peace. He had promised to arrange a four-power summit and to visit Russia in the spring.

Khrushchev returned to Moscow a changed man. In speeches at the airport and immediately afterward at the Central Lenin Stadium, he said he believed that Eisenhower "sincerely wishes to see the end of the Cold War" and that together they could "do a great deal for peace." He ended each address with a hurrah for Soviet-American friendship that would have been unimaginable a year earlier. Towns and villages the length of the country began primping and planting in case the Eisenhowers—who had been told that nowhere was off limits—decided to drop by. "You could sense an elated mood in Moscow," Sergei Khrushchev wrote. "It was like the atmosphere in a home which awaits the arrival of a dear and hoped-for guest."

The hopefulness grew. Some Russians dared to call the spring of 1960 the American spring. Khrushchev's biographer, William Taubman, has written that it was in danger of turning into "a massive, spontaneous, public ideological defection."

It never came to that, but it was real, and it was underpinned by one of the boldest decisions of Khrushchev's career. In January 1960 he slashed the size of the Soviet armed forces by 1.2 million men. Eisenhower concluded that his new friend in the Kremlin was serious about disarmament.

* * *

Not everyone agreed, however. One of the doubters was another former fighter pilot, Colonel Thomas Lanphier Jr. (retired), without whose tireless work Gary Powers might never have made his last flight over Russia.

Unlike Powers, Lanphier had his chance to prove himself in World

War II, and took it. In April 1943 he was stationed at Henderson Field, a forward U.S. air base on Guadalcanal in the South Pacific. He was already a prolific fighter ace with four confirmed Japanese kills, including three in a single day earlier that month. At midnight on the seventeenth he was summoned to a cabin being used by Admiral Marc Mitscher, commander of all airborne U.S. forces in the Solomon Islands, to be told he would be ambushing a Japanese air convoy expected to come within range the following morning. Mitscher had received his intelligence on the convoy directly from the navy secretary in a top secret document that ended: "MUST AT ALL COSTS REACH AND DESTROY. PRESIDENT ATTACHES EXTREME IMPORTANCE TO MISSION."

Lanphier was smart, fearless, loquacious, and an exceptionally gifted pilot. Born in the Panama Canal Zone in 1915, he was the son of another military pilot, Thomas Lanphier Sr., whose close friends included the aviation pioneer Charles Lindbergh. A degree from Stanford adorned the younger Lanphier's résumé, but flying was in his blood.

Fortified with Spam, dried eggs, and coffee, he took off from Henderson Field at 7:00 a.m. on April 18 in an attack formation of four twin-engine P-38 Lightnings backed up by twelve more Lightnings to provide cover. All sixteen planes flew for two hours toward their expected rendezvous with the enemy, skimming the waves to avoid detection by radar. A formation of Japanese bombers and fighter escorts appeared above them exactly as predicted, flying southwest toward the island of Bougainville. Lanphier climbed, chased one of the bombers inland, and brought it down with a long burst of cannon fire that tore off one of its wings. "The plane went flaming to earth," an army intelligence report said afterward. Among the casualties was Admiral Isoroku Yamamoto, mastermind of the attack on Pearl Harbor.

Years later other pilots on the Yamamoto raid began disputing Lanphier's version of events, but he stuck by his like the fighter he was. After the war he worked briefly in newspapers in Idaho, but he retained a fierce loyalty to the air force and the national defense. When invited to Washington to serve as special assistant to the secretary of the air force, he accepted. His new boss was Stuart Symington, the future senator. They worked formally together for only two years but kept in touch. By the late 1950s Lanphier, now living in Southern California, was one of Symington's most valued sources on the missile gap. He had maintained excellent contacts in air force intelligence and had gone one better: from 1951 to 1960 he was a vice president of Convair, maker of the mighty Atlas missile that Willie Fisher may have seen trundling over its last few miles to Cape Canaveral from San Diego under an enormous shroud.

The phrase "conflict of interest" barely begins to describe Tom Lanphier's rabidly partisan approach to advising one of the most powerful congressional allies of the American military-industrial complex. Yet he was in good company. Air force intelligence was crammed with highly competitive analysts who believed they were in a zero-sum game not only with the Russians but also with the army and the navy. If they could make the missile-gap theory stick, America would have to respond with a crash ICBM program of its own. The dominance of the Strategic Air Command in the U.S. military hierarchy would be complete—and Convair would profit mightily. It is hardly surprising that the information Lanphier fed to Symington and Symington to every politician and columnist who would listen was authoritative, alarming, and completely, disastrously wrong.

Symington's "on the record" projection of Soviet nuclear strength, given to Senate hearings on the missile gap in late 1959, was that by 1962 they would have three thousand ICBMs. The actual number was four. Symington's was a wild guess, an extrapolation based on extrapolations by air force generals who believed it was only responsible to take Khrushchev at his word when, for example, he told journalists in Moscow that a single Soviet factory was producing 250 rockets a year, complete with warheads.

Symington knew what he was doing. He wanted to be president and believed rightly that missile-gap scaremongering had helped the Democrats pick up nearly fifty seats in Congress in the 1958 midterm elections. But everyone was at it. The 1958 National Intelligence Estimate had forecast one hundred Soviet ICBMs by 1960 and five hundred by 1962. In January 1960 Allen Dulles, who should have known better because he did know better, told Eisenhower that even though the U-2 had shown no evidence of mass missile production, the Russians could still somehow conjure up two hundred of them in eighteen months. On the political left a former congressional aide called Frank Gibney wrote a baseless five-thousand-word cover story for *Harper's* magazine accusing the administration of giving the Soviets a six-to-one lead in ICBMs. (Gibney also recommended putting "a system of really massive retaliation" on the moon.) On the right, Vice President Nixon quietly let friends and pundits know that he felt his own boss didn't quite get the threat. And in the middle, Joe Alsop wrote a devastating series of columns syndicated to hundreds of newspapers in which he calculated that the Soviets would have 150 ICBMs in ten months flat and suggested that by not matching them warhead for warhead the president was playing Russian roulette with the national future.

Alsop, who lived well but expensively in a substantial house in Georgetown, was the Larry King of his day—dapper, superbly well connected, and indefatigable in the pursuit of a good story. His series ran in the last week of January 1960. Khrushchev read it in translation and resolved to steal the thunder of the missile-gap lobby, which was threatening to land him with an arms race that would bankrupt Communism. Before the four-power summit, which was now scheduled for Paris in mid-May, he would offer to dismantle his entire ICBM stockpile. No one needed to know how big or small it was; they just needed to know that he was serious about disarmament. He revealed his plan to the Presidium of the Central Committee of the Communist Party of the Soviet Union at a secret meeting in the Kremlin on February 1. It was bold, crafty, and conciliatory all at the same time. It was vintage Khrushchev, and it marked the high point of his power.

Eisenhower read the Alsop columns and fulminated. He called the missile-gap men "sanctimonious, hypocritical bastards." But he also bowed to mounting pressure from his own senior staff to beef up the evidence that the missile gap did not exist. This was why he allowed two more U-2 flights before the summit. It was an understandable decision, and a disastrous one.

It was understandable because the CIA had at last confirmed from other sources that the small stock of ICBMs Russia did have was being installed at Plesetsk, 150 miles due south of Archangel—and not in the northern Urals. Time to photograph them before they were hidden in their silos was fast running out, the Americans believed, and the more Ike knew about Khrushchev's true nuclear disposition, the less shadowboxing he would have to do in Paris.

It was disastrous for two reasons: Eisenhower was right that the loss of a U-2 over Russia would destroy his priceless reputation for honesty. But he was wrong if he thought that Khrushchev's silence on the subject of spy planes at Camp David meant he was resigned to them. On the contrary, privacy was now more central than ever to the Soviet leader's strategy. His extravagant bluffing about the size of his nuclear arsenal had to work, because without the impression of a meaningful stockpile, there could be no meaningful disarmament. What Khrushchev wrote later about arms inspections applied equally to overflights: the Americans "would simply have been given the opportunity to count our weapons and see that we were weak!"

He did not believe, after Camp David, that Eisenhower would allow his confounded U-2s to violate Soviet airspace again. But if reactionary forces within the administration sent them in anyway, they would *have* to be brought down.

* * *

The loggers and graders had arrived outside Kosulino the previous summer. They had come to other villages too, and on a map those villages made a tight ring round Sverdlovsk. Trees were felled and tracks cut into the woods that were suitable for heavy trucks but not much else. No one in the villages was told what was going on, but star-shaped patterns in the forest could be seen from civilian flights on final approach to Sverdlovsk Airport. Richard Nixon was on such a flight in late July. So was Ray Garthoff, a junior State Department staffer assigned to travel with the vice president. Nixon had asked to be allowed to use his own plane for the domestic side trips tacked onto his Moscow itinerary that year, in order to take pictures. The request had been turned down for the same reason, but Garthoff snapped some of star-shaped patterns in the forest anyway. Were *these* the long-sought ICBM sites that Stuart Symington knew all about?

Not quite. Until September they were nothing but clearings. Then soldiers arrived to dig in for the winter. Kosulino's battalion was led by Major Mikhail Voronov, a proud veteran of the Great Patriotic War and a confident leader of men. He had no rockets yet, but he had subordinates to train and by Lenin he would train them.

Voronov was born in 1918 in a village in western Russia too small to have a school. When Hitler's tanks rolled into Minsk he was a sergeant at war college in the Caucasus, and after two months of accelerated officer training he was dispatched to the front. At the battle of Tula he broke his leg. He was patched up in Tashkent, returned to the front, and apprenticed in the terrifying art of shooting at dive-bombers as the Fascists advanced on Stalingrad. At the battle of Kursk he commanded his own antiaircraft battery as wave upon wave of German fighter-bombers tried and failed to dislodge the Red Army. At Kursk he also met his wife, Valentina, who fought with him all the way to Lublin and still lived with him on the Black Sea coast sixty-three years later. The war prepared him for everything that followed, he said, including the events of May 1, 1960. That day felt "like a small war, just for me."

* * *

In terms of miles covered, it was a big war.

As the star shapes were being carved out of the forest round Sverdlovsk, a thousand miles to the south the new commander of the Turkistan Air Defense Corps set out on an urgent journey to the roof of the world.

It was a journey that probably began by air, over the giant white rampart of the northern Pamirs. Behind the rampart, in the late 1950s, snow leopards reigned supreme and the world's biggest nonpolar ice cap sent glaciers carving and tumbling toward China, Afghanistan, and the deep, fast-flowing River Pyandzh.

The commander's plane would have skirted to the west of the main Pamir massif and dived into the gorge dug by the Pyandzh to land on a thin concrete strip wedged between the river and Khorog. Then he needed a truck.

He was driven into the mountains along the legendary frontier road to Osh, leaving trees, warmth, and all trace of civilian life behind. Beyond the first high pass, where border guards kept vigil over one another and eventually managed to grow a few tomatoes in a greenhouse warmed by hot springs, the road descended a short distance onto a vast brown plateau. For an hour the truck followed the plateau's northern edge. To the left the lumpen shoulders of Pik Kommunizma, the highest mountain in the Soviet Union, stood back under their mantle of ice and snow. To the right, yaks grazed on oxygen-starved grass. Eventually the truck bumped off the road and headed south toward a cluster of white domes, barely visible at first but proof of a human presence in this moonscape.

The man in the truck was General Yuri Votintsev. Two years earlier he had led the showstopping procession of Dvina missiles through Red Square. Now he had come to shake things up at the closest Soviet early-warning station to Pakistan.

The U-2's flight planners in Washington believed that if they could smuggle the planes into Soviet airspace with no initial radar contact their chances of being tracked and shot down later in their missions would be drastically reduced. Votintsev and his superiors in Moscow knew from experience that this was true. They knew the monstrously impertinent routes flown by Cherbonneaux and Jones in 1957, even if they didn't know the pilots' names. They had an inkling about Knutson's route in 1959, even if Stan Beerli thought it had gone undetected. In December that year and again in February 1960, before Eisenhower's authorization for a final pair of flights before the Paris summit, more U-2s from Peshawar had photographed the pockmarked proving grounds of Kazakhstan from Kapustin Yar in the west to Sary-Shagan in the east. Votintsev was informed, but too late for a coordinated response.

"It took me two months to become familiar with the [radar] units, including the personnel of individual companies stationed along the Osh-Khorog road," Votintsev wrote. "I concluded that the effective strength of the corps deployed on the country's southern borders was not capable of accomplishing the assigned missions."

His men had been staring at their screens and seeing occasional high-flying specks, and yawning. Only the Andijon fighter squadron had shown any alacrity, but its pilots had not come within ten thousand feet of the intruders even in a zoom climb. Votintsev spent a year replacing dud officers with the best men at his disposal and installing powerful new radars along the Osh-Khorog road. It made a difference. U.S. aircraft flying along the Soviet border detected the new radars and their findings were fed into a National Intelligence Estimate of March 1960. The estimate said the only gaps left in the southern radar defenses of the entire Sino-Soviet bloc were in southwestern China.

Even so, project HQ thought the U-2s would still get through.

* * *

On April 8, 1960, Frank Powers and Bob Ericson, another Agency pilot still based at Adana, climbed into a C-130 and took off with the Quickmove team for Pakistan. Ericson was the mission pilot. Powers was his backup. Beerli was back in Washington as Bissell's head of operations. His place in charge of Detachment B had been taken by William Shelton, an air force colonel who was never quite obsessive enough about secrecy for Beerli's taste. As Beerli put it, cryptically and yet quite clearly: "Quickmove did not have such an impact on Shelton. . . . He was more or less Air Force rather than CIA."

The previous two missions had not provoked protest notes, but Powers knew the window of the U-2's invulnerability to Soviet rockets must be closing. "We could not shake the feeling that time was catching up with us," he wrote. He would find out soon enough that rockets had been fired at an air force U-2 on a ferret run along the coast of Chukotka in the Soviet Far East. They missed, but a Dvina missile had already brought down a Taiwanese spy plane at 63,000 feet near Beijing; and in Washington another National Intelligence Estimate, this one barely a week old, had concluded that the Dvina had "some capability" up to 80,000 feet.

In Kosulino and the other villages around Sverdlovsk, the rockets had at last arrived.

In central Siberia, a luxury log cabin was being built for President Eisenhower and his family on a headland overlooking Lake Baikal.

In a secluded piece of parkland outside Moscow, for the same honored guest, engineers and landscape artists were constructing the Soviet Union's first golf course.

* * *

Ericson took off at dawn on April 9 and was 150 miles into Soviet airspace before being spotted. For six hours he zigzagged over every top secret site in Kazakhstan, leaving chaos in his wake. It was a greatest hits tour, as if the pilot and his paymasters somehow knew that time was running out for Soviet overflights and he wouldn't be back: Sary-Shagan, Semipalatinsk, Sary-Shagan (again), Tyuratam (yet again). For six hours fighters were scrambled to intercept him, some armed, some unarmed, none with much hope of success. For six hours Marshal Sergei Biryuzov, head of all Soviet air defense forces, maintained a miserable, silent vigil in front of a giant map of the Soviet Union at his Moscow headquarters.

The most excruciating snafu was caused by the very nuclear security that Ericson was violating. The challenge was to get new Sukhoi Su-9 fighters into the air near the U-2, since they could zoom much higher than more readily available MiG-19s. Ericson seemed to dawdle forever over the Semipalatinsk site, but the nearest Sukhois were a thousand miles away in Perm and would need refueling before heading for the stratosphere.

Years later, Sergei Khrushchev pieced it all together:

> *The Semipalatinsk test site had its own airfield, but ordinary air force pilots were not permitted to land there. A special "atomic" pass was required. The local military headquarters sent a request to Moscow. Since it was the middle of the night, naturally only the air defense duty officer was there....*
>
> *The duty officer followed regulations. He woke up [Marshal] Biryuzov. Biryuzov informed the defense minister, Marshal Rodion Malinovsky....Malinovsky telephoned Yefim Slavsky, the minister of medium machine building [the official euphemism for nuclear defense]. He was the only one who could take responsibility for allowing "uncertified" pilots to land at his airfield. While all this telephoning was going on, time passed and it was 7 am before the unit finally received permission to land at Semipalatinsk. By then the U2 had finished photographing the nuclear test site and was heading toward Lake Balkhash....*

As Ericson finally headed south from Tyuratam, a seething Biryuzov broke his silence to order two MiG-17s to chase him into Iran if necessary. The planes were scrambled from Merv in southern Turkmenistan, the site of an especially horrific massacre by Genghis Khan in 1221. No one died there on April 9. One of the Soviet pilots spotted the U-2 as it sailed over the border and gave chase. But he ran low on fuel and turned back before Ericson started his descent.

Both Khrushchevs were in the Crimea for a spring break. Why not send a protest note this time? Sergei asked his father. "Why give our enemies the satisfaction?" was the reply. The Soviet premier then retired from public view for eleven days to nurse his rage.

* * *

Three weeks later the Americans did it again. Authorization for the mission came from the very top and was given with extreme reluctance on account of the looming Great Power summit in Paris and Eisenhower's hopes for it:

## TOP SECRET

April 25, 1960

MEMORANDUM FOR THE RECORD:

After checking with the President, I informed Mr. Bissell that one additional operation may be undertaken, provided it is carried out prior to May 1. No operation is to be carried out after May 1.

*A.J. Goodpaster*

The first person outside the White House to know about Mission 4154, apart from U-2 program director Richard Bissell, was Stan Beerli, the former Detachment B commander since reassigned to Washington. On April 26 he was told to pack for Norway. On the twenty-seventh he put on his usual dark suit and caught a flight from Dulles to Oslo. "I went commercial," he remembers, "via Copenhagen." He arrived on the twenty-eighth, checked into a hotel, and waited.

Barbara Powers knew something was up almost as soon as Beerli. On the twenty-seventh, a Wednesday, Gary asked her for a good-sized pack lunch, and that was something she could provide with or without a broken leg. She filled one thermos with hot potato soup and another with coffee. She made him six sandwiches filled variously with tuna, Spam, and pimiento cheese. She packed them all into a red plaid carrying case and filled the gaps with olives, cookies, and sweet pickles, because high-altitude weather recon could be a hungry-making business.

Her husband took off in a Hercules that morning, confident he'd be back by Sunday evening. The communications chief was going home, and "an appropriate sendoff had been planned."

Barbara was left with the one companion she knew loved her unconditionally—Eck, the German shepherd.

***

In Moscow, Marshal Biryuzov was still smarting. Comrade Khrushchev had chewed him out over the phone from the Crimea as only Comrade Khrushchev knew how. What did it say for the country's defenses against nuclear bombers if they could not bring down an unarmed spy plane? Where had all the billions for surface-to-air missiles gone? Was half the Soviet military asleep? Biryuzov passed the kicking down the chain of command.

"It was a terribly nervous time," said Colonel Alexander Orlov, namesake of the great illegal, who had spent the early hours of April 9 with Biryuzov in the air defense headquarters on Frunze Embankment. Orlov found out that a Soviet listening post in the Caucasus had picked up encrypted American radio chatter about the Ericson flight "several days before it happened" but had failed to pass it on.

Heads rolled at the listening post. Votintsev was reprimanded by the defense minister. In Kosulino, Voronov received orders to start sending his soldiers on live-fire exercises with the Dvina.

In Washington, the president had given permission for a second overflight and was not consulted again. It was up to Richard Bissell to choose between two spectacularly high-risk flight plans. One started in western Greenland and flew halfway around the Arctic Ocean before loitering for three hours over northern Russia and landing in Norway. The mission planners called it Operation Time Step. The other started from Peshawar and crossed the entire Soviet landmass, also ending in Norway. This was Operation Grand Slam. Both had one main target: Plesetsk, which still had not been photographed and still nourished air force fantasies of a massive Soviet ICBM strike force to be countered with an even more massive American one.

Bissell chose the Grand Slam route and left town for the weekend.

***

"We were trying something new," Powers wrote later.

It was a small thing; a variation on Quickmove devised by Colonel Shelton and General Bill Burke, another air force man who was serving as Bissell's deputy in Washington. If the weather was bad over Russia and the mission delayed, the U-2 would be flown back to Adana rather than hidden in a hangar in Peshawar.

"Rudolf Abel" was arrested in his underpants in a room in New York City's Latham Hotel on June 21, 1957. At his subsequent arraignment and trial he played up to the image of Soviet superspy by hardly saying a word. (*Time & Life Pictures/Getty*)

Powers in his U-2 helmet. The faceplate frosted over the moment he released his canopy after the aircraft broke up over Sverdlovsk on May 1, 1960. (*Time & Life Pictures/Getty*)

The early U-2 pilots trained at a top-secret Nevada base that they called the Ranch, also known as Area 51. More than half a century later it remains strictly off limits to civilians even though the neighboring nuclear test site has long since fallen silent. (*Getty*)

Except to the few who saw it up close, during the cold war the U-2 only ever appeared as a thin black line against the sky. (*Time & Life Pictures/Getty*)

The U.S. air base at Adana in southeastern Turkey as seen from a U-2 in 1958.
(© *Stan Beerli/Courtesy of the author*)

Former lieutenant Nikolai Batukhtin in Sverdlovsk, now Yekaterinburg, with an S-75 missile of the kind that his unit used to bring down Powers. (*Courtesy of the author*)

Former captain Mikhail Voronov, eighty-nine years old, at his home on the Black Sea, recalling the moment that the missile fired on his order detonated near the tail of Powers's aircraft, changing the course of history. (*Courtesy of the author*)

The wreckage of Powers's U-2 remains on permanent display in Moscow's Central Armed Forces Museum fifty years after it was first exhibited to the public, and to bashful U.S. diplomats, in Gorky Park. (*Courtesy of the author*)

The Bridge of Spies today. (*Courtesy of the author*)

Upon his release, Pryor flew back to the United States with his family, determined to put his "Rip van Winkle" experience behind him. He strode through the airport flanked by police, looking like an investment banker. (*Time & Life Pictures/Getty*)

No one could be exchanged on the Glienicke Bridge until Frederic Pryor was handed over to his parents at Checkpoint Charlie, the legendary crossing point between West Berlin's American sector and the East. (*©SuperStock, Inc.*)

This was not how Beerli would have done it. Beerli was a hide-everything-and-everyone-in-the-hangar man—but he was no longer in charge. He was in Oslo, waiting.

Soon after midnight on Thursday, April 28, the U-2 for Operation Grand Slam dropped out of the blackness and coasted to a halt on the concrete at Peshawar. It was the plane known as Article 358, the most reliable in the detachment's inventory. Powers had arrived the previous afternoon in the C-130. He'd eaten some of Barbara's soup and turned in early—not that there was much chance of real sleep on a camp bed in a corner of the hangar. "It was hot and noisy," he wrote. "As usual, I tossed and turned, sleeping only sporadically."

He was woken at 2:00 a.m. to eat, suit up, and start prebreathing for a 6:00 a.m. takeoff. There was no steak in Peshawar, but there were eggs, bacon, and toast. If it took an effort of will to hold down such Anglo-Saxon staples while wrestling with preflight nerves, no U-2 pilot admitted it. Powers just called it "a good, substantial breakfast," as if bacon and eggs at two in the morning at the foot of the Khyber Pass were the most natural thing in the world.

About 3:00 a.m.—the middle of the evening rush hour on the East Coast—the CIA's weather analysts in Washington postponed the mission by a day. The message was encrypted, sent to Germany, bounced from there to Turkey, and bounced again over the Hindu Kush to Pakistan. Powers came off the hose and Shelton had the U-2 ferried back to Turkey.

The same thing happened on Friday and Saturday. It was too cloudy over Russia to use the precious presidential permission slip for a mission that might yield nothing. Each day the U-2 commuted to Adana and back—except that by Friday night, Article 358 had flown two hundred hours since its last major inspection and was due for another. On Saturday, Article 360 was flown in instead. No one in the detachment liked Article 360. Powers called it "a dog."

* * *

By 6:00 a.m. on May 1 it was already "scorching hot" on the Peshawar flight line, and there were plenty of good reasons to cancel Mission 4154.

The mission's cover was almost certainly blown. There had been seven U-2 ferry runs in three days between Turkey and Pakistan. To make them possible, Shelton had been forced to fly in extra fuel from Adana, and for no obvious reason he had broken Beerli's rule of only using C-130s, loading the fifty-five-gallon drums into a conspicuous double-decker C-124 instead. Quickmove was a distant memory. The airport watchers who the CIA assumed were retained by Moscow to monitor U-2 movements in Peshawar and Adana can seldom have been busier. The same was surely true of the Soviet listening post in the Caucasus, caught napping by Orlov earlier in the month. "Can you think of any better way to telegraph to the Russians that we were coming?" Beerli would ask.

Article 360 was, moreover, a lemon. It had run out of fuel over Japan the previous year, leading to a belly landing and extensive repairs back in California. But one set of wing tanks was still not always feeding fuel to the engine properly. As Powers put it, "something was always going wrong," and his good friend Bob Ericson agreed. Ericson was in the hangar as Powers's backup and did not believe the plane would get to Norway.

Even in a perfect plane, the odds against success would have been daunting. Grand Slam was the first mission to try to cross the Soviet Union from one side to the other, which would mean flying in a straight line for hours at a time. Ericson had shown on April 9 that continuous changes in direction helped to throw off pursuers; Powers would not have that luxury.

The Soviet air defense forces were now on near-permanent alert. Despite its zigzags, the April 9 mission had been tracked by Soviet radar and followed by Soviet fighters for eight and a half of its nine hours. The National Security Agency may not have been able to eavesdrop on Khrushchev's furious reaction, but it was reasonable to assume that Marshal Biryuzov and his men would do their utmost not to let another U-2 get away. Furthermore, the CIA knew the Russians had plugged its radar gaps in the Pamirs.* It had also come to believe the Russians were

* It may not have known yet that Lee Harvey Oswald, who later shot President Kennedy, had offered Moscow information on the U-2 when trying to defect the previous year. Oswald had worked as a radar operator at a base used by U-2s in Japan, but his security clearance there was low.

close to solving the guidance problems that made surface-to-air missiles so unreliable at very high altitudes, and it knew that S-75 Dvina missiles had been installed around Sverdlovsk. Officially the pilots were not privy to this intelligence, but they had collected much of it and knew full well that the window of opportunity for overflying Russia was probably closing.

They did not know in any detail what they were supposed to be looking for, but Allen Dulles did, and as director of central intelligence he had admitted to Eisenhower in January 1960 that if the Soviets really had a crash ICBM program of the kind the U-2 was seeking, it would have been found already. Nonetheless, final planning continued for a May 1 overflight, even though it was a major Soviet holiday. Most military and civilian air traffic would be grounded for the festivities. An intruder, especially at seventy thousand feet, would stick out like a UFO.

If Powers crashed or was brought down, Eisenhower's hopes for a resolution to the Berlin crisis at the Paris summit—not to mention his shared vision with Khrushchev of large-scale nuclear disarmament—would almost certainly crash with him. Ike had thought this through in clairvoyant detail. "The President said that he has one tremendous asset in a summit meeting," General Goodpaster wrote in another memorandum for the record on February 8. "That is his reputation for honesty. If one of these aircraft were lost when we are engaged in apparently sincere deliberations, it could be put on display in Moscow and ruin the President's effectiveness."

But the truth was no one in Washington was listening to the arguments against overflights anymore. By the end of April even Eisenhower had given up. He considered himself a good judge of character but had completely misinterpreted Khrushchev's silence on the subject of the U-2 at Camp David and the absence of protest notes since. His science adviser, George Kistiakowsky, thought the Russians were "practically inviting us" to continue with the overflights, and the president was coming around to the same view.

The U-2 mission planners, now just two blocks from the White House on H Street, were still trying to prove a negative—the absence of a giant missile factory. This was not easy in a country the size of the USSR, and they still hadn't photographed Plesetsk, the suspected ICBM site north of the Arctic Circle. They knew about the heightened risk now posed by surface-to-air missiles, but they used it as an argument for risk, not restraint; for cramming in as many missions as possible before overflights really did become suicide runs. At the latest meeting of the president's Board of Consultants on Foreign Intelligence Activities, in February, General James "Jimmy" Doolittle had gotten in on the act. The hero of the Doolittle raid was now secretary of the air force and hardwired, like his predecessors, to press relentlessly for action. Toward the end of the meeting the sober Goodpaster, who knew his master's mind more intimately than anyone else in the room, reminded those present of a brand-new spy plane in the Skunk Works pipeline that would be available soon and would fly higher and much faster than the U-2, making it almost impossible to intercept. Doolittle pounced. "The reliability of the new airplane is bound to be much lower," he pointed out. "This is a special factor in this connection, since the embarrassment to us will be so great if one crashes." The logic was contorted, but it had ground Ike down. He had given permission for a flight and they were going to use it.

* * *

Powers had spent Friday night playing poker. By Saturday night the waiting was getting to him, and so was the knowledge that he would be flying a less-than-perfect plane if the go code ever came through. But he was at least drowsy enough to get some sleep.

In the Urals two pilots of the 45th Fighter Regiment of the Soviet air defense forces, Captain Boris Ayvazyan and Lieutenant Sergei Safronov, turned in expecting to have Sunday off. They were stationed outside Perm, an unlovely, smog-choked factory town west of the Urals on the Trans-Siberian railway. Two months earlier, Ayvazyan had shot an American spy balloon out of the sky. Statistically, the chances of his being called upon to land another blow on the American aggressors quite so soon were slim.

A third pilot, Captain Igor Mentyukov, was en route from Novosibirsk to Belorussia in one of two brand-new Sukhoi Su-9s being delivered to an air base at Baranovichi. It was a long flight and hard to do in a single day given its low priority and the need for multiple refuelings. There was also a discouraging thunderstorm over the Urals that evening. Mentyukov and his partner were spending the night in officers' lodgings in Sverdlovsk.

In the woods outside Kosulino, Mikhail Voronov had let three of his officers go home for the holiday, but his rockets were still manned. One of those still on duty was Lieutenant Nikolai Batukhtin, graduate of the Gorkovsky Radio-Technical Institute in Samara and now the proud operator of the transmitter that sent in-flight guidance signals to the rockets. The fiasco of April 9 had stung them all, but by the thirtieth, he insists, "we were ready."

For the radar stations along the Osh-Khorog road, May Day would not mean family. No family could endure the endless cold and desiccated air of the Pamir plateau, never mind the stories whispered by the mountains of the man-eating *snezhnyi chelovek*—the abominable snowman. But there might be vodka, and that would take the edge off the boredom.

In Adana, Barbara Powers was resigned to not having Gary back for Sunday evening. It would not be the first party she had enjoyed without him.

In Washington, Richard Bissell (by this time thoroughly distracted by plans for toppling Castro in Cuba) was weekending with Walt Rostow, an old friend and a future liberal apologist for the Vietnam War. Bissell's deputy, air force colonel Bill Burke, was handling U-2 matters.

The weather over Russia looked better, though not perfect. Eisenhower's permission was unclear as to whether a flight could happen on May 1 but quite clear that it could not happen after. That would be too close to the summit. It was now or never. Burke said afterward that he consulted with Allen Dulles before issuing the go code, and Dulles concurred.

The code took a long time to reach Peshawar.

Powers was woken at 3:00 a.m. His routine restarted: long johns, breakfast, suit, hose. As he started purging his system of nitrogen, he received his flight plan. It was 4:30 a.m. and the first time he knew he would be heading for Norway. A few months later he wrote wryly that he was glad he'd already had his breakfast because after looking at the map he would have been too nervous to eat. Before he pulled on his helmet and started shutting out the rest of the world, Shelton came over and asked if he wanted to take a pin.

Approved suicide methods had moved on from the L pill. For a reported three million dollars, the CIA had produced a needle dipped in highly concentrated curare poison from the South American jungle and hidden in a silver dollar. The coin was made to look like a souvenir brooch. One end of the pin protruded, ending in a flange. A quick twist and the whole thing came apart easily enough. Then a decisive jab anywhere in the body would bring on total, permanent anesthesia with no need for the sharp intake of breath required with cyanide.

"OK," Powers said. Shelton gave him the silver dollar and he put it in an outer pocket.

He was told takeoff would be at 6:00 a.m. Normally the go code would come through four hours before that, but Powers was nearly an hour into his prebreathing and still it hadn't come. Ericson helped him out to the plane anyway and strapped him in.

Six o'clock came and went, and still no go code. As the sun came up, Powers waited and sweated. Ericson, who was waiting with him, took off his shirt and spread it over the canopy.

Powers was convinced the mission would be scrubbed, and Shelton was getting anxious. He came over to say they were still waiting for clearance from the White House, which wasn't true. It was past eight o'clock in Washington and all the approvals were in. Burke had sent the go code. It had reached Germany, and Turkey, but the communications chief there was having trouble retransmitting it. The CIA later identified the problem as ionospheric interference, which was not a euphemism for a hangover. It was a seasonal early-morning radio hitch, and it left only one option—to send the go code in unencrypted Morse on the aircraft emergency frequency, where at 6:20 a.m. on May 1 the comms crew in Peshawar eventually found it.

Anyone else listening in could have found it too, but Powers was not to know this, and if Shelton knew he didn't say. Powers started his engine, noted a half-hour delay in his logbook, and closed his canopy.

At 6:26 a.m. the giant black crow carrying Barbara Powers's husband, a fully loaded Hycon B camera, 1,300 gallons of fuel, and a two-and-a-half-ton Pratt & Whitney J-75 engine turned slowly onto the scorching runway. Powers was soaked in his own sweat and unable to wipe his brow because of the helmet clamped hermetically onto his suit. For the next nine hours he would be moving without moving, doing without thinking (he could think when it was over). But at least he had his orders, direct from his commander in chief. If this wasn't proving himself, nothing was. He throttled up. Outside, they heard the familiar rising scream. Inside, he left most of the noise behind but felt the power in his back and then beneath him as the great black crow succumbed to its outrageous excess of lift over drag and hurled him into the sky.

* * *

There was no trouble getting the signal to Oslo. In his hotel, Stan Beerli took the call that said the mission was a go. The CIA station chief had a plane ready to take him to Bodo on the Arctic coast, where he was to be joined by a Quickmove recovery team in a Hercules that had been waiting in Germany since the twenty-seventh. The team consisted of a pilot to bring Powers's plane back to Adana, Lockheed mechanics to ensure it was still airworthy, and enough fuel in fifty-gallon drums to keep the mission self-sufficient and thus secret.

Beerli had fond memories of Bodo. He had spent three weeks there with Powers and others in 1958, waiting for the weather to clear over Plesetsk and getting to know the local Norwegian intelligence chiefs (whom he indulged with Scotch and, on one occasion, a crate of lettuce flown in from Germany). Now it was spring, and long, limpid evenings had come to the fjords. In other circumstances there would have been fishing and maybe hiking in the backcountry. This time Beerli was confined to the Norwegian air force base that filled most of the flat land between the mountains and the water.

He had told the head of Norwegian intelligence in Oslo that the mission he was going to meet would be a signals run along the Soviets' north coast. In Bodo, his point person was a General Tufti Johnson, and he had to be even less forthcoming with Tufti: they were doing atmospheric sampling. That was the line, he says, "but they weren't fooled a bit. They knew." And they knew the whippet-thin Beerli never brought enough to eat. "So this is May 1," he remembers. "We're sitting in the hangar, staying out of sight, not doing anything. And who should come walking in but Tufti Johnson with a tray full of hors d'oeuvres. And it's on a big silver platter, so I know what he did. He just picked it up from the mess hall and brought it over. I'll never forget that."

* * *

The miner's boy from Pound pricked the great imaginary bubble of Soviet airspace at 67,000 feet, flying more or less level. As his fuel load lightened, he would climb another 3,000 feet. Turning his head an inch or two inside his helmet, he could make out the brilliant, sculpted white of the high Pamirs nine miles beneath his right wing. Ahead, an ocean of cloud covered the cotton fields and the parched nothingness of Soviet central Asia. Everything else could have been anywhere else—Nevada, Turkey, California; the blue black of the stratosphere was a constant. So were the suit, the yoke, the reassuring slab of instruments, the soft hiss of the oxygen.

Powers clicked his radio on, then off. Bob Ericson was listening out for it in the Peshawar radio van. He sent a click back, and Powers was on his own with 3,788 miles to go.

"Everything was working perfectly," he would write in prison five months later. "No excuses for aborting the mission and no returning. I had to continue."

He guessed he'd been airborne for thirty minutes. In fact the radar station on the Pamir plateau picked him up and logged him as an intruder after just ten. The calls started at 5:36 a.m. Moscow time: the Pamir station to Tashkent, Tashkent to the duty officer on Frunze Embankment, the duty officer to Marshal Biryuzov, Biryuzov to Marshal Malinovsky.

It fell to Malinovsky as defense minister to wake Khrushchev on the secure Kremlin line. The call was patched through to his residence in the Lenin Hills, where the phone on the premier's bedside table rang at 6:00 a.m. It was happening again. All units had been alerted. They would do their utmost....

Khrushchev came down for breakfast looking like thunder. "He sat at the table in silence," his son remembered. "There was only the sound of his spoon clinking against the sides of his glass of tea."

For an hour Powers flew north over the Kara-Kum and Kyzyl-Kum deserts, unobserved for all he knew, but in Moscow they knew his location to within a few miles.

Chauffeurs had been woken even earlier than Biryuzov and his senior staff to speed them through empty streets to the air defense forces' command center, where they watched the U-2's progress on the same map that had recorded the April 9 humiliation. The map was printed on a wall-sized glass screen. Behind it, a uniformed sergeant silently pushed a black cross toward Tyuratam as each new fix on Powers's position came in.

Over the Cosmodrome the cloud thinned and Powers switched on his cameras. Far below he saw the first contrails of pursuit planes, supersonic, first heading south, then with him to the north. He wasn't worried. He pressed on.

With Biryuzov was Alexander Orlov, whose tasks in the previous tense weeks had included plotting potential future U-2 routes. This was not one of them. The Americans usually flew loops over central Asia. True, they had taken a look at Sverdlovsk before, but why again? (It was a good question to which there was no good answer. To Stan Beerli, routing Powers over Sverdlovsk when the Agency knew it had recently received S-75s was asking for trouble, and it still rankled decades later.)

The first alarm woke Mikhail Voronov at seven o'clock: "Was I asleep? Of course I was asleep. It was the first of May. I was planning to walk over from the barracks to give my soldiers their traditional May Day congratulations. Instead I ran. We all did. We rushed to our positions and when we got there I told my commander that my battalion was ready to fire, ready to push the button."

For most of Voronov's men this meant scrambling out of tents and into uniforms on the one day of the year when they could have expected an extra hour in their sleeping bags. It was a rude awakening, especially considering this was almost certainly a drill.

Word came through that it was not a drill. Voronov passed it on: there was an intruder twenty thousand meters over the Aral Sea with who knew what in its bomb bay. The control cabin filled up: Voronov, Lieutenant Batukhtin, and five other guidance-control officers, one for each rocket.

Silence fell over the encampment.

Was this how it started? Was this what the Americans wanted on the first of May? "We were bewildered and shocked," Batukhtin says. "We couldn't understand how in the middle of the country an enemy plane had simply appeared in the sky. It was like a strike from the blue."

Yet no one panicked, least of all Voronov. The veteran of Kursk and Tula knew a thing or two about morale. As the silence stretched the nerves of the younger men in the cabin, he got back on the radio and asked his commander, a Colonel Gaiderov two villages away, if they could all have breakfast. Gaiderov gave them ten minutes.

* * *

Boris Ayvazyan, the pilot from the 45th Fighter Regiment, lived two hundred miles from Kosulino but only thirty-two minutes from his base. He knew this because he commuted by motorbike. (As in Miramar, so in Perm: no self-respecting top gun went to work by bus.) He didn't have a phone, though—he was scrambled Soviet style by a soldier banging on his door.

By the time he got to his MiG-19, his wingman, Sergei Safronov, was already there and suited up. They took off, then received their orders: fly to Sverdlovsk and refuel. Back on the ground they waited for what felt like hours. They demanded breakfast.

***

Three hours and thirteen hundred miles into Mission 4154, Powers's autopilot quit. He had expected fuel-feed problems if Article 360 chose to act up, but this was almost as serious. Instead of staying automatically within the narrow speed and altitude ranges that kept the plane flying economically and in one piece, it started pitching up and slowing down. He had 2,400 miles to go. Six hours. Flying the plane manually for those six hours while also navigating, operating the cameras, and constantly checking instruments would be a whole new sort of marathon. But the skies ahead had cleared and he could see no contrails below. Turning back would be no picnic. "I continued as planned."

***

Marshals Biryuzov and Savitsky were staring at the glass wall, thinking about ceilings. Biryuzov was Khrushchev's most senior man in uniform. Savitsky had command of every fighter squadron in the country and knew better than anyone that unless the intruder had to lose height because of a malfunction, Ayvazyan and Safronov stood little chance of reaching him. No one had flown a MiG-19 higher than 17,500 meters even in a zoom climb (which Savitsky claimed to have invented). His only hope was a Su-9, but his only Su-9s within range of the impertinent black cross were the two being delivered by Igor Mentyukov and his partner to Baranovichi. They were unarmed, but they would have to do.

Their pilots were summoned. Mentyukov could not be found, so his partner was sent up alone, vectored south toward the closed nuclear city of Chelyabinsk, and ordered to jettison his drop tanks for extra height. He ran out of fuel so quickly that he had to force land in a field.

The search for Mentyukov had not been abandoned. The legend of Mentyukov, in fact, was only just beginning. By some accounts he had put on his uniform and was heading into town to join the festivities when apprehended at a bus stop. By his own account he stood waiting at a bus stop *after* being found at his hotel; for all the urgency of the moment, a bus was his only way of getting to his plane.

The result was the same: by the time Mentyukov reached the airport, Marshal Savitsky (code name "Dragon") had run out of patience. Mentyukov was ordered to take off at once. He obeyed, strapping himself in without pressure suit or helmet and taxiing past Ayvazyan and Safronov, who were wolfing down their breakfast while listening in over their headsets.

Mentyukov took off still not knowing what he was supposed to do.

Sverdlovsk's ranking air force commander, General Yuri Vovk, took the microphone.

> *Vovk:* Can you hear me?
> *Mentyukov:* Loud and clear.
> *Vovk:* Your course is Chelyabinsk. You have a real target at high altitude. Your mission is to destroy it.
> *Mentyukov:* I'm ready. I'm totally ready.

There was a problem, though. He had no weapons. He knew that Vovk knew, which could only mean one thing.

> *Vovk:* Your mission is to intercept the target and ram it. That's an order from Dragon.

Mentyukov lit his afterburner and pointed his plane toward the heavens. "I quickly knew I had no way out," he said much later. "If I refused that would have been the end—of my career, my reputation, everything. It was better to die well, so I asked them one thing—to look after my pregnant wife and mother."

The legend says Savitsky personally assured him over the live link from Moscow that his family would be well cared for. Ayvazyan, who was still listening, says he never heard the line about the pregnant wife and that no fighter pilot busy putting his life on the line would pause to say such a thing. But it is not disputed—because it was seen on so many radar screens—that Mentyukov then climbed through 65,000 feet without a pressure suit, and kept on climbing, and closed on Powers from behind at twice the speed of sound.

Ground control cut in. "Target ahead, twenty kilometers."

Reliving these few seconds at the age of seventy-seven, Mentyukov had a clear recollection of his altitude—20,090 meters—and his speed: 2,185 kilometers per hour. This meant he was traveling a thousand miles an hour faster than the U-2, shrinking the gap between them by a mile every three seconds.

"Target, fifteen...target, ten...target ahead! Look, look! Can you see him?"

He could not. He was looking for a line in the sky. It would be no more than that, and it would be gone in a flash.

In Moscow, Savitsky could see his plan unraveling. He told Sverdlovsk ground control to order Mentyukov to cut his afterburner. Mentyukov refused: maximum power was the only way he could maintain maximum height. The order was repeated. It was Dragon's order! Mentyukov cut his afterburner and fell like a stone.

***

Khrushchev finished his tea and left for the Kremlin. From there, a little later, he would walk out of the Spassky Gate to take his place on the reviewing stand in front of Lenin's mausoleum. There would be gymnasts, dancers, soldiers, missiles, tanks, veterans of the Great Patriotic War, young pioneers, and banners—endless triumphal banners in the red and gold of the revolution. All the pride of world Communism, real and manufactured, would be concentrated for him, right in front of him, here in Red Square over the next two hours.

His power was unchallenged. Stalin and Stalinism were history. The putschists of 1957 had not dared try again. The skeptics of his new coziness toward America had not yet broken cover. The golf course and the magnificent retreat above Lake Baikal—they would be finished in time for the Eisenhowers' visit. The new era was not yet at hand, but it was achievable, and it would be Khrushchev's achievement. Yet his mind was fogged with anger.

On May Day Khrushchev normally drove his own family into town. Today he had left them to make their own way and come with his driver. On May Day Biryuzov would normally be with him on the stand. Today he was in his command center watching helplessly as another spy plane peeled back another layer of the thin wrapping that covered the Soviet Union's nuclear nakedness. Khrushchev had already lost his temper with Biryuzov on the telephone. Now all either of them could do was wait.

* * *

Mentyukov had overshot and was almost out of fuel. As his altimeter unwound he was ordered back to base.

Ayvazyan and Safronov, fed and refueled, took off again and spiraled to gain height over Sverdlovsk, awaiting further orders. But Savitsky was at a loss to know what to do with them. It was the rocketeers' turn.

Voronov's men had breakfasted, then waited in silence as medium-range radar stations to the south tracked Powers heading north. As he sailed over Chelyabinsk, one hundred miles south of Sverdlovsk, Voronov switched on his target-acquisition radar and for the first time saw the intruder as a green dot on his screen.

For a few minutes the dot continued north. Then it turned sharply to the right. There was one kink in Powers's route, and this was it. Two years earlier the cooling system for a nuclear-waste tank near Kyshtym, north of Chelyabinsk, had exploded, releasing more radiation than Chernobyl and a surge in strontium-90 levels that the CIA had been able to detect as far west as Alaska. Bob Ericson had flown over the site the previous summer. Rightly or wrongly, the Agency wanted another look.

The right turn took Powers over a network of fuel-enrichment and nuclear-waste plants east of Kyshtym and out of range of Voronov's rockets. *That's it,* Voronov thought, *he's escaped.*

* * *

Powers knew nothing about the Kyshtym disaster. For half a century the countryside below him would remain one of the most irradiated places on earth, but from thirteen miles up on a fine spring day the scars and smokestacks of the Armageddon industry blended innocently into a two-dimensional spread of forests, lakes, and farmland.

Powers thought it looked a bit like Virginia. He took his pictures and made a ninety-degree left turn that pointed him back toward Sverdlovsk, Scandinavia, and safety.

At this point, he would write in his prison diary, he was "feeling fairly good":

> *I was on course, the aircraft was working very good with the exception of the autopilot, and the weather was clear and navigation was fairly easy. I had been in clear weather for thirty minutes or so.*

Voronov's targeting officer saw the left turn at once. The dot was coming back into range, and the Kosulino battery was going to have the best shot. An order came through from the regimental command post to fire if the guidance system could lock on.

"I followed the dot till it came in range," Voronov said. "Then I gave the order. *Pusk.*"

Nothing happened. For some reason Eduard Feldblum, the launch-control officer, was hesitating.

"Fire!" Voronov yelled, and Feldblum pressed the button.

It was 8:52 a.m. Moscow time; nearly one in the morning in Washington. Three of Voronov's six rockets were supposed to spurt fire and streak heavenward, defying gravity and America and the slippery upper atmosphere in a supersonic firework extravaganza for the ages. If they had, Frank Powers would have been done for and every assertion by Eisenhower's advisers that a high-altitude U-2 shoot-down was not survivable would have proved accurate. But only one rocket ignited. It shot up toward seventy thousand feet on a whoosh of flame, creating its own radar dot and converging at Mach 2 on the dot that was Article 360. For a full minute the men in the cabin watched their screens and everyone else waited—Ayvazyan and Safronov in their spiraling MiGs, Vovk (and now Mentyukov) on the ground, Biryuzov and Savistsky and their underlings in the command center, Khrushchev in the Kremlin, Beerli—not that he was worried yet—in Oslo.

The Dvina had two boosters. The second would give out at twelve and a half miles, after which everything depended on ballistics and luck. In principle the missile's fins would still have some purchase up there on the final, quiet yards of its trajectory. In principle the warhead would detonate automatically when it came within two hundred feet of its target. But above twenty kilometers anything could happen. Or, as likely, nothing.

"We watched the two dots," Voronov says, bringing his two old hands together above the table in his front room near the Black Sea. "And then we saw them hit each other." In Moscow it was 8:53 a.m.

Powers felt it as a WHUMP. Not a bang or a crump, but a whump. It was not a word he would have used if he were making it up. He had made his left turn and noted down his speed and altitude and exhaust gas temperature when the sky went orange and the whump hit him in the back. "Good Lord," he said to himself and maybe to his helmet. "I've had it now." He knew the plane would probably break up, but for a few seconds it stayed in one piece. His right wing had dipped, so he pulled left on the yoke and seemed to be flying level again. Then his nose started dropping, so he pulled back on the yoke, but this time it kept on dropping and the aircraft started to describe a big, slow arc from the horizontal to the vertical, gradually losing all its forward speed and converting some of it to downward speed in the sickening inverse of a zoom climb, leaving Powers looking straight down at Russia and realizing he had probably lost his tail. Those five-eighth-inch bolts were not designed to survive a missile blast any more than he was.

Both wings tore off, and what was left of the U-2 started to spin, first nose down, then nose up, dragged earthward by its two-and-a-half-ton engine. Powers spun inside it, painfully, his body forced up out of his seat against his seatbelt, his helmet smashing against the inside of his canopy. His first thought was that he would have to eject, but the g-forces building in the cockpit made thinking hard and pushing back into his seat even harder. Something else was making movement difficult. His pressure suit had inflated. And something else again was nagging at the back of his mind. He was supposed to throw the self-destruct switches that would destroy the camera in the payload bay below him. So for a few long seconds of his life Frank Powers was wedged up against the canopy of an airplane that had lost its wings and tail, in a suit that was supposed to save his life but felt as if it were squeezing the life out of him, weighing strategies for getting out alive and keeping America's most precious secret all at the same time.

Arcing over his legs, in front of his nose, was a titanium canopy rail.

The front edge of the removable part of the canopy slotted into it. If he could reach down between his legs and pull the eject cord right now, his rocket-powered seat would bust through the canopy, but nothing would bust through the rail, which looked as if it would cut his legs off somewhere above the knee. That much was knowable in the blur of sky and sensation that threatened to tip Powers into panic as his bullet-shaped black fuselage fell backward through 34,000 feet.

Thirty-four thousand feet was still an Everest and a half, but it was shrinking at ten thousand feet a minute. He had to think, to stop and think. That was more than an idea. It was a highly specific piece of advice from someone who had been through this sort of serious equipment failure and worked the problem and come out dangling from his parachute and not even too shaken up. (Jack Nole? Bob Ericson? Powers would thank whomever it was in his memoirs, though not by name.)

So he used some of the precious time he had earned by falling from such a great height to think, and in doing so he saved himself. He realized he didn't have to eject. He could climb out. He opened the canopy by hand and was flung sideways into a freezing hundred-mile-an-hour wind rushing up at him from the fields around Kosulino.

Powers's faceplate frosted up instantaneously. He was still connected to the cockpit by his oxygen tube, and the cockpit was still spinning, so he was spinning with it, on a lanyard. (The physical remnants of this moment are museum exhibits and black-and-white photographs, but they are photographs of the man in borrowed lounge suits and of his airplane in pieces. They scarcely convey the astounding fact that all this actually happened; that for a few seconds in May 1960, as the Western world slept and the Soviet Union tried simultaneously to celebrate the American spring and the triumph of international socialism, a fine young man from a small town in Virginia, with every good intention but no visa, was to be found tumbling toward Sverdlovsk in a fully inflated pressure suit, loosely connected to the dismembered fuselage of a U-2.)

He had not forgotten the destruct switches. By his own account he tried to pull himself back toward the cockpit to activate the seventy-second timer that, the Agency had promised, would give a pilot time to get clear before the two pounds of cyclonite explosive detonated. But the switches were hard to get at and the g-forces were too strong, he said—and he was there. "And then I thought: I've just got to try to save myself now. Kicking and squirming, I must have broken the oxygen hoses, because suddenly I was free, my body just falling, perfectly free."

For a few more seconds the body of the plane fell next to him. Then, at fifteen thousand feet, his parachute opened automatically. With time to think again, he pulled off his frozen faceplate. He considered using the poison pin on the way down but thought better of it. Why now? Escape was still conceivable, and if he tried it he might need the pin as a weapon.

He floated past a set of power lines and landed hard in a field, where a farm worker who had been watching his descent from a tractor walked over and started to fold the parachute. A Moskvich car bumped over the field from the direction of the nearest village. The driver got out and helped Powers to his feet. "Are you OK?" he asked in Russian. No reply; just a troubled look from a man in shock.

"Are you Bulgarian?"

A crowd was gathering, drawn by the fireworks and the sight of Powers's orange and white parachute on its long descent, and now by the sheer strangeness of his alien presence in their field. He carried a pistol in a holster outside his suit. A passenger from the Moskvich took it and gestured to Powers to get into the backseat. His seat pack went in the trunk. In it was a message printed on silk in fourteen languages: "I am an American and do not speak your language. I need food, shelter, assistance. I will not harm you. I bear no malice toward your people. If you help me, you will be rewarded." The Moskvich drove off, heading for Kosulino. Powers was offered a cigarette and took it. The passenger with the gun studied it for a while, then traced the letters "USA" in dust on the dashboard. Powers nodded.

* * *

Around ten o'clock there was a sudden ripple of movement in the row of dark overcoats on the reviewing stand in Red Square. Diplomats noticed it from their seats opposite the mausoleum. Khrushchev's son noticed it from the family's seats to the right. A man in air force uniform was pushing through the politburo toward Khrushchev himself, then whispering in his ear. It was Air Marshal Biryuzov, with the news.

* * *

"We were expecting him at noon," says Stan Beerli, who was waiting in Bodo with the Hercules and the Quickmove recovery crew. "We started clicking about a half hour before that."

A single click in reply was all they needed in the communications van in Bodo. They would know Powers was throttling back somewhere over the Arctic Ocean and starting his long glide back to earth with two drum-sized bobbins of nuclear secrets wound tightly in his Hycon B. But the click never came. They waited for a couple of hours, then started packing up. The Quickmove Hercules took Beerli back to Oslo, where he called the Agency's extension at the U.S. embassy. Three words: "The party's over." Then Beerli headed back to Washington.

Powers was already in Moscow. He spent that night in a cell beneath the Lyubianka, having been strip-searched, well fed, questioned for several hours, and relieved of his poison pin by a KGB man with a briefcase. As it was taken away, he asked an interpreter to make sure it was handled with great care. The KGB later put out the story that it was tested on a dog and that the dog perished in ninety seconds.

# part three

# CAUGHT IN THE ACT

# 8

# CITY OF COWBOYS AND INDIANS

In 1959 the official Soviet count of Western espionage, "terror," and propaganda organizations based in West Berlin was forty-eight. The generally accepted Western estimate of the number of Communist agents operating out of East Germany at the same time was sixty thousand.

Berlin was crawling with spies, sometimes literally. They had to crouch low to reach the end of the quarter-mile eavesdropping tunnel built by the British and Americans under the Soviet sector that had been dug up by the Russians when the snow melted in 1956.

Even at the end of the decade there was still no wall, so spies could mingle. They mingled in the bar at the brand-new Hilton and in raincoats at the airports. They mingled in uniform at the Allied military missions in Babelsberg, the international diplomatic enclave surrounded by Soviet-controlled territory on the west bank of the River Havel, and they mingled incognito in the glass-walled cafés along the Ku'damm. They traded stories with the Reuters men (and with Annette von Broecker, the beguiling Reuters editorial assistant) in the restaurants near the news agency's West Berlin bureau on Savignyplatz, and they traded hard information for hard currency in the CIA's rented villas in Zehlendorf.

The British hung out of the cockpits of RAF Chipmunks flying low over Soviet bases in the eastern suburbs and took pictures with handheld Minoltas. The French military attaché worked for the East German secret police or the KGB—no one was sure, or sure if the distinction mattered. The Russians practiced tradecraft in the ruined city center that they refused to rebuild as a way of reminding Germans of the price of Fascism. The Americans refused to recognize East Germany, but their mission to West Berlin was bigger than most of their embassies and bristling with antennae.

Willy Brandt, the West Berlin mayor and future West German chancellor, called his city's spies "grown-ups playing cowboys and Indians." As ever, he was being gracious. They were not always grown-ups. Students on both sides of the East German border were frequently offered assistance with their travel expenses in return for running errands and taking "interesting" photographs.

It was into this milieu that Fred Pryor parachuted after escaping from Yale. The graduate of Oberlin College and the Society of Brothers in remotest Paraguay was personable, funny, smart, and self-reliant. He was well traveled and interested in Communism, but everyone who knew him agreed he would have made a lousy spy. The idea was "amusing," says one Oberlin contemporary who went on to work for the CIA. He was "just too flaky and unreliable." Then it became more than idea, at which point, another friend remembers, "we all laughed."

Looking back, Pryor doesn't find it all that funny. "They knew who I was, the secret police," he says. "They had a file on me, even before."

Of course the Stasi knew who Pryor was. He was the American in the red Karmann Ghia, the lanky one at the Free University. He was the Yale PhD student with the deep and unusual interest in East German foreign trade. He was the one who had assiduously polished his German and was now crossing into the Soviet sector every few weeks, against the tide of East Germans flooding out, to interview the country's top economists and read their theories in the Hochschule für Planökonomie.

And the Stasi? They were the obsessives, the men in gray leather jackets with faces of stone and one informant or full-time agent for every thirty-eight adult East Germans. They were the most overstaffed security force in history, the Ministry for State Security. As the exodus of young professionals from East Berlin to West intensified in the spring and summer of 1961, they were obsessed in particular with the fear of an economic blockade should new border controls be introduced. To make a blockade hurt, the West would have to understand the country's foreign trade. And who knew more about that than the young American who liked to breeze through Checkpoint Charlie in his scarlet sports car? That he knew nothing and cared less about tradecraft and covert intelligence mattered little to the Stasi. They would have expected Pryor's interviews to report their contact with him to the authorities, and every one of them did. Even before the wall went up, it was inconceivable that the Stasi would not have a file on him.

* * *

The same was probably true of Marvin Makinen, though in the end it was not the Stasi who caught him.

Unlike Pryor, Makinen was one of those students who did get the call, whose personal contrails had singled him out as of interest to one of the forty-eight espionage, propaganda, and terror organizations operating in Berlin, and who was consequently invited—rather than forced—to join the grown-ups in a game of cowboys and Indians. In terms of life choices and intellect, he was not unlike Fred Pryor: a young man with spectacles and a precocious mind, at large in the world, intensely aware of its variety and not intimidated by its borders. But there was less of the innocent abroad about him, and more of the maverick.

Pryor and Makinen were contemporaries at the Free University but didn't know each other. Makinen was a fourth-year undergraduate exchange student from the University of Pennsylvania, majoring in chemistry but with political science credits still to earn. His dean had told him he would learn more political science in a year in Berlin than in a three-credit course in Philadelphia, and his dean turned out to be right.

In his first spring in Europe, in the break between winter and summer semesters, Makinen visited relatives in Finland. He had planned to ski with them in Lapland, but a distant cousin told him about a new package tour to Leningrad and Moscow, so he took that instead. Back in Berlin his Soviet visa had a certain cachet. In the ritual comparisons of passport stamps as students returned from France, Greece, Switzerland, and Yugoslavia (if they were daring), Makinen's stood out. People knew where he had been, including people whose business it was to know. "So I got the call," he said, "and I accepted."

He met two men from U.S. Army intelligence in a restaurant near the *Studentendorf* in Dahlem where he was living. They gave him a late-model Pentax, showed him how to use it, and suggested that he take advantage of the new camping routes through western Russia being advertised by Intourist. For the first time, westerners were allowed to take their own cars, and the men from army intelligence said they would lend him one. All he had to do was take a lot of pictures, and if he happened to take any of airports, bridges, military installations, passing tanks... well, that was all to the good.

Makinen left Berlin that summer bound for Prague, Budapest, Kiev, and points east if his traveler's checks allowed. He would be gone some time.

# 9

# A FIRST-CLASS PANIC

Norton, Virginia, is a few miles farther from the Appalachian watershed than Pound and altogether more established. The hills stand back from Route 23 as if a town is actually meant to be there. Main Street is straight and broad instead of having to follow every twist of the river, and although the side streets have to climb a little, they still allow the construction of respectable business premises that might suit a cobbler, or a lawyer, or, in hard times, both at the same address.

The late 1950s were hard times in Norton on account of the mechanization of the mines and the job losses that followed. Still, it was home for Carl McAfee, a young lawyer who set up there in private practice at the end of 1958 after a tour of duty in the army.

Norton also seemed to Oliver Powers a more auspicious place than Pound to open a shoe shop.

In the spring of 1960 McAfee and his partner had a none-too-onerous amount of lawyering to do, but they did maintain an office. "It was on the second deck in back of the bank," he remembers, "and Oliver had his shoe shop directly underneath. And believe it or not, in those days telephones were not rampant, and we had one line. I never will forget the number. Eight one three."

"I became acquainted with Oliver because he had a lot of time to spend, no clients or anything, and he and I became quick friends," McAfee continues. "I used to sit and chat with him, and he would tell me about Gary because Gary and I were the same age. He'd gone to Milligan and I'd gone to Lincoln Memorial, both in Tennessee. I didn't know him, but Oliver used to tell me that Gary was a pilot in the air force, and that went on through '59 and continued on into 1960 . . . and anyway he came running up there one morning and said, 'Carl, my son's been shot down over Russia.' And I said, 'Surely not,' and anyway, we chatted, and he said, 'Yeah, he has been.' "

Oliver was not mistaken. Two men from the CIA had done the nine-hour drive from Washington to bring the news on May 3, a Tuesday, which was the day the U.S. government first put out a press release admitting a U-2 was missing. The press took a while to catch up because that first release said nothing about Russia, but when they did catch up all hell broke loose.

"All of a sudden people were trying to reach Oliver," McAfee says. "He didn't have a telephone. I don't think he even had a telephone in his home, but somehow or another they got my telephone number, so I started getting all these calls to ask if I would get a hold of Mr. Powers—there were newspapers galore, and they wanted to talk to him."

The agency people would have preferred Mr. Powers to leave the talking to them, but—"well, you'd have to know Oliver," Mr. McAfee goes on. "If he wanted to talk, he was going to talk. That's the problem the government had with him. I thought the world of him, and he was not one to sit back and have somebody tell him, 'You've got to keep quiet, and you can't do this or you can't do that.' Because he was a person of action."

At about the time that two agency men turned up at the Powers home in Pound, two more called on Barbara Powers and Eck von Heinerberg, the family dog, on superhouse trailer row outside Adana. They told her Gary was missing and took her to the base doctor for an injection to calm her down. Three days later they came back and told her to pack for an emergency return to the United States. Her heavier belongings—her rugs, Gary's shotgun, the silver-gray Mercedes—would be shipped later. Eck could join her on the plane.

It was as if the Agency's top secret global reach was all facilitated with bungee cord: one long, sudden, jarring flight and Barbara's two-and-a-half-year Turkish interlude was over. She was going back to Milledgeville and her dyspeptic mother. The Agency men "fed me liquor to help ease my nerves," she later claimed. They flew with her through the night to New York, where they changed planes in a hurry and flew on to Atlanta. Eck went on by a different route in a crate, so as not to give away Barbara's arrival to the waiting press. In Atlanta her traveling companions rented a car for the drive to Milledgeville, but halfway there they stopped and asked if she would like to buy a gift for Mother's Day. That would be the next day, Sunday, May 8. Barbara clambered out with her one good leg and her other still in plaster. She saw her picture and Gary's on the front page of a newspaper and fainted on the spot.

* * *

Stan Beerli was not unduly worried as he flew south in the Hercules, back to Oslo. He knew Powers could have been shot down, but thought the most likely explanation for his no-show was that the mission had been scrubbed. He still thought so on the plane back to Washington and on his way into work on Tuesday, May 3. But when he walked into project HQ on H Street, he found "a first-class panic" under way.

The night duty officer in the early hours of May Day had been Carmine Vito, "the lemon drop kid." As a U-2 pilot over Eastern Europe, Vito was said to have sucked on an L pill for a while before realizing it wasn't one of his preferred lemon drops (not true, he later said; he only got as far as looking at it). But he really was the first man in Washington to know something might be wrong with Mission 4154: at around 4:00 a.m. Eastern Standard Time he took a call from the NSA saying that a surge in Russian military radio chatter starting more than three hours earlier had ended suddenly soon after one o'clock. Then Beerli's message had arrived via the Oslo station chief.

Vito phoned Bob King, one of Richard Bissell's special assistants. "Bill Bailey didn't come home," Vito said. "You'd better find the man, quick."

"The man" was Bissell. King knew he was out of town but didn't have Walt Rostow's number and had to tell the operator it was a "goddamn national emergency" before she gave it to him. By the time he got through, Bissell had left anyway. When he landed in Washington he went to the office—it was not far out of his way and there was a mission in progress, after all—to find the place in chaos.

Bissell was much admired on H Street for his cool head and his troubleshooting genius. His staff were relieved to see him. He practically sauntered in, Bob King recalled, "and everybody said (if not out loud, at least to themselves), 'Whew, now we're off the hook because he'll take charge of this mess.'... He came in as if he were about to assemble a Monday staff meeting—'Hmmm, hmmm, yeah, OK, we'll talk about it.' Not excited."

Inside, he felt "a sense of disaster about the entire affair." No end run round the air force was going to help him now. No quiet personal plea to Goodpaster or Dulles could put a U-2 back in the air once it was in pieces in the Urals. He was pretty certain the whole program would be canceled. He was also pretty certain the pilot would be dead. That being so, regrets apart, the next step was clear. The president had to be informed and asked to sign off on the preexisting cover story. Goodpaster was alerted at home in Alexandria. The Army Signal Corps put him through to Eisenhower at Camp David. Bissell passed on the news, and the president chewed it over in silence as he flew back to the White House on Marine One. He approved the cover story the next morning. The gist was a terse statement to be used as the basis of a press release issued from Adana:

> *U2 aircraft was on weather mission originating Adana, Turkey. Purpose was study of clear air turbulence. During flight in Southeast Turkey, pilot reported he had oxygen difficulties. This last word heard at 0700Z over emergency frequency. U2 aircraft did not land Adana as planned and it can only be assumed is now down. A search effort is under way in Lake Van area.*

Lake Van was 1,500 miles from Sverdlovsk, where the CIA was already reasonably certain Mission 4154 had ended. "Oxygen difficulties" could only get a plane so far off course. "If the Soviets claimed it had crashed not near the border but in the middle of the country, we planned to accuse them of moving it to a site that they had selected for propaganda purposes," Bissell wrote later. "All of this might have worked if Powers had not survived." *Might* have—but he was already clutching at straws.

***

The Soviet chatter picked up by the NSA on May Day did not stop when the two dots collided on Major Voronov's screen. In fact, at that moment it intensified. The screen dissolved into a blur of reflections that Voronov at first thought might be chaff thrown out by the intruder to confuse the missile. In any case he was preoccupied by the failure of two of his three rockets to fire.

After the cold war that failure was used to embarrass the veterans of the Soviet rocket troops: their vaunted surface-to-air missiles (SAMs) were like guard dogs that could not even be relied on to growl; or, in one version, two out of three shots had to be aborted at the last second because they would have obliterated the control cabin in the middle of the complex. But Nikolai Batukhtin explains the failure as a success: there was indeed a risk of destroying the cabin, but it was averted automatically, as Grushin had intended. The rockets were designed to fire at an angle to the ground of not more than sixty-three degrees. Any closer to vertical and their billowing exhaust, with nowhere to go, would incinerate their launchers and much else nearby. Only one rocket was given a suitable launch angle by its guidance system—and it did the trick.

After it had been fired, Batukhtin and three other lieutenants ran outside to see its exhaust trace and debris from an explosion drifting earthward through the clear blue sky. But Voronov stayed in the cabin and told Colonel Gaiderov, the Sverdlovsk air defense commander, that he could not confirm the target had been hit.

A neighboring battery was ordered to fire at anything within range, and did. Captain Ayvazyan and Lieutenant Safronov, the MiG pilots scrambled from Perm and still circling over Sverdlovsk, suddenly found themselves under attack. Realizing they were friend, not foe, ground control ordered them to lose height urgently. Ayvazyan understood what was happening and put his MiG into a vertical dive from 34,000 feet, pulling out at less than 1,000 feet and landing at once. Safronov was not so quick. Hit by one of three more missiles that were fired that morning, he ejected but was found dead next to his parachute.

At last the radar screens began to clear. Voronov realized he had probably hit the target with his one and only rocket, and shortly before 9:30 a.m. Moscow time, he got back on the radio to say so. The message was passed on from Sverdlovsk to Moscow, and a stunned calm returned to the airwaves above Russia.

Powers was lucky—and unlucky. "If we hadn't got him he would have made it to Scandinavia," Batukhtin says. "There was no other missile complex like ours on his route, or even in the country."

* * *

In his cell in Moscow, Powers ate nothing for a week. He had arrived in the bowels of the Lyubianka with an irregularly beating heart, a raging thirst, a headache, and an oppressive tiredness. In a scene that could have been written by Woody Allen, not one but three women doctors in white coats pronounced him fit, but he could not bring himself to eat. One of the doctors gave him two aspirin—and (could it have been?) a sympathetic glance. Another gave him an injection that he feared would be truth serum or a prelude to the brainwashing that the CIA believed would figure high on the KGB's menu for apprehended spies. It wasn't. He concluded it was a routine inoculation, or to help him sleep.

For all his tiredness, sleep came hard. The cot in his cell was a narrow metal frame with metal bands instead of springs and a couple of army blankets. A light above the door was never switched off and an eye in a peephole underneath it never went away. Each day he was taken to a large interrogation room, above ground, with natural light and a long table at which up to twelve people sat. They included, to begin with, Aleksandr Shelepin, head of the KGB, and Roman Rudenko, who smoked Western cigarettes and had been chief Soviet prosecutor at the Nuremberg trials. Periodically the questioning would pause for officials to talk among themselves. Powers began to form the impression that they did not know what to do with him, but this was an insidious idea that sat uneasily in his head alongside a more firmly established one—that sooner or later he would be taken out and shot.

His first faint hopes were quickly encouraged. On Monday he was taken on a tour of Moscow. He had been gone from Peshawar barely twenty-four hours and was being shown Red Square, Saint Basil's, and a ski jump high on the west bank of the Moscow River from the back of a Zil limousine. Truly this was not a tour that could be booked through Thomas Cook. If the idea was to confound his assumptions and make him believe anything was possible, it worked. "Perhaps I wouldn't be shot after all," Powers wrote. "Perhaps they were trying to impress me, both with their city and their kindness, because they were soon going to release me."

It was not a ridiculous thought. Again and again he was asked the obvious question: why had he been sent? More than once there was a follow-up that struck Powers as much less obvious: was it to ruin the Paris summit?

He was barely aware of the summit. The thought had not occurred to him, but now the fact of the meeting stuck in his mind. As the Zil headed back toward the Lyubianka, scenes started swimming in his mind of Khrushchev presenting him to Ike in Paris as a sign of goodwill and forgiveness—and proof of the astonishing performance of Russian S-75 rockets.

Powers was onto something. He understood that unless he was indeed going to be shot or hidden forever in a remote corner of the Gulag, his chief value to his captors was for propaganda. But to maximize that value they needed urgently to know if Washington knew he was alive. So the other question to which Shelepin and Rudenko kept returning was whether he had radioed his base before bailing out. Powers refused to answer, knowing that if he said he had, they might be able to prove he was lying by studying the remains of the U-2's radio, whose range was only three hundred miles; and knowing that if he told the truth—that he had not sent out a Mayday as he plummeted to earth—the Kremlin would still have the option of killing him and covering it up without much fear of an international scandal.

On Tuesday the questioning got tougher and Powers's hopes shrank back to zero. His minders started to worry about his appetite. The interpreter asked if there was anything that he would eat—anything at all. He asked for something to read, including a Bible, and was promised the interpreter's own copy of *Gone with the Wind.*

* * *

For three days, Eisenhower thought he might have gotten away with it. There were no diplomatic notes, no indignant Tass exclusives, and almost no U.S. editors interested in the anodyne press release out of Adana, Turkey, on the missing weather plane. The *Washington Post* ran it as a brief.

Ike's son, John, said later there was not "one scintilla" of doubt in his father's mind, when they discussed the missing plane at the beginning of the week, that its pilot was dead. Allen Dulles had assured them so often since 1956 that a U-2 shoot-down was not survivable that his wisdom was now gospel. It was sad, of course, and in its own special way. It was hard to think of a lonelier way to make the ultimate sacrifice, getting blown apart or asphyxiated up there over Russia; and it was hard to think of a set of circumstances less likely to allow the remains to be brought back to the grieving family for a proper burial. But it was a noble sacrifice and the president would acknowledge it in the right way in due course. In the meantime it looked as if Khrushchev was going to take the intrusion on the chin again, and that, too, was impressive. Preparations for the summit could continue. A nuclear test ban treaty was not out of the question and would be a crowning achievement of Eisenhower's presidency. He would recognize Khrushchev's role in it by presenting him in Moscow with a jet-powered hydrofoil.

Would it have been possible for Khrushchev to hush the whole thing up for the sake of world peace? Ike assumed so, and both President de Gaulle of France and Prime Minister Harold Macmillan of Britain would later encourage him to believe it. But none of them knew much about the pressures that the U-2 program had imposed on Khrushchev, or those he had brought upon himself. Thanks to Marshal Biryuzov's briefing on the reviewing stand in Red Square, the entire Soviet military establishment now knew about the overflights at least as a subject of gossip, and they knew that one had been brought down. The insult had been intolerable, but having been avenged it could be rewritten as a triumph. Khrushchev's control of the media was firm but not absolute. The group with least to gain from the summit—the military—had the most to gain from publicizing the fine work of whichever battery commander had pressed the button. One way or other, the story would get out.

Khrushchev knew it must be his way.

The Supreme Soviet was in session. Fifteen hundred dutiful appointees from every oblast, *okrug, krai,* and far-flung autonomous republic were assembling each day in the Great Hall of the Kremlin to rubber-stamp new laws handed down by the politburo and to applaud the far-sighted inspiration of the party's first secretary.

On Thursday morning Llewellyn Thompson, the U.S. ambassador to

Moscow, was invited to the Great Hall to hear Khrushchev's set piece speech to the Soviet. The two men knew each other well. The Thompsons had spent a winter weekend sledding at the premier's dacha. Some politburo members were even muttering that since returning from Camp David Khrushchev seemed to trust the ambassador more than his own ministers.

The speech could have been about Uzbek folklore and it would have been rapturously received. In fact it was a significant statement of Khrushchev's intent to reorganize the Soviet economy in favor of civilians and at the expense of the military. Slickly titled "On Abolishing Taxes on Workers and Employees and Other Measures to Improve the Well-Being of the Soviet People," it lasted nearly four hours (with an intermission). For the first two and a half Thompson listened politely, wondering with a trace of unease why he had been seated in a box above the podium. The answer came near the end of hour three, when Khrushchev moved suddenly from his hopes for the Paris summit to a thunderous exposé of the entire overflight program, including the May 1 debacle. As he switched subjects, witnesses said a shaft of sunlight angling in from a window high in the Great Hall lit up Khrushchev's face. The May 1 mission had been "an aggressive provocation aimed at wrecking the summit conference," he declared. The command had been given to destroy the plane. The command had been fulfilled.

The hall erupted. Delegates and the Soviet press hurled shouts of "shame!" at the imperialists' ambassador. Thompson's face remained a mask, but inwardly he marveled at Khrushchev's showmanship. He had seized the moment. In order not to sacrifice the future, he carefully blamed American "militarists" rather than Eisenhower. Equally carefully, he omitted to mention that the pilot was still alive.

Teletype transcripts of the speech reached Eisenhower at a National Security Council meeting in a secure bunker outside Washington. In a huddle afterward it was agreed that a more detailed cover story would have to be issued, still on the assumption that Powers was dead.

That evening, at an Ethiopian diplomatic reception, Thompson overheard a deputy Soviet foreign minister tell the Swedish ambassador that as far as he knew the pilot was being questioned. Thompson rushed to his office to cable Washington. Four minutes before his message reached the State Department, NASA issued its new press release—five hundred words of detailed nonsense about a plane that could fly "for as long as four hours at altitudes of up to 55,000 feet" and spent its time collecting information on "convective clouds, wind shear, the jet stream, and such widespread weather patterns as typhoons."

No one could fault NASA for conviction, but every spurious detail compounded the lie. When the State Department spokesman saw the release he turned ashen. When the press saw it and started comparing it with Khrushchev's version, the game was up. All at once it was open season on the U-2.

For years, senior executives at the networks and most East Coast newspapers had known the broad outlines of the U-2 story but kept it out of the headlines in deference to the administration's pleading. But since overflights had restarted in 1959, mere reporters had been getting wind of the program. Now the Moscow bureaus had the scoop from none other than Khrushchev and the Washington press corps would play catch-up with a vengeance. Like a startled deer, the CIA set about covering its traces.

First, the Agency settled on a fall guy in case the president wanted one. It would be Dick Newton, Colonel Shelton's executive officer in Adana. He would take responsibility for sending Powers on such a reckless mission at such a sensitive time but would not be available for comment. (He was spirited from Turkey to Wiesbaden, and kept there until the tornado blew itself out.) In case the excitable British press should remember the fleeting presence of U-2s at RAF Lakenheath in the countryside north of London in 1956 and suspect a British angle now, that angle was swiftly smoothed over: three RAF pilots pulling duty with Detachment B at Adana were overnighted back to England, where they refuse to discuss their Turkish assignment to this day. The Oslo station chief went to ground so that no one at the U.S. embassy there could help the Norwegians with their investigation. (Bodo? Where?) Plans were even made to welcome Tufti Johnson, Stan Beerli's friend and bringer of hors d'oeuvres, into comfortable American anonymity should Norway decide it needed a scapegoat from its own side.

Ninety miles from there, the Atlanta federal penitentiary's most cerebral *New York Times* subscriber—the Soviet master spy and silkscreen printer still known as Rudolf Abel—first read about the lost U-2 on Friday, May 6. He couldn't miss it: "SOVIET DOWNS AMERICAN PLANE; U.S. SAYS IT WAS WEATHER CRAFT; KHRUSHCHEV SEES SUMMIT BLOW." It was the three-line banner format normally reserved for coups and assassinations, and it was not encouraging. Without a live pilot the only news relevant to Fisher was that the summit was in jeopardy. The slimmer the chances of détente, the slimmer his chances of going home.

That day was hell for Oliver Powers and his ailing wife, who Gary feared would already have suffered a heart attack over his disappearance. It was their third day knowing he was missing without knowing if he was alive. "Distressed? We all were," Gary's childhood friend Jack Goff remembers. "It was more like a bad dream than anything." The family gathered at the home Oliver had built beneath the sugar maples outside Pound and prayed.

At the end of the worst week of his political career, Eisenhower faced three choices: to continue to deny the entire Soviet story, to admit it and blame his subordinates, or to admit it, explain it, and hope the world would understand. None of them was appetizing, and the decision itself was almost impossible without knowing what had happened to the pilot. That afternoon, therefore, a car left the U.S. embassy on Moscow's inner ring road and made the short drive to the Ministry of Foreign Affairs. A bland and plaintive note was handed over. It stuck to the weather reconnaissance fiction but acknowledged Khrushchev's accusations without denying them. "In the light of the above," it ended, "the United States Government requests the Soviet Government to provide it with full facts of the Soviet investigation of this incident and to inform it of the fate of the pilot."

The next day, Khrushchev obliged. Back in front of the Supreme Soviet, he dispensed with lengthy preliminaries and came quickly to the point. "Comrades, I must tell you a secret," he said. "When I made my report two days ago I deliberately did not say that we have parts of the airplane, and we have the pilot, who is alive and kicking!"

The applause was wild and spontaneous, and Khrushchev could not resist it. He had brought with him the fruits of Powers's first six days of interrogation, and a bulging folder for show and tell. He named Powers. He named Colonel Shelton, the new Detachment B commander (who was quickly reassigned to a remote base in northern Michigan).

He named Peshawar (and warned both Pakistan and Norway that they were "playing with fire"). He held up fake pictures purporting to be those Powers had taken, and a real one of the poison pin. He made hay with the idea of using a pistol or handing out gold watches at seventy thousand feet—were they for Martians?—and mentioned in passing that he thought it would be appropriate for Powers to stand trial "so that world opinion can see what actions the Americans are taking to provoke the Soviet Union."

He repeated his belief that Dulles and the militarists were responsible, not Eisenhower. But if that was intended as an olive branch, it was a prickly one. He could not even leave unsaid the obvious corollary—that Ike was no longer in charge. "When the military starts running the show, the results can be disastrous," he mused. Such as? A hydrogen bomb from them, and "a more destructive hydrogen bomb in return."

There. He'd said it. Armageddon had been explicitly invoked. It was the zenith of Khrushchev's career as a performer—"a masterpiece," said one junior diplomat who watched it live on television. But it was also the beginning of the end of Khrushchev as a politician. Later, out of power and under virtual house arrest, he told a visiting American that from the moment of the shoot-down he felt "no longer in full control."

* * *

At the Powers home, the news on Sunday that Gary was alive brought waves of relief, then indignation. Oliver would later rely heavily on Carl McAfee, his "boy lawyer," for help communicating with heads of state and their intermediaries, but not today. He drove into Pound and fired off a telegram to the White House in his very own syntax: "I WANT TO KNOW WHAT ALL THIS IS ABOUT MY SON FRANCIS G. POWERS THAT IS GOING ON AND I WANT TO KNOW NOW. ANSWER."

Then he rolled on down the Trail of the Lonesome Pine to Norton and walked up to McAfee's office behind the bank and started taking calls. One was from the *New York Times.* Powers senior had left school after fourth grade, "but that man read *everything,*" his daughter Jessica remembers. He had already done some reading on Khrushchev and told the reporter from New York that he was "going to appeal to Mr.

Khrushchev personally to be fair to my boy. As one coal miner to another, I'm sure he'll listen to me."

When Gary was shown the clipping a few days later in the long interrogation room in Moscow, he broke down and wept.

(The KGB no longer had anything to gain by withholding from Powers the knowledge that his parents knew he had survived, since Khrushchev had made sure that the whole world knew. But Powers's interrogators still wanted to know if he had sent a distress signal before going down. If he had, they reasoned, he could also have *received* radio messages in flight, including one alerting him to the SAM sites near Sverdlovsk. That might explain the strange kink in his route north of Chelyabinsk—but it would also point to a highly placed mole in the air defense establishment. When he finally told them he had maintained radio silence throughout his flight, they were more baffled than ever.)

In Milledgeville, the Agency men on the Barbara Powers detail bowed to the inevitable when the news broke that Gary was alive. They sat her down in her mother's kitchen and told her she was going to have to give a press conference. A doctor was on his way "to give you something to ease your nerves," they said, and she was grateful. The Baldwin Hotel downtown was already full to bursting with out-of-town reporters, and now they descended on the pilot's mother-in-law's front yard. Barbara faced them from a swing seat on the porch and proudly joined the ranks of CIA-affiliated obfuscators.

"I do not consider my husband a spy," she told the throng. "He was assigned to reconnaissance flights, period. To me this is a big difference. Gary is definitely not the cloak-and-dagger type."

It was only a matter of time before someone asked about her leg, and she didn't miss a beat. "I broke it in a waterskiing accident," she said.

* * *

For nearly a week the men of Mikhail Voronov's S-75 battery talked quietly and curiously among themselves. Having been alerted to the orange and white parachute on May 1, Voronov had sent an officer and two men to find the pilot, but the Moskvich car got to him first. Batukhtin and ten others from the regiment were assigned to cordon off the debris field but were told nothing about the debris. By the evening, reasonably sure they had scored a hit without starting a war, they celebrated with a few hundred grams of vodka.

A Tupolev carrying a fearsome concentration of senior air force and KGB officers had touched down in Sverdlovsk soon after midday. Some returned to Moscow with the prisoner. Others supervised the search for evidence and summoned a crane to heave the U-2's engine from a swamp. No one in Kosulino was told anything. Voronov's first confirmation that he had shot down an American who was still alive came from Khrushchev himself, in his second speech to the Supreme Soviet.

By then the remains of Article 360 were in Moscow, where the best and brightest of the Soviet aviation design bureaus would try, without much success, to reverse engineer it into a stratospheric dragon lady of their own. But first it was put on show.

Khrushchev the exhibitionist was on a roll. For a few more days his "fetish for secrecy" (Ike's grumpy sound bite) was subordinated to his fetish for propaganda. The dismembered U-2 was displayed in the Hall of Chess in Gorky Park, with captions in Russian and English and helpful wall-mounted displays on its route, cameras, pilot, and dastardly purpose. The pressure suit and pistol were there. So were the parachute and the poison pin. One of the first to take a look around was . . . Khrushchev. Trailing almost as many reporters as he had eight months earlier on Roswell Garst's corn farm, he paused in front of the crumpled fuselage just in case anyone had any questions. As far as he was concerned, the summit was still on, he said. But was the same true of the Eisenhowers' visit? At this he paused for fully half a minute. Those present thought he was genuinely thinking it through. "Put yourself in my place and answer for me," he said at last. "I am a man, and I have human feelings." If the visit happened, it was not going to be much fun.

The next VIP ushered into the Hall of Chess was Powers, on his second and last outing before his trial. Shelepin wanted to squeeze him for technical information on the plane that many of the Soviet Air Force's top brass had said could not exist despite the evidence of their own radar screens. Powers decided his strategy would be to "examine it curiously, as if seeing it for the first time." In a sense he was: he had never seen the plane turned inside out and had no idea until then how many of its parts bore their manufacturer's name. Words like "Hewlett-Packard" and "Pratt & Whitney" jumped out at him as shamelessly as if Kelly Johnson had etched "Made in USA" across the tailplane.

Powers studied the tail with particular care. He saw no scorch marks or even scratches in the paint, leaving him more convinced than ever that he had been the victim of a near miss, not a direct hit.

Then he was driven back to the Lyubianka and the floodgates were opened. The public formed queues that snaked endlessly through Gorky Park, and the squads of military attachés at the U.S. embassy were as curious as anyone. Professionally, they needed to find out if the wreckage was genuine and, if possible, how the plane had been brought down. Personally, they were fascinated by a piece of equipment that even they had not been cleared to know about. But they were also known to the KGB and did not want to give Mr. Khrushchev any more excuses for grandstanding. So instead of going themselves they sent a young political officer who had good Russian, an open, friendly manner, and next to zero knowledge of aeronautics. His name was Frank Meehan.

"The line seemed to be miles long," Meehan remembers. "I knew I could go to the head of the line and show my diplomatic ID and they would let me in. But I thought to myself that maybe they'd decide to make an incident of me. They were perfectly capable of doing that if they wanted to.

"So I did a Hamlet. I argued with myself. I walked down the line, on and on and on, will I do it, won't I do it. I finally got the courage up and went to the head of the line, and there was a *militsianer*—a cop. He looked at me, and I produced my ID, and he looked at me some more, the way they did, very cold, and he had some questions. I thought he was going to throw the book at me. And then he said, 'Pozhalusta'—it's your plane. Be my guest."

Meehan did his best, looked around, peered at the captions, wrote it up. "But what did I know about any plane? What I produced was an ignoramus's report on what it looked like. Without the captions I wouldn't have known which bits were which."

His report was fed into the embassy's larger report on the exhibition and the state of the plane, which concluded that it was in "remarkably good condition" given that it was supposed to have smashed into the ground, having fallen apart at seventy thousand feet. That conclusion, in turn, fueled fast-growing rumors in Washington that Powers had not been downed by a missile at all; that he'd had a flameout and descended to restart his engine before being hit at about thirty thousand feet; or even that he'd landed, defected, and spent the evening in a Sverdlovsk nightclub.

Kelly Johnson didn't believe the missile story. Nor did Allen Dulles. Nor, later, did his successor, John McCone. They all knew that the Kremlin had an interest in letting it be thought that its surface-to-air missiles were lethal even at an altitude of thirteen miles. That would go some way to negating the threat posed by the U.S. Strategic Air Command's fleets of nuclear-armed bombers. Allen and McCone were also privy to NSA decryptions of Soviet communications from the morning of May 1 that seemed to indicate someone had descended to thirty thousand feet before being hit at *that* altitude and bailing out. Someone had, of course—the ill-fated Sergei Safronov in his MiG-19—but no one outside Russia was to know that until after the cold war.

In due course Powers would have to confront the men who thought they knew more than he thought they knew. That would test his patience and nearly destroy his reputation. But first he had to reconcile himself to the accusation of ruining détente.

* * *

In the second week of May, Powers and Khrushchev must have been the two most anxious men in Moscow. Nothing Shelepin or his minions said or did in the interrogation room persuaded Powers that they would spare his life. On the contrary, soon after his visit to the wreckage of his plane he was told he would be tried for crimes against the Soviet state, which carried a maximum penalty of up to fifteen years in prison, or death. So he spent his days playing mental poker with his captors—telling the truth when he thought they already knew the answers to their questions and lying when they came back, as they so often did, to the U-2's ceiling and the history of its overflights. He spent his nights in gloomy anticipation of a secret trial and a bullet in the head.

Half a mile away, in his office in the Kremlin, Khrushchev's public and private faces were coming unglued. In meetings with aides and ministers he was a parody of frothing indignation. In private he still desperately wanted a grand bargain in Paris, massive disarmament to fund fridges for the Soviet people, and a quiet shelving of the Berlin issue. After that, he still wanted to consecrate the deal on home turf with Eisenhower.

A few days before leaving for the summit, he took an evening walk with his son near their dacha outside Moscow and "suddenly began talking about Eisenhower's farm" at Gettysburg. They had visited the farm and admired Ike's cows while staying at Camp David. So the president should come to the dacha and see the Khrushchevs' vegetables, then take a boat ride on the Moscow River. "There was no indication that the visit might be canceled," wrote Sergei Khrushchev, his father's closest confidant.

Nor was there any sign that Khrushchev senior had begun to doubt his own assumption that Powers's flight had been planned and authorized by Dulles, not the president. Yet at the same time he was genuinely furious that so much hope and planning had been put in jeopardy. Had he not just laid off more than a million soldiers, including 250,000 officers? This was the one Soviet constituency with nothing at all to gain from détente, and the May Day outrage had given them the perfect opening to step up their mockery of Khrushchev's trust in Ike, not to mention their challenge to his authority in general. Small wonder that on May 9, at a reception at the Czech embassy in Moscow, he made a beeline for Llewellyn Thompson. "I must talk to you," he whispered in the American ambassador's ear. "This U-2 thing has put me in a terrible spot. You have to get me off it."

What he meant was clear enough: throw me something—an apology if you can, or at least an undertaking not to send *more* planes across my country's most sensitive nuclear sites. Thompson said he would try, but it was too late. In Washington a statement by the new secretary of state, Christian Herter, had already been approved for release. Instead of apologizing for the overflights, it defended them as essential given the Soviet drive to force the free world to choose between "abject surrender or nuclear destruction." Instead of forswearing more flights, it pointedly failed to rule them out.

At this, Sergei Khrushchev said, his father "simply boiled over." Before taking off for Paris he huddled with his farewell committee under the wing of his Tupolev and decided to open the summit with an ultimatum: Eisenhower must apologize, punish those responsible for the Powers mission, and promise not to repeat it. Or the Soviet delegation would walk out. On the short flight, his speech to the summit's opening session was rewritten as a harangue. He had brought forward his departure by two days, initially to give time for private talks with Eisenhower to put the unhappy U-2 business behind them. Eisenhower had also wanted to clear the air, but Herter advised against, saying the idea would be seen as a sign of weakness. The American invitation was never sent. Khrushchev told de Gaulle and Macmillan what he planned to say in advance but otherwise spent the weekend before the summit sulking in his Paris ambassador's residence, hoping for a response from Eisenhower and not getting one. For his own part, Ike landed at Orly saying there was "too much at stake for profitless bickering" and then refused to respond to an ultimatum he had not received.

Monday, May 16, 1960, was the day the laser was invented (by Theodore Maiman at the Hughes Research Laboratories in Malibu). It was also the day the leaders of the world's four nuclear powers could have stopped the arms race in its tracks. Instead, three of them listened patiently while the fourth unleashed a forty-five-minute tirade against, among others, the "small, frantic group in the Pentagon and [U.S.] militarist circles who benefit from the arms race and reap huge profits." Khrushchev was not in fact paranoid. This was precisely the group against which Eisenhower warned the American people in his final televised address from the Oval Office. The only difference between the two leaders' perceptions of the group was one of scale. Ike called it the military-industrial complex. Certainly, it was never so obliged. Goaded on by the silent, glowering presence of defense minister Malinovksy at his shoulder, Khrushchev issued his demand for an apology. He suggested that if he didn't get one the summit be postponed for eight months (in other words, until after the U.S. presidential election). He rescinded Eisenhower's invitation to Russia. He went even pinker than usual. Ike went red with anger. De Gaulle told Khrushchev not to shout, noting that the acoustics in the intimate dining room they were using in the Elysée Palace were perfectly adequate. Macmillan, whose idea the summit had been, found the whole thing "a most unpleasant performance." At lunchtime they went their separate ways, the wasted opportunity dissipating almost visibly across the parquet.

Looking back twelve years later, Macmillan called that day "one of the most agonizing as well as exhausting which I have ever been through except, perhaps, in battle." Yet his agonies weren't over. The following afternoon he and de Gaulle were still trying to get the nuclear behemoths back to the negotiating table—but the Russian was in the bath at his ambassador's house, refusing to respond in writing to a fresh invitation until the others made clear whether it was for a preliminary session or the summit proper. He was, in his own half-crazed way, still begging for an apology, which he had admitted "our internal politics requires." But Ike was in no mood to give it. In desperation, the British foreign secretary asked Herter why not. Herter: "Because he is not sorry."

And so the summit proper never happened. Khrushchev flew home via East Berlin, where he tried to make a virtue of having faced down the aggressors. In reality he betrayed the depths of his now-forlorn hopes for détente by refusing to renew his Berlin ultimatum. Eisenhower enjoyed a layover with the new Portuguese dictator, and Macmillan wrote to the Queen, saying he would not try to conceal his "shock and disappointment" at the way things had turned out.

Not everyone was so dismayed. Notable for his high spirits at the Paris parties that had punctuated the abortive summit sessions was none other than Joe Alsop, the columnist who had done so much to inspire fear about a supposed missile gap between the United States and the Soviet Union. Back in Washington he had greeted the U-2 story with a column headlined "The Wonderful News," praising the CIA for having taken the missile threat seriously enough to take such risky pictures. It was a neat way of changing the subject from an actual gap to the idea of a gap and of appearing to own up to his own distortions while doing no such thing. In Paris he was in "wonderful" form, wrote Marina Sulzberger, wife of the *New York Times* correspondent C. L. Sulzberger. More than that, he was "optimistic as never before and glorying in the company of... all those beautiful women he always has up his sleeve."

Alsop in 1960 was as guilty as Bush or Cheney in 2003 of ignoring the available intelligence about the enemy's WMD for the sake of a compelling story. Not that he was bothered. His conscience never seemed to suffer any more than his reputation, which was helped enormously by the fact that Powers came down where he did. Sverdlovsk was eight hundred miles southeast of Plesetsk. Article 360 was still two hours from its main target when it fell apart, with the result that Richard Bissell's air force never did photograph the only place left in the Soviet Union where it might have found operational ballistic missiles capable of reaching North America. Had Powers reached the site, switched on his cameras, and carried them safely to Stan Beerli's waiting Quickmove crew, he would have provided the first documentary evidence of the number of ICBMs in Khrushchev's stockpile—all four of them. That was it; that was the extent of the intercontinental nuclear arsenal with which the Soviet premier seemed to have threatened to bury the West. The missile gap did not exist—a vital piece of information for politicians and military planners alike, and one that the U-2 never quite established.

To most people the point was academic, especially when the CIA's Corona satellites at last finished the job. But it was not academic to Alsop, or to Allen Dulles, or to history.

As a journalist, Alsop could adapt his views to reality, and he did, eventually hailing the absence of a missile gap as a sort of personal victory—a bullet dodged thanks to alarms raised by people like him. As a political player, Dulles could not be so cavalier. Having given Eisenhower wildly conflicting signals as to the advisability of continued U-2 flights before the Paris fiasco, Dulles had the grace to offer his resignation. Ike turned it down but was still so angry that he asked his son to ensure that he and Dulles were never again left alone together.

Dulles did not take it personally. In fact, his political antennae were already trained elsewhere. As the Eisenhower presidency wound down, in August 1960, he paid a call on the Democratic nominee for that year's general election. It was ostensibly a courtesy that the director of Central Intelligence would have granted any nominee, but in this case it was more than a courtesy. He visited John F. Kennedy at the Kennedy compound in Hyannis Port, and when the subject of the missile gap came up, Dulles looked Kennedy in the eye and said that in view of the failure of the Powers mission he could not categorically confirm that the gap did not exist. It was, in essence, the very opposite of the advice he had given to Eisenhower seven months earlier. It did untold violence to reality but was not an out-and-out lie. More to the point, it was what

Kennedy needed to hear. He was able to continue to use the issue of the missile gap in his campaign, and three months later he won the White House by the narrowest margin in U.S. presidential history.

In January 1961, on the night of his inauguration, Kennedy attended the customary round of balls and then, still in white tie, called on an old friend in Georgetown. Joe Alsop opened the door himself, and they talked into the early hours over warm turtle soup.

# 10

# SOVIET JUSTICE

Kennedy owed Powers. He owed Powers from the perspective of what actually happened over Sverdlovsk on May Day, 1960—a shoot-down that wrecked a summit and kept alive the idea of a missile gap until the presidential election—but also from the perspective of what *might* have happened. Had Article 360 gotten through to Bodo, the Paris summit might very well have proceeded constructively if not cordially. A sort of superpower peace, uneasy but still a vast improvement on nuclear brinkmanship and morbid mistrust, might very well have been Eisenhower's triumphant legacy. And Nixon might very well have ridden his predecessor's coattails into the White House. Such an analysis sits ill with the Camelot-as-destiny approach to presidential history, and it affords a journeyman American pilot and a dutiful Russian antiaircraft gunner unfashionably large roles in world affairs. Neither consideration makes it wrong.

Kennedy owed Powers, but it was not a debt he had a mind to acknowledge. In fact he showed Powers nothing but disdain. According to one rumor that reached Powers's hometown of Pound from Washington, and that was broadly accurate, the new president could have asked for Powers's release at his first meeting with Khrushchev in Vienna in 1961 but chose not to. According to another rumor heard by Carl McAfee, far from admiring Powers's heroism, "Kennedy wanted to prosecute his ass."

McAfee's recollection was only slightly skewed. It was Bobby Kennedy, the new attorney general, who wanted to try Powers for treason on his return to the United States. But the president undoubtedly shared his brother's contempt for the way Powers handled himself after having the temerity to survive his crash. Like many Americans, "Kennedy looked at this as a disgraceful incident," McAfee remembered. Like many Americans who became indignant about Powers's behavior as a prisoner, Kennedy second-guessed it without making the slightest effort to understand it.

* * *

When Powers was told he would be tried for espionage, he imagined a perfunctory hearing behind closed doors, followed by death. He was in for a surprise. The Hall of Columns occupies a large oblong of prime Moscow real estate on what is now Teatralnaya Ploshchad—Theater Square—but in 1960 was named, aptly, for Sverdlovsk. Wedged between the Lyubianka and the Kremlin, it was perfectly located for the show trial of an American spy. It was less than five minutes' walk from the defendant's cell, the prosecutor's office, and the colossal Sovetskaya Hotel, where a carefully assembled cast of foreign observers would be accommodated. But the Hall of Columns was the obvious venue regardless of location. It was a showpiece of czarist splendor co-opted and refurbished by the Soviet Communist Party to intimidate the many and terrify the few. It was in the Hall of Columns that Bukharin had refused to prostrate himself to the Military Collegium of the Supreme Court of the Soviet Union (and the shadow of Stalin himself, watching from a high concealed window) at the zenith of the purges in 1938. Bukharin, and so many other loyal Bolsheviks, were taken back to the catacomb of tunnels beneath the Lyubianka and shot in the head within minutes of their sentences being pronounced. And it was the Military Collegium that would try Powers.

In his honor, the hall was repainted in green and white. A gold-colored hammer and sickle set within a crest the size of a hot tub was hung above the stage and polished until it shone. A press center was set up in one of the hall's cavernous anterooms, complete with two long tables of typewriters, an international cables desk, and a newfangled international phone booth. In another anteroom more tables would groan beneath the weight of caviar, smoked fish, cold cuts, pickles, layered sponge cakes, and pungent mineral water from the Caucasus.

The fourth estate was to be kept fed and happy, and the majesty of Soviet justice was to be revealed according to a strict timetable: the complex was booked for three days and no more. Anyone hoping that any aspect of the trial's timing, content, or outcome would be left to chance, or even to the force of unrehearsed argument, would be disappointed.

Powers fell into that category. By the time he took the stand on Wednesday, August 17 (his thirty-first birthday), he was underweight, depressed, lonely, confused, and thoroughly frightened. The first two of these were linked. His involuntary fast was long since over, but even though his prison food was reputedly delivered from a canteen where KGB generals ate, he did not eat much of it. This was why, shortly before the trial, his digestive tract was examined from the bottom up in full view of "an audience of doctors, nurses, guards and interpreters." Powers later called it the ultimate indignity, and it was surely intended as such.

His loneliness and confusion were also linked. Having been denied any visits from the U.S. embassy, he had not met a single compatriot since his fall to earth. As a result, his minders were his only source of information on what was known of his fate back home; on how his actions were being judged there; and on whether the CIA understood that he had divulged only what he thought the KGB already knew. He had played exhausting mind games with his interrogators, trying to keep his lies consistent on how high the U-2 could fly and how often it had overflown the Soviet Union. He assumed those games would only get tougher at his trial and hoped against hope that the Agency would notice them.

As for his fear, the cause was simple. He faced the death penalty.

After the trial the British reporter James Morris (who covered the first ascent of Mount Everest for the *Times* of London but had since defected to the *Manchester Guardian*) wrote that Powers had "presented himself as a poor deluded jerk from Virginia, a part that I suspect did not require much playing." It was a cruel assessment. It was also inaccurate in that the appearance of being deluded by his Agency paymasters was precisely the part of Powers's trial persona that did require acting. But Morris touched on two truths: Powers had been violently deracinated and then dragged along a psychological assault course for which the CIA had left him completely unprepared.

Like Kennedy after him, Eisenhower was unsympathetic. He complained in the first days of the crisis that Powers seemed to have started talking "the moment he hit the ground." As the trial unfolded, squads of editorialists who had never been shot down or spent a day in solitary confinement pitched in with clichéd references to Nathan Hale and some marginally more apt ones to Rudolf Abel. Hale's silence was golden. Powers was a blabbermouth.

Powers was, in fact, a diligent pilot and a dependable follower of orders. That is why he found himself soaring over the Hindu Kush early on May 1 when common sense would have sent him back to Turkey. That is why he flew on toward the Urals even when his autopilot failed, and that is why, had the CIA instructed him to keep his mouth shut if captured, he would undoubtedly have kept his mouth shut. Instead, he dressed for his trial and made the short journey to Sverdlovsk Square on August 17 with one overwhelming fear—of execution—and one coherent piece of Agency advice to cling to: "You might as well tell them everything, because they're going to get it out of you anyway."

Those had been the exact words of the intelligence officer at Adana when Powers had asked what he should do if captured in Russia. They were a recommendation to pursue the very strategy that the KGB itself urged Powers to follow: cooperate.

Yet this was not in fact the strategy that Powers chose. A simpler soul in his position might have seen only a binary decision to make—to talk or not to talk. But the "deluded jerk from Virginia" assumed from the start that if he was to have any chance of saving his life, his honor, and the U-2's most precious secrets, he would have to use his wits.

He agonized for months about the chess game in which he found himself a pawn. "Barbara, I don't know what is going to happen to me," he wrote when first allowed to send a letter to his wife. "I will be tried in accordance with Article 2 of their criminal code for espionage. The article states that the punishment is 7 to 15 years imprisonment and death in some cases. Where I fit in I don't know...I only know that I don't like the situation I am in or the situation I have placed you in."

***

Oliver Powers didn't like the situation he was placed in either. He had seen his only son quit medical school for the air force and hadn't liked it. He had seen him quit the air force for something that could not be named but smelled like the FBI and hadn't liked it. He had found out from a pair of men in suits who showed up on his doorstep one fine day in May that what smelled like the FBI was in fact the CIA, and he'd liked that even less, not only because the CIA had lost his boy over Russia without a plan to get him back but also because when he formed a plan of his own the Agency had tried to muzzle him. He was fired up and apt to lose his temper.

The plan in question was as simple as it was audacious. As things turned out, it gave rise to one of the more cinematic rituals of the cold war—that periodic pause for breath when each side was forced to level with the other and confess to small secrets in the hope of preserving larger ones and agree to a rendezvous somewhere quiet and secluded, preferably in fog, for a furtive human swap. It was not originally Powers's idea. It had first been suggested in the *New York Daily News* eleven days after the shoot-down. But there is all the difference in the world between suggesting and doing, and Oliver Powers was a doer.

Inevitably, the boy lawyer above his shoe shop became involved.

"Bless his heart," McAfee says. "Oliver was no dummy. He came up here one day and said, 'Hey, listen, have you heard of Rudolf Abel?'"

McAfee replied that he had; that he remembered the trial and the conviction. Abel was a Russian spy.

"Well," said Powers, "he's pulling time in Atlanta and I'd like to see if he's willing to be exchanged for my son."

McAfee suggested writing a letter. Powers suggested that McAfee was the one to write it. "So I found out where he was," McAfee said. "I prepared the letter, in which I told him who I was and asked if he would be prepared to be exchanged for Gary Powers. I get a letter back saying would you please contact my wife in East Berlin. And not long after that some guy walks into my office and says he's with the CIA and I am not to make any effort to contact Rudolf Abel again."

The Agency's reaction to the letter "miffed Oliver to no end." But contact had been made. A paper trail had been started, and Oliver Powers now had more than a hunch that the way to force the pace in the freeing of his son was to make sure he forgot to ask the CIA's permission for anything.

He observed the same rule when arranging to attend the trial. When the date was announced, he and McAfee slipped out of Norton, telling no one their destination. They headed north up Route 81, along the eastern foothills of the Appalachians toward the nation's capital. They called in person at the consular section of the Soviet embassy on Wisconsin Avenue the next day and applied for visas to visit Moscow, which were granted in short order.

A stampede followed. When Barbara Powers heard that her father-in-law and his lawyer were going to the trial, she decided to go too. When Ida Powers, Oliver's wife, heard that Barbara was going, she told Oliver she would have to make the trip despite her angina and her emphysema. Instead of trying to dissuade her, Oliver asked his wife's doctor to join the party. When Barbara learned that Gary's mother would be going, she told her own mother to get packing, and her mother's doctor for good measure.

There was "a chasm" between Barbara and her in-laws, McAfee recalls. But on each side of the chasm the same question hung over the prospective Moscow-bound adventurers: who would pay? The CIA wanted to buy everyone's tickets, and their loyalty, but Oliver was having none of it. He had already accepted an offer from *Life* magazine for his entire party's expenses and a five-thousand-dollar fee in return for an exclusive story. The deal had been brokered by Sol Curry, a Norton department store owner, whom *Life* sent along for the ride and tasked with keeping their exclusive exclusive. He had his work cut out.

The Agency did bankroll Barbara's party, without her knowledge. It used the Virginia Bar Association as a proxy to expedite her visa applications, underwrite her travel expenses, and smother her with the attention of responsible grown-ups. Two of these were respected Virginia lawyers, an Alexander Parker and a Frank W. Rogers, ostensibly added to the group to help with Gary's defense. In reality their main assignment, apart from keeping an eye on Barbara, was to try to debrief Powers for the Agency. Parker's wife joined the party to help hold Barbara's hand, sometimes literally, and Sam Jaffe, a CBS News correspondent based in New York, was unwittingly enlisted to the cause. He was given privileged access to the histrionic Mrs. Powers that delighted his editors but also forced him to participate as a restraining influence in her vodka binges, which he found acutely embarrassing.

The ill feeling between the two Powers camps was intense throughout. Barbara and Oliver were each determined to be seen as Gary's true protector, which meant constant efforts to upstage each other in the press and an undeclared race to get to Moscow.

McAfee was first out of the blocks. Delayed by the task of securing visas for his wife and her doctor, Oliver Powers sent his lawyer on ahead to try to make contact with Gary. McAfee was willing and not easily intimidated, but he was new to the jet set. Apart from his travels in the navy, he had never left the country. At thirty, he had never even been to New York City until he changed planes there to catch a night flight with SAS to Copenhagen.

It was delayed.

"I got into Copenhagen late," he says "Missed the flight from there to Moscow and pleaded with those people telling them I had to be in Moscow the following day. They sent my ass up to Helsinki."

The boy lawyer cooled his heels in Finland for an afternoon and reached Moscow at four the next morning. He had been expected the previous afternoon. No one was there to meet him, and as a result there were now two bewildered young men from Virginia in the Soviet capital. As Powers fretted in prison, McAfee fretted at the airport until Intourist could be alerted. Forty-eight sleepless hours after leaving Norton, he was swept into town in a Zil limousine and installed in the Sovetskaya's Lenin suite.

The rest of the Virginia contingent arrived in waves. Barbara's team flew Sabena via Brussels, reaching Moscow on August 13. She and her mother were assigned a suite occupied by Vice President Nixon the previous summer. An uneasy Sam Jaffe was billeted on the same luxury floor. Oliver and Ida Powers and the family doctor came on a separate plane, which upset Gary when he heard about it but was the only arrangement his father would consider.

Four days later, having consulted her older sisters and bought her own ticket, Jessica Powers-Hileman emerged alone and unexpected from passport control at Moscow's miserable Sheremetyevo Airport. She hoped to be taken to her ailing mother, and eventually she was. "I'd given a telegram to someone I thought was a reporter in Stockholm," she remembers. It had not been delivered. "It was my first time outside the United States. It was dark, it was midnight, and no one knew what to do with me. We thought the Russians had two heads and forked tails and all that, and I thought, 'Gee, I'll never be seen again.'" In desperation she showed a taxi driver her passport and pronounced her name. He understood—"Who didn't know that name?"—and took her to the Sovetskaya. Looking back, she reckons she grew up quite a bit that day.

* * *

Why had they all come? For Barbara it was complicated. There was not much love left in her marriage, but she still had a husband to support, at least in public, and a father-in-law to stand up to. And she had little to do in Milledgeville besides drink and mope. For Ida there was a son to be prayed for and a daughter-in-law to be outnumbered. For Oliver the point was simple—to bring Gary home.

At Oliver's instruction, McAfee had assembled a fat dossier of affidavits testifying to Gary's good character. He had also collected photographs illustrating Gary's humble upbringing. He had even buried his nose in textbooks on international law and developed a theory that the Soviet Union had no jurisdiction thirteen miles up, having already conceded that it had no jurisdiction thirteen miles out to sea. McAfee and his client were going for broke. If the CIA wouldn't let them arrange a swap of Gary for Rudolf Abel, they would try their luck with the KGB, asking for an acquittal on the basis of no case to answer.

It was bold, imaginative, and doomed. McAfee was not allowed to visit Gary, but he did meet Gary's Soviet defense lawyer, Mikhail Grinev, who accepted the affidavits and the photographs of blue-collar America but did not give the "no jurisdiction" theory a second look.

Like Roman Rudenko, the prosecutor general, Grinev was a veteran of the Nuremberg trials. He was also a picture of gloom and a professional loser. A heavy mustache seemed to press his mouth into a perpetual grimace. If an unscripted thought ever sprang to life behind his hooded eyes, he did not let it out. His appointment to the case as Rudenko's notional adversary was part of a general effort to remind the world of Nuremberg, where it was generally accepted that Soviet lawyers and due process had managed to coexist. But this did not give Powers much cause for hope. As *Life* magazine's Moscow correspondent pointed out to McAfee, every German whom Grinev represented at Nuremberg was executed.

On the stage of the Hall of Columns, fully six feet above the stalls,

Grinev was to sit at a desk facing Rudenko. Powers's place would be behind him in a dock that the *New York Times* said looked like a playpen. Between the lawyers and above them, behind a long table draped in red cloth, three senior generals would make up the Military Collegium.

The hall started to fill up early on the morning of the seventeenth. It was gray outside and drizzling, but crowds gathered anyway. The press had reserved seats in a raised tier round three sides of the hall, and both groups of Powers supporters were driven to the hall from their hotel in plenty of time to talk to them. Oliver said the court would find out that his son was a good old boy and always had been. Barbara, in a black silk dress and black cloche hat, said he was the most wonderful person she had ever met. Most American reporters wrote generously that her eyes were red from weeping. Sam Jaffe noted later that a night of almost unremitting booze had played its part. (The drinking had been interrupted by a 3:00 a.m. taxi ride to the Lyubianka and back. Barbara had intended to find a door and bang on it until they let her in to see her man, but at Jaffe's suggestion she made do with a sniffle and a prayer in the backseat of the cab. Debriefed after the trip by the FBI, he said that on their return to the hotel she grabbed him and kissed him and that on this, as on many other occasions, he could have "been intimate" with her but wasn't.)

A few minutes before 10:00 a.m. a bell rang in the hall. Forty-four chandeliers blazed down on a crowd of two thousand. Interpreters took their seats in soundproof booths to provide simultaneous translation via headsets in English, French, German, and Spanish. The Powers family and entourage were ushered into a box behind the press gallery. In the sea of heads in front them were those of Khrushchev's daughter Yelena (her father was watching on television in the Crimea) and many of his ministers. Guy Burgess, the exfiltrated British spy, was there. So were senior diplomats from most of the embassies. It was, McAfee says, "like going to the Super Bowl."

At ten o'clock the generals took their seats behind the long red table and Powers entered, stage left, in a too-big double-breasted blue serge suit. Barbara started sobbing at once. The audience, which had risen for the entrance, now sat down. Powers sat too. The presiding judge ordered him to stand and stay standing for the reading of the indictment, which covered seventeen pages and took nearly an hour.

Grinev had given him no warning about the setting. Powers wrote later that he felt as if he were being tried in Carnegie Hall and was extremely nervous. He hid it as best he could behind a mournful look that stared out from a thousand front pages the next day.

There might have been aerial gunnery graduates of Turner Air Force Base who would have relished this strange moment in the glare of Soviet klieg lights, who would have deflected Roman Rudenko's propaganda with a firm jaw and the glint of a fighter jock's eye. Powers wasn't one of them. He was the pilot who had suffered stage fright as a schoolboy but felt a preternatural calm in the cockpit. Even in rare group pictures of the Detachment B pilots in their pressure suits, helmets clutched like trophies under their right arms, he is the one who looks somehow uncomfortable. In the Hall of Columns he was miserable.

Along with Powers, the indictment named Dulles, Nixon, and Christian Herter (the new secretary of state). They were its real targets—the instigators of the "gangster flight" dispatched expressly to wreck the Paris summit. In case anyone missed the point watching the trial, that day's *Izvestia* carried a cartoon of Nixon, Herter, Eisenhower, and a generic uniformed villain from the Pentagon sitting in the dock next to Powers in his suit and helmet.

He had read the indictment in his cell. Nearly half of it was an attack on the United States, not him. As he listened to it being read out by Rudenko, he looked "painfully ashamed," one Soviet commentator said. Painfully alone would have been closer to the truth. When Rudenko finished, he pleaded guilty. A recess was announced. As he was being led out, he spotted Barbara waving from her seat and choked up.

What he failed to understand was that almost nothing he could say at his trial would change its outcome, because nothing about it, or contemporaneous with it, had been left to chance. By way of countdown to that morning's proceedings, a series of other American "spies" had been unmasked and expelled. Edwin Morrell, a student, had been thrown out in July. Colonel Edwin Kirton, air attaché at the embassy, had gone the previous Wednesday. The next day it had been the turn of Robert Christner, a tourist, and the next James Shultz, another student.

America was incorrigible, shameless, obsessive in its meddling.

And Russia?

Fast-forward to day three of the trial. The verdict is near. The world waits to know Powers's fate. The press room is full of newsmen banging out backgrounders. Some who have already filed are filling their bourgeois bellies with kielbasa and caviar in the refreshment room. Suddenly (according to Radio Moscow's live commentary) "somebody brings joyous news. . . . I hear a correspondent dictating an account of the court proceedings on the telephone who interrupts his dispatch and almost shouts into the mouthpiece: 'Stop. I have a flash. A new Soviet spaceship.'"

The wizard of Baikonur has done it again. Sergey Korolyov has put into orbit a five-ton space capsule carrying not one but two live dogs and has brought them safely back to Earth. Never mind that five tons is the weight of an exceptionally large H-bomb complete with guidance system and heat-resistant nose cone. The man from Radio Moscow calls it "yet another peaceful star" and commiserates with Powers for sitting in the dock when he could be in training for space. Russia is irrepressible.

Powers spent nearly seven hours on the stand. He fought rearguard skirmishes with Rudenko about his altitude when shot down—he stuck with 68,000 feet to remind the CIA that he was keeping the secrets that really mattered—and about the amount of advance warning he had been given before his mission (he said he had none). He impressed some of the American diplomats in the audience with his outward calm, even though by the end of his first four-hour session on his feet he was, he said later, quite ready to scream at the judges that they should "sentence me to death and end this farce."

He made two other claims in his memoir ten years later that hint at the pressure he felt to inject some heroism into the role history had given him. He wrote that in a break on the trial's first day he saw a chance to escape when taken into a yard with an unguarded exit to the street, and that he nearly took it—"I tensed my legs, leaned forward slightly"—only to be foiled by a heavy hand on his shoulder. He wrote that in his cell before the trial he had visions of himself refusing to testify and of going down in history with Nathan Hale. He rejected these as "the heroic fantasies of a young boy," convinced they would have cost him his life.

Would they? Maybe not. With the luxury of half a century's hindsight it seems likely that Powers could have "pulled a Milt," like Willie Fisher in Brooklyn three years earlier. He could probably have said nothing, put his trust in geopolitics, and returned eventually to the United States not as the spy who spilled his guts but as the stoic son of Virginia who kept his mouth shut. It would have saved him a great deal of trouble.

The purpose of his testimony was not to reveal anything the KGB did not already know. It was to provide a prelude to Rudenko's closing harangue, which was in turn designed to shift the blame for the wrecked summit from Khrushchev back to the Americans. It wasn't subtle. Rudenko was a fat-faced ideological yes-man who had reached the top of the ziggurat of Soviet justice by floating there on the shifting winds of change. As the *New York Times* put it: "He has purged and he has purged the purgers. He had helped to concoct false confessions and fantastic indictments, and he has dealt affably and studiously [at Nuremberg] before a tribunal run in the Anglo-Saxon manner."

Rudenko now reverted, on the morning of Friday, August 19, to a full-blown Marxist-Leninist critique of American militarism. This trial, he told his comrade judges and a vast live television audience, exposed not only the crimes of spy-pilot Powers, but also "the criminal aggressive actions of United States ruling circles, the actual inspirers and organizers of monstrous crimes directed against the peace and security of all peoples." He let rip at the "bestial, misanthropic morality of Mr. Dulles" (for expecting Powers to jab himself with the curare pin); at Eisenhower for promising to end overflights of Soviet territory and then allowing another one by a stripped-down Boeing RB-47 on July 1; and, most forcefully, at the unnamed masters of the American military-industrial complex who had reared and bred Powers and his fellow Powerses "in conditions of the so-called free world" to do their murderous bidding and ask questions later.

"It is precisely these Powerses," he proclaimed, "who would have been ready to be the first to drop atom and hydrogen bombs on the peaceful earth, as similar Powerses did when they threw the first atom bombs on the peaceful citizens of the defenseless cities of Hiroshima and Nagasaki."

It was preposterous, of course, and it made Powers "sick at heart" to listen to. But it was not much more preposterous than William Tompkins's undisputed claim at Willie Fisher's trial that Fisher's offenses posed a threat to "the free world and civilization itself." Nor was it outlandish to suggest that Powers would have dropped a nuclear bomb if ordered to. He had been trained to do just that at Sandia Air Force Base in New Mexico in 1953 as a successful participant in "Delivery Course DD50." Nor were Powers's "masters" entirely innocent of contemplating a preemptive nuclear war. It was General Curtis LeMay of the Strategic Air Command who became famous for totting up potential casualties in the tens of millions and judging them tolerable. In fact Rudenko's attack on the American military-industrial complex was strikingly similar to the more famous one by Eisenhower himself, but that was still five months in the future.

In the case of pilot Powers, Rudenko asked for fifteen years' imprisonment, but not death. Powers felt suddenly that he could breathe again. "I wasn't going to be shot!"

His father, in a dark suit and bow tie, stood up at the back of the hall and shouted, "Give me fifteen years here, I'd rather get death!"

Barbara Powers wished afterward that she had told him to sit down and shut up but was "almost doubled up in our box, crying convulsively." She was also heavily sedated.

After a recess, Grinev wound up for the "defense." To that point he had not challenged a single assertion by the prosecution or any of its expert witnesses (among them the KGB vet who had administered Powers's poison pin to a dog and then, it turned out, to a mouse, which also died). Grinev was not about to change his tactics now. He merely requested sympathy for his client, noting his working-class origins, his upbringing in the shadow of "mass unemployment," his seduction by the dollar, and his penitent cooperation as a prisoner. He asked for seven years.

Powers had the last word. Grinev had told him again and again that his life depended on the sincerity of his expressions of regret, and in the end he stuck to a script the two of them had agreed, even though he knew he no longer faced execution. He started by saying he knew he had committed a grave crime and must be punished for it. He finished by asking to be judged "as a human being who is not a personal enemy of the Russian people... and who is deeply repentant and profoundly sorry for what he has done."

Carl McAfee spoke for everyone who had made the journey from Pound when he said later: "I think Gary should have said whatever it took to save his hide."

Ed Stevens of *Life* magazine spoke for most Americans when he leaned over and muttered in McAfee's ear: "That remark is going to cost him."

The court took another recess. It reconvened at 5:30 p.m., past midnight for viewers of continuing live coverage in the Soviet Far East but well within deadline for reporters from New York and London. Lieutenant General Viktor Borisoglebsky, the presiding judge, delivered a final tirade against reactionary Americans leading the world to war, then, as a gesture of socialist humaneness, sentenced Powers to ten years' confinement. On cue, most of the two thousand people in the hall stood and applauded.

Powers managed not to flinch. He and Barbara could not see each other for photographers. She tried to take in what the sentence meant—only the first three years were to be served in prison, and only the locals understood that this meant the next seven would be in a labor camp. Gary was led offstage. Moments later, the family were taken to join him in one of the judges' anterooms, where Gary finally broke down and sobbed in his parents' arms.

A posse of Russian photographers was on hand to record the reunion, ensuring that the tables of hors d'oeuvres provided by the Military Collegium remained in focus in the background. ("That was my first taste of caviar," says Jessica Powers-Hilcman. "I never did like it.") The pictures were distributed by Tass that night, as were the musings of an obliging Danish Supreme Court justice, Christian Wilhelm Hargens. He called Grinev "outstanding" and the conduct of the trial as a whole "unimpeachable." Above all, he said, "I am impelled to compare it with the Rosenberg case," in which two people were sentenced to death on the strength of an indictment "the strength of which does not bear any comparison with the lawful character of the charge against Powers."

In London, the *Times* and the *Daily Telegraph* were predictably scornful of the Soviet parody of due process, but the *News Chronicle* called it "a coherent and cogent indictment of US aggression." In New York, reporters went onto the streets and asked people what they thought of the verdict. One woman said that considering what he'd been paid, Powers had been lucky to receive such a light sentence. "You don't get that kind of money for parting your hair." On balance—and especially considering the timely return of canines Belka and Strelka from outer space to Kazakhstan—it was a banner day for Soviet propaganda.

* * *

Returning to his cell after an hour with his family, Powers realized he had brainwashed himself into expecting the death penalty. He also realized that having been spared it, the prospect of ten years in a Russian jail was, if anything, worse. But he had not reckoned with the depth of socialist humanitarianism, nor with the tenacity of his father and his father's lawyer.

His captors showed their true empathy a week after the trial. Barbara had stayed on in Moscow for a few days to shop in the GUM department store on the east side of Red Square and to petition Khrushchev for leniency on the west. She was not allowed to see the general secretary, but she was allowed to see her husband one last time, "without guards."

The conjugal visit has a long-established place in Russian penal policy, but it can seldom have been granted to two more surprised or grateful spouses than the Powerses. Gary was conspicuously coy in his description: "We were left alone three hours."

Barbara threw modesty to the wind. Left alone with him in a new cell with a couch, sheets, blankets, and an easy chair, she first kissed him and held him close, she wrote, tracing with a pin on the palms of his hands some messages from the CIA that Messrs. Parker and Rogers had asked her to pass on without being eavesdropped. She did not say what they were or whether Gary understood them, but they made for exquisite foreplay:

> *With the preliminaries over, Gary and I began to make love. In nothing flat, Barbara Gay Powers was standing stark naked in a Russian prison cell.... And just that quick we were bouncing up and down on Gary's cot, enjoying the true union of man and wife.*
>
> We had intercourse three times in those three hours.
>
> *Gary hadn't been able to bathe for twelve days, and he smelled like a Billy Goat! But I didn't mind. I was swallowed up by our passion. It*

*felt like my husband was* raping *me. Once, between love sessions, Gary whispered—"You do realize the guards may be watching?"*

*"I don't give a good damn!" I retorted.*

Sated for the time being, she left for New York via Paris the next day.

Carl McAfee, the young lawyer from Virginia, had less fun but more luck in pressing Powers's case for leniency. Ed Stevens had advised him that the man to approach was not Khrushchev but the president of the Presidium, Leonid Ilych Brezhnev. A meeting was arranged, and the boy lawyer swept through the Kremlin's northwest gate to attend it in the by-now-familiar Zil. Brezhnev received him in "the rinky dinkest office that I have ever seen," McAfee remembers.

The beetle-browed president, who would later ruin the Soviet Union in the arms race that Khrushchev was so anxious to avoid, listened graciously as the young Virginian pleaded through an interpreter for a shorter sentence for his client's son. Looking back, McAfee does not recall Brezhnev offering much hope—"and if he did it was in Russian and I don't know what the hell he said." But the visit was probably not pointless and was certainly unique in the annals of freelance diplomacy.

The same was true of Oliver Powers's efforts to arrange an exchange. He had not told his son about his letter to "Abel" in Atlanta, because the reply had been discouraging. What he did not know was that on the day Fisher sent it he also wrote a letter to his lawyer that was "electric with excitement."

# 11

# THE MAN IN THE SCARLET SPORTS CAR

When the Berlin wall went up, it cut the world capital of spying in half, but it still caught the West napping.

On March 16, 1961, an American reporter named George Bailey predicted in a Washington political magazine that Khrushchev would soon "ring down the Iron Curtain in front of East Berlin—with searchlights and machine gun towers, barbed wire and police dog patrols." Why? Because for sixteen years the young, the energetic, and the qualified had been voting with their feet and their suitcases, moving west in such large numbers that in the country they left behind "the mass of the population is either retired or approaching retirement." East Germany was scarcely viable, let alone the socialist economic powerhouse that Khrushchev had been assured would overtake the West German economic miracle. Nothing tried so far had slowed the outflow. Something new and drastic had to be done. President Kennedy read Bailey's article but did not act on it.

On June 4 Kennedy received a new Berlin ultimatum from Khrushchev at their first meeting in Vienna. The Soviet Union would sign a peace treaty with East Germany in six months that would cut off NATO's special access routes to West Berlin.

*Khrushchev:* It is up to the United States to decide whether there will be peace or war.
*Kennedy:* Then it will be a cold winter.

On June 15 President Walter Ulbricht of East Germany issued an unsolicited denial to the press that he would "mobilize the construction workers of the capital...for the purpose of building a wall." Many of his top advisers knew then that this was precisely what he planned to do, but no Western reporter took the hint.

On June 21 the commander of Soviet forces in East Berlin approved a plan to establish physical control of the borders of "Greater Berlin." Stockpiling of barbed wire began in Soviet army warehouses close to the city.

On June 25 Kennedy issued his response to the new ultimatum. He told the world from the Oval Office that West Berlin had become "the great testing place of Western courage and will," where American commitments and Soviet ambition "now meet in basic confrontation." But was it militarily tenable? "Any dangerous spot is tenable if men—brave men—will make it so."

On June 26 Khrushchev cabled his ambassador in East Berlin to tell Ulbricht it was time to lay "an iron ring" around the city. "If this drags us into war," he said, "there will be war."

On August 1 Khrushchev met Ulbricht in Moscow and gave him two weeks to make the iron ring a reality.

On August 3 the leaders of every Warsaw Pact country were summoned to join Ulbricht in Moscow and told of the plan.

On August 11, Erich Mielke, the East German minister for state security, briefed senior Stasi officials on the details of "Operation Rose," the delicate euphemism chosen for the building of the wall.

On August 12, shortly before midnight, Ulbricht let his own cabinet in on the secret at a meeting at his country house in Wandlitz. Until then, fewer than two dozen people in East Germany had known what was about to happen.

On August 13, a Sunday, Soviet tanks mobilized at one minute past midnight thundered toward the city as East German soldiers began digging trenches and unrolling barbed wire along the ninety-six-mile border of West Berlin. Fred Pryor was on holiday in Denmark. He would hear about the closure on his car radio on his way home later that day. He was as surprised as President Kennedy, who was called to the shore of Cape Cod and handed a one-paragraph telex as he stepped off the family motor launch at Hyannis Port seventeen hours after Operation Rose began. Much earlier, George Bailey, in Berlin for *ABC News*, had seen his forecast come true in the person of an East German police captain with a jackhammer, tearing up the pavement in Potsdamer Platz at four in the morning. At about the same time, an East Berlin lawyer, not widely known but with a persuasive charm and a long list of friends and associates in the West, approached the Brandenburg Gate in his car. His wife was in the passenger seat. They were on their way home after a late dinner with friends in West Berlin. West German police advised them to turn back; ahead of the Vogels the border was now a tangle of coiled wire, and behind that, East German *Volkspolizei* armed with machine guns were silhouetted by searchlights. The lawyer thought for a long moment, then drove on through a gap in the wire into a city being turned, as it slept, into a prison. His name was Wolfgang Vogel.

"I belong here," Vogel told one of many Western interviewers who later beat a path to his door on the eastern side of the wall. Hundreds of victims of the Stasi would be grateful for the choice he made that night, but the first of them was Frederic Pryor.

The wall did not appear at once. On day one and day two of the new era of hermetic ideological segregation, there was no hint of concrete; only wire and police and, a block or two back from the border, the Soviet tanks. Ulbricht and Khrushchev were waiting to gauge Kennedy's reaction, which was one of anger—but his anger was directed more at the CIA and State Department for failing to warn him than at the Communists. The operation was a shock, and it was devastating for the families it split in half, but in truth it was easier for Washington to cope with than a unilateral peace treaty between the Soviet Union and East Germany. Kennedy told Vice President Lyndon Johnson and General Lucius Clay to be ready to fly in to sustain morale. He denied a request from U.S. commanders in Berlin for permission to bulldoze the wire.

Daniel Schorr of CBS News was on Bernauer Strasse, whose northern sidewalk formed the border, when the concrete first appeared. It came in slabs, at first just four feet square but then much bigger, slotted by cranes into the trenches that the soldiers and the *Vopos* had been digging. Schorr mused into his microphone that he was reminded of the Warsaw ghetto.

That was on Tuesday morning. On Tuesday afternoon a nineteen-year-old East German army sergeant named Conrad Schumann, distressed by the sight of a daughter handing flowers to her mother across the border wire, took a run at it and jumped. He cleared it neatly, like a well-trained pony. His right boot pressed the wire down. He kept his left foot high and his gun strap taut so that nothing snagged. At that instant a shutter clicked, recording his escape on the single most iconic square of thirty-five-millimeter celluloid of the cold war—and Schumann ran on into a waiting West Berlin police van.

Johnson and Clay reached Berlin at the end of the week and found themselves mobbed by grateful, hopeful crowds all the way from the airport to the Schöneberg district city hall. The next day, 1,500 American troops rolled along the autobahn from their barracks in Helmstedt, one hundred miles away across the West German border, to reinforce the U.S. Army's Berlin garrison. Kennedy kept his closest military adviser up all night to check every twenty minutes that the convoy had not triggered the Third World War. When it arrived safely, Mayor Willy Brandt said he believed the threat of war had passed, and the White House began to breathe again.

The following Friday—August 25—Khrushchev invited the American journalist Drew Pearson to his summer house in the Crimea to explain his actions in Berlin. Ulbricht had a similar urge on the same day, but he satisfied it with a speech rather than an interview. It was to be delivered near Alexanderplatz, in the heart of East Berlin, and was widely publicized in advance. It is likely that a tall, fair-haired English spy named David Cornwell was there. Though posted to Bonn, he spent the last week of August in Berlin quietly researching a novel, *The Spy Who Came In from the Cold,* that he would publish as John le Carré. And it is certain that Fred Pryor was there, the budding expert on Soviet foreign trade. He wanted to know how Ulbricht would justify the wall. He also wanted to test the East German promise that access to East Berlin for westerners would be unaffected by the new border controls.

Pryor had no trouble getting in. As usual, he crossed into the Soviet sector at Checkpoint Charlie in his car, the red VW. It was his farewell visit to the East. He had a development job lined up in Pakistan, and his doctoral thesis was complete. In fact, he had a few copies on his passenger seat. After listening to the speech, he planned to deliver them to people who had helped him with it. And after that he hoped to say good-bye to a young economist, a Fräulein Bergman, who had worked with him on a separate project comparing textile firms in the two Germanys. Maybe he would even ask her out to dinner.

Pryor did not see le Carré in Alexanderplatz. Not to recognize, at any rate. He did see a westerner whom he knew, though. A fellow Oberlin graduate from the class of 1955 was in the crowd and several inches taller than most of the East Germans around him. Martin Skala, in what he calls his postcollege "idealistic phase," was visiting from Austria. He had crossed the border with some money for a church group hidden under his clothes and was hanging around for the speech before returning to West Berlin for the night. The two men listened as Ulbricht blamed ideological weaklings and Western provocateurs for forcing his hand on the thirteenth. Then they chatted about how small the world was, and Pryor gave Skala a ride to Checkpoint Charlie. Skala got out; Pryor headed back to East Berlin.

Fräulein Bergman was not at home. Nor was her landlady at liberty to tell Pryor where she had gone. Finding out these meager facts took him out of his car and up several flights of stairs. When he returned to the car he found it surrounded by East German police.

"They asked where I had been. I told them. They asked what I was doing there. I said I went to see somebody but they weren't there."

Bergman had fled to the West, and the Stasi had staked out her apartment. Pryor was arrested on suspicion of helping her flee and attempting to recover her possessions. He was taken first back to Alexanderplatz, to police headquarters. There he tried claiming that he had gone to the wrong address, but no one believed him. That evening he was moved away from the city center, beyond the reach of any conceivable quick rescue, out of the category of unfortunate misunderstandings and into the vortex of Stasi paranoia. He was moved to the Hohenschönhausen Investigation Prison, a world unto itself in a remote northeastern suburb that never appeared on an East German map. The streets leading to it simply stopped. It was a prestigious place to work but a soul-destroying place to live: a complex of fifty-four squat brick and concrete buildings ringed by its own wall and monitored by its own octagonal watchtowers, where right-thinking people locked up wrong-thinking people and tormented them until they confessed.

Pryor was never told what the Stasi wanted him to confess to, but he had a pretty good idea. "I was arrested for the wrong thing," he says.

"But once they discovered the dissertation in my car they got excited. I realized after a couple of days that I would be in prison for the next ten years."

He was put in a cell with a cell mate who worked diligently as a stooge, and he was interrogated every day for five and a half months. Every two days he was led down the yellow-lit corridor of his cell block, across perhaps five meters of open space and into a "tiger cage"—the prisoners' term—to exercise. The cages were concrete boxes four meters long and two and a half meters wide, open only to the sky. That gave those in them an occasional view of Soviet jets descending toward East Berlin's Schönefeld Airport, but the view was obscured by an armed guard on a metal platform, one for each four cages. The platforms were positioned above the cages where their corners met, enabling guards to shoot prisoners at point-blank range in the unlikely event that they attempted to do anything other than prowl. Sessions lasted fifteen to twenty minutes.

Prisoners sometimes found loose lumps of asphalt in the cages and lobbed them into neighboring cages to advertise their existence. The recipient of such a lump could take it back to his cell, but it would be confiscated at his next cell inspection.

Pryor's cell was five paces long and two wide, with two pine bunks, a small window filled with glass bricks, a sink, and an open toilet bowl. Under the window were a small table and a chair, both bolted to the floor.

He was not tortured, but his interrogation made those of Willie Fisher and Gary Powers look perfunctory by comparison. "I had nothing to hide, so I answered their questions," Pryor says, which was one reason the questions did not stop. There were two other reasons: having read his thesis, the Stasi tried to build a case of economic espionage against him under Article 14 of the East German criminal code. And having researched his background they became convinced that his father was a personal friend of Robert McNamara, the U.S. secretary of defense and a fellow homeowner in Ann Arbor, Michigan. This would make Pryor one of the most valuable bargaining chips to have fallen into the Stasi's web since its creation. The result was an epic two-way conversation about nothing, recorded in minute detail.

When he returned to Berlin to read his Stasi file in 1994, Pryor found that it was 10,000 pages long, including a meticulous German translation of his thesis, transcripts of interrogations of everyone he had interviewed, 350 pages of notes and suggested questions handwritten by his cell mate, and seventy-two items taken from his wallet.

One of these items was his Yale library card, stamped with the words SPECIAL STUDENT—ONLY ROOM 413.

To his interrogator, "special" was a special word.

> *Interrogator:* I thought you said you were a regular student.
> *Pryor:* I was.
> *Interrogator:* What's the special room?

"We spent about a week on that," Pryor says. "Then finally I remembered that in my last semester I hadn't paid my tuition on time. Room 413 was the economics seminar room, the only room in the library I could use until I paid my bill."

A week's work done, the interrogator let it go. He was a professional, after all; a graduate of the Stasi's own university in Potsdam, the Harvard Law of Eastern Bloc interrogation schools. He had other ways to wear young Pryor down.

Another week, he asked about a girl Pryor had met half a dozen times in East Berlin. She was a medical student. The relationship had been strictly conversational, he says, a series of dates at which they talked about the endless differences between growing up in Ohio and East Germany. It had ended at her request when she explained that it might start to look bad on her records to have had such frequent contact with a foreigner. Pryor did not explain this in the interrogation room, for her sake, but "they kept pushing, pushing, pushing, and suddenly I got the notion of what they were really after."

Just as Pryor understood that "fear of the Stasi" was not acceptable to the Stasi as an explanation for ending a relationship, so his friend did too. They must have got to her, and she must have said something else.

"So after three days I said, 'I confess, I tried to screw her.' 'Tried to screw her.' He wrote it down. And the questioning stopped."

Thirty-three years later, going through his file, Pryor looked at the transcript of her interrogation. "She said roughly the same thing as I did: 'I had to break up with him because he tried to violate my socialist virginity, *meine sozialistische Keuschheit zu verschmutzen.*' And so our stories agreed."

He was fed well—"three squares a day." The Stasi called it the tubercular diet, and Pryor assumed he was put on it because his mother was Jewish and it would look bad if when he was eventually released he raised his shirt for the press and said, "Auschwitz." But feeling full did not make him a happy prisoner. He was told he would stay in Hohenschönhausen, denied all contact with the outside world, until he confessed to spying. Parcels and letters from his parents were not delivered. His interrogator told him his girlfriend in West Berlin had betrayed him, and he could never quite dismiss the idea that this might be true. When his cell mate intimated that he would have to stand trial for espionage, Pryor had visions of a German version of the farce that Powers had endured in Moscow and said he would sooner commit suicide.

"I meant it," he says later, matter-of-factly, toward the end of his career as an economics professor in Pennsylvania. "I didn't want to be used as a tool in cold war propaganda." How he would have killed himself was a tricky question given the scarcity of implements in his cell. But he got as far as thinking about biting through the veins in his wrist, and his kamikaze warning to his cell mate may have shaken a few bureaucratic screws loose higher up the Stasi chain of command.

Soon afterward, on a cold February day in 1962, he had a visitor. They were given a room for a private conversation that was inevitably recorded and transcribed in full for Pryor's file. The man who joined him there was a lawyer who evidently did well for himself. He was youngish, compact, dapper, and guardedly optimistic. He pointed first to the ceiling as a warning that microphones would be hidden there. Then he introduced himself as Wolfgang Vogel and handed Pryor a note in handwriting he recognized immediately as his father's. It consisted of five words: "You can trust this man."

# *part four*

# ANATOMY OF A DEAL

# 12

# POKER FOR TABLE STAKES

Christmas 1961 was not a good time to be in jail as a spy in the Eastern Bloc. It was cold outside, miserable inside, and godless everywhere. Snow blanketed northern Eurasia, covering its prison exercise yards and hiding the missile silos that the U-2 had never quite photographed.

Khrushchev and Ulbricht hid most of their intentions. Khrushchev had released the two American survivors of the RB-47 shot down over the Soviet Arctic the year before but had received no answering gesture from Kennedy. Kennedy thought Khrushchev a perplexing maverick and did not want to be any further in his debt. In Berlin, the wall was four months old. It was no longer a direct threat to peace, but it was still a livid scar and East Germany was still unrecognized by the free world. Westerners sucked in by the Stasi could not be reached by official channels, and the unofficial ones were largely untested.

Being a spy in prison in Atlanta was warmer but not much more uplifting. In his fourth annual Christmas message to his lawyer, the inmate known as Rudolf Abel asked as usual for his four-pound ration of milk chocolate, then let his guard down and admitted that life on the inside was becoming "an affliction."

And yet, within two months, something had changed. It was not that the tectonic plates of geopolitics had moved. On the contrary, the superpowers were digging in for thirty years of proxy wars and breakneck missile construction. The change was almost imperceptible. The movement was the movement of human restlessness, between the plates, as people began finding new ways around them—people like Fred T. Wilkinson, U.S. deputy director of prisons, who late on the night of Thursday, February 8, 1962, received a message in his Manhattan hotel room to drive down West Street to the corner of Eleventh Street in Greenwich Village and wait. It was snowing. He drove carefully, stopped at the corner, and rolled down his window. A man emerged from the darkness and asked: "Are you ready to make the trip?" Wilkinson nodded and drove back to his hotel.

* * *

Willie Fisher had kept faith with the Cheka, and the Cheka had kept faith with him. For five years he had admitted nothing, either in prison or in court. For five years Russia had denied all knowledge of his Abel alter ego, dismissing Reino Hayhanen's stories about him as a tissue of lies. But for nearly four of those years a young KGB officer posted to Berlin had been working the angles, trying to pry him loose—and impersonating his fictitious cousin.

For the purposes of this marathon charade, the young KGB man called himself Cousin Drewes. His real name was Yuri Drozdov. He was lean and strong, with a long, thin nose. He looked, James Donovan eventually decided, like Otto the Strangler. At that time he lived with his wife and two small children in a modest flat in Karlshorst, near the KGB's East Berlin headquarters. He later became a general, then a private security consultant, and was still in business in comfortably appointed offices in central Moscow in 2009.

At first Drozdov didn't have much luck as Cousin Drewes, nor as Hellen Abel, Rudolf's wife, whose part in the negotiations was played by a real woman when necessary but whose letters to America he tended to write; he was fluent in German and English as well as Russian, and the ranking polyglot on the case.*

These early letters were addressed to Donovan as Abel's lawyer and postmarked Leipzig (the KGB was still not ready to admit Abel was

* She looked plump and matronly, like Mrs. Khrushchev, one collaborator thought; nothing like the real Mrs. Fisher.

one of theirs). They begged for leniency, offered nothing in return, and dripped with fake self-pity. Donovan had seen letters from the real Mrs. Abel during her husband's trial. He had been moved by their spare descriptions of the flowers and changing seasons at the family dacha and could tell the difference at once. He forwarded the phony ones to his client, and to the CIA, and thought little of them.

The capture of Gary Powers changed everything—not just world history, but Willie Fisher's chances of seeing his family again. The Russians, as Donovan noted immediately, had found some bait.

Oliver Powers was just as quick to see the opportunity. He jump-started the new dialogue with his letter to "Abel" from Pound while his son was still awaiting trial. "Dear Colonel Abel," Powers (and Carl McAfee) wrote. "I am the father of Francis Gary Powers who is connected with the U2 plane incident of several weeks ago. . . .

"You can readily understand the concern that a father would have for his son and for a strong desire to have my son released. . . . I would be more than happy to approach the State Department and the President of the United States for an exchange for the release of my son. By this I mean that I would urge and do everything possible to have my government release you and return you to your country if the powers in your country would release my son and let him return to me. If you are inclined to go along with this arrangement I would appreciate your so advising me and also so advising the powers in your country along these lines."

The letter was wildly optimistic and it annoyed the CIA, which assumed it had a lock on American spy swap negotiations. But it thrilled Fisher because it gave Donovan a reason to write something concrete back to "Mrs. Abel" and her lawyer—a certain Wolfgang Vogel.

Unlike "Drewes" and most of his accomplices, Vogel was a real person. Still only thirty-three, he had been appointed to the Abel case a full two years before he met Fred Pryor, in response to a KGB request to the Stasi for a go-between.

Vogel was a lawyer, the hardworking, god-fearing son of a Catholic schoolteacher from Lower Silesia. But above all he was a player. In 1953, when East Germany's Communists enlisted Soviet force to crush a rebellion on the streets of Berlin, he was the protégé of a justice minister who defected to the West and tried to take Vogel with him.

Then, as in 1961, he stayed in the East. As his biographer wrote: "Faust made his bargain with the devil. Vogel made his with the Stasi." The Stasi called him Secret Informer "Georg." In his reports to them he preferred to sign off as Eva.

He liked antique watches, Western cars and suits, and other people's secrets. He earned them with charm, discretion, and the highly sensitive antennae of a natural deal maker. In due course he would persuade the West German government to part with six hundred million deutsche marks for the freedom of nearly a quarter of a million people from behind the Iron Curtain. He also dabbled in high politics, setting the agenda and taking the notes at a delicate summit between the leaders of the two Germanys in 1982. But in 1961 his main chore was meeting Yuri Drozdov for coffee in East Berlin and crafting letters to Jim Donovan.

It took Vogel and Drozdov a while to answer Oliver Powers's prayers: they took their cues from Moscow, and there could be no progress toward an exchange in the frosty aftermath of the Vienna summit or during the building of the wall. But on September 11, 1961, they delivered. In Brooklyn, a letter reached Donovan from "Mrs. Abel" saying

> *On your advice I visited the Soviet Embassy in Berlin.... I am glad to tell you that as before the Soviet representative showed great understanding of my case and reassured me of their willingness to help.... I gathered from our talk that there is only one possible way to achieve success now—THAT IS SIMULTANEOUS RELEASE OF BOTH F. POWERS AND MY HUSBAND WHICH CAN BE ARRANGED.*

"There it was," Donovan wrote. "That is what I had been waiting to read."

He forwarded the letter as usual to the CIA, which digested it like a cold-blooded monster with glacial metabolism and four months later produced its response: a phone call to Donovan. Would he come to Washington?

Would he ever. Donovan was earning good money traveling the length and breadth of the United States defending the insurance industry against irritating claims from outraged policyholders. But the work was dull. It was not a good reason to be staying up so late, smoking so many cigarettes, and seeing so little of his family. Spying was a far better one. It reminded him of wild times with the OSS during the war, and the case of Rudolf Abel in particular was sufficiently high profile—when allowed into the headlines—to help build the Donovan brand in the minds of Democratic voters; he hoped that one day they might back him as a New York senator.

The CIA was in agreement with the KGB. The time was right for an exchange. As they told Donovan, it would be in the national interest. That shorthand covered a multitude of motivations: since Abel had made it abundantly clear he would not talk, and since any intelligence he could provide on the United States on his return to Moscow would be five years out of date, his continued presence in Atlanta was merely a burden on the taxpayer. As for Powers, the U-2 affair could not be consigned to history as long as he was stuck in Russia. (Nor could the Agency give him the merciless grilling it felt he deserved about what really happened over Sverdlovsk.)

As Donovan knew, the Soviets appeared ready to do the deal. So the Agency asked: would he be willing to undertake a mission to East Germany to make it happen? If so, he would have the full logistical support of the CIA but was to make it look like a business trip and tell no one its true purpose, even in his own family.

Donovan was a man of broad experience and deep convictions who took the world almost as seriously as he took himself. He was a grown-up. Even so, he could barely contain himself.

From his hotel in Washington he immediately composed and sent a letter to "Frau Abel" in "Leipzig." It was dated January 11, 1962. He proposed a meeting at the Soviet Embassy in East Berlin at twelve noon on Saturday, February 3. If this was agreeable, he asked her to cable his law office the three words "Happy New Year."

Two weeks later—late but not too late by the Russian calendar—the New Year's greeting arrived. "The meeting in Berlin was set," Donovan wrote. On January 27 he attended the annual luncheon of the International Association of Insurance Counsel at the Plaza Hotel in New York and told anyone who would listen that he would soon be traveling to London to discuss an unspecified merger. He made free with promises of Liberty scarves for members' wives. Then he booked a suite at Claridge's and a first-class seat to London on Pan Am.

Business trips did not come much better than this.

***

The man Donovan was to rescue was in less salubrious accommodation. After his sweaty romp with Barbara in the cell with the easy chair and the bouncy cot, Gary Powers had been driven out of Moscow, through farmland and forest, to the prison where all high-value foreign enemies of the revolution ended up. It was a walled complex of cell blocks and workshops 150 miles east of the capital outside the town of Vladimir.

After the war, probably in 1947, it was to Vladimir that the most celebrated prisoner taken by the Red Army in its devastating march on Berlin, Raoul Wallenberg, was brought and left to die. Wallenberg should have been borne aloft on the Soviet troops' shoulders to Moscow, Yad Vashem, and eventually home to Stockholm, for he was the Swedish Schindler, the young diplomat who saved thousands of Hungarian Jews from the Holocaust by giving them exit visas and free passage to his country. He was the very opposite of a Fascist. But having allowed him to disappear, probably through simple clerical error, neither Stalin nor any of his successors would admit it. Wallenberg was almost certainly still alive in cell block 2 in 1961, but no entreaty by the Swedish government or those he saved has ever elicited conclusive proof of his fate from the Kremlin or the KGB.* His bravery was rewarded with decades of solitary confinement and an unmarked grave.

Vladimir prison was also the home for most of his adult life of Tamas Andras, a Hungarian prisoner of war who arrived there without papers in 1945 and was simply forgotten. He spoke no Russian, and no one at the prison spoke Hungarian. Guards and officials thought his mutterings were those of a madman, and he was sequestered in a special wing for the insane, out of earshot of anyone who might understand him, for fifty-five years. He was rescued and repatriated in the spring of 2000 after a Hungarian television journalist overheard his rantings while researching a feature on post-Communist Russian prisons.

* And thereby hangs another long and heroic tale: that of Marvin Makinen's exhaustive cell-occupancy analysis of cell block 2, part of a ten-year investigation by the Swedish and Russian governments into Wallenberg's fate in which Makinen took part after spending two years in Vladimir himself for photographing troop movements and military installations on his car trip through Ukraine in 1961.

No such atrocities were visited on pilot Powers. Not one of the horror stories he had heard from his employers about the Soviet treatment of spies came true. In fact, as he wrote repeatedly in his prison journal—for the censors who might read it but also for posterity—he was treated better than he dared hope. He was allowed to write and receive mail. He was sent monthly care packages by the U.S. embassy in Moscow, their contents chosen by Barbara before her departure (to include lump sugar, cigarettes, pipe tobacco, instant coffee, and Pream powdered milk). He was allowed a long, hot shower every ten days and as much reading material as he could devour. *Time, Life,* and *Newsweek* were banned in favor of the *Daily Worker,* but the entire English-language fiction section of the Moscow State University Library was available to him, and since most of it predated the revolution it included the classics. He read Shaw, Dickens, Galsworthy, and Thackeray, and Voltaire and Tolstoy in translation. He liked especially Pushkin's *Tales of Ivan Belkin.* Nor did the cross-cultural education of Gary Powers end there. He asked for and was given an English-speaking cell mate, Zigurd Kruminsh, who taught him Russian and quilt making, won his lasting friendship, and never let him suspect that he was in fact a stooge. Together they attended prison screenings of Soviet films that Powers described briefly in his journal: "October 15: Saw my second movie—about a quarrel on a collective farm. Not real good." "October 29: Saw another movie about construction of a railroad bridge in Siberia. Fair."

When a visiting KGB colonel asked how he rated what he had seen of Soviet cinema, Powers said he thought it compared with American B-movie westerns. The colonel was so dismayed that he had a sixteen-millimeter print of a Bolshevik classic on the conquest of Russia by barbarians sent specially from Moscow. A private screening was arranged for the two men in cell 31.

Despite his gentle handling, by his second Christmas in Vladimir Powers was going quietly out of his mind. This was partly because he thought his preferential treatment meant he could be released at any time: the longer he remained inside, the more personally he took his sentence. But there were other reasons. The previous Christmas he had received ninety-six cards, thanks to a seasonal drollery from Herb Caen, the *San Francisco Chronicle* columnist: "Let him know that U-2 haven't forgotten." But 1961 brought no syndicated reminders for American readers and hardly any cards. Was the world forgetting?

Worse than that, was America turning against him? His first inkling came in an issue of *Time* that a new prison guard inadvertently let through the post room. It contained a short mention of an initiative by Robert Maynard Hutchins, president of the Fund for the Republic, to discover whether the differences between Airman Powers and Nathan Hale, America's first spy, pointed to "signs that the moral character of America is changing." What the devil did that mean, he asked Barbara in a letter. But she wasn't writing back, and that was what bothered him most of all. He spent the long, cold nights of his second winter in prison lying awake in his cell, replaying in his head the worst scenes of their marriage and thinking of divorce. "I am a nervous wreck because of this," he wrote in the last entry in his journal, dated January 31, 1962. "As hard as I try I cannot keep from thinking about it. I need help badly! But who can help?"

A week later the colonel who had tried so hard to turn Powers into a Soviet movie buff appeared unexpectedly in the corridor outside his cell. He asked how Powers would feel about going to Moscow the next morning, "without guards," and Powers said he would feel just fine.

* * *

Donovan's final CIA briefing before his departure for London took place at the Harvard Club in midtown Manhattan. The briefer was a friend and fellow Harvard alum, so it looked perfectly natural. Two men. Two armchairs. One wintry afternoon.

They talked about the first meeting in Berlin, scheduled for the third. Originally Donovan was to have made the trip through the wall to the Soviet embassy with a minder from the U.S. mission, someone fluent in German and Russian, unlike him. But the Agency had rethought that. Donovan was to go alone, no gun, no wire. And if anything went wrong, he would have "no official status at all."

Donovan's friend rephrased himself. If anything went wrong, the government would naturally take a very grave view of the matter, and at the highest level. But there had been too many awkward incidents since the wall went up, and if an official U.S. representative were somehow trapped inside a country the United States did not recognize, it would be "embarrassing."

Speaking of incidents, he continued, there was one other thing. He explained about Fred Pryor. It was the first time Donovan heard the name, and the first time he heard that Vogel claimed to represent Pryor as well as "Mrs. Abel." Not only that, Vogel had sent a message to the U.S. mission saying Mrs. Abel was confident that if her husband was released in exchange for Powers, Pryor would be freed as well. No one at the mission knew whether to trust Vogel, but if Donovan could fold Pryor into the deal the family would be grateful.

Donovan said he'd try. He took a cab back to Prospect Park West and packed.

* * *

The first person to know Pryor was missing was his girlfriend, Eleonora. She had expected him to return to his room on Viktoria-Luise-Platz on the evening of Ulbricht's speech about the wall. She did not panic when he failed to show. This was Fred, after all. Paraguay Fred. Between answering his ad and typing up his thesis and starting to fall in love with him, she had learned a fair amount about his proclivity to roam. He was legal in the Soviet sector. He had that car. He spoke good German now, thanks partly to her. He would be fine.

By the following week there was still no word from him, and Eleonora began to worry. She telephoned his twin brother in Connecticut. He telephoned his parents in Michigan. They were retired and had plenty of time to watch the news on television. For two weeks the footage flown back nightly from Berlin of Soviet tanks back in the city they had "liberated" sixteen years earlier and of families jumping from the windows on Bernauer Strasse to escape them had been harrowing enough even for parents without sons caught up in the chaos. Now their son seemed to be lost in it.

"My father was a very take-charge sort of person," Pryor remembers. It was true, as the Stasi suspected, that Millard H. Pryor was acquainted with Robert McNamara, the defense secretary, since they had homes in the same neighborhood in Ann Arbor. He was also friendly with another neighbor, a Professor William Haber of the University of Michigan, who in turn was an old wartime comrade of the great Lucius Clay, Kennedy's crisis manager in West Berlin. But, his son insisted, "he was not the kind of person who would leave it to the authorities to get me out of prison."

What Pryor senior did instead was book tickets for himself and his wife to West Berlin. He was well-to-do after a long and successful career in business, interrupted only by a spell as a navy commander in the Pacific. His sons were—more or less—through college. If he could only get Fred out of this mess, they would both be fending for themselves. He had money. If this is what it turned out to be for, then he would spend it. On arrival, Millard and Mary Pryor checked into the Kempinski.

Their first call was to the U.S. mission on Clay Allee, a low-rise complex of gray office buildings on a boulevard named after the most powerful man inside them. Considering their contacts, the Pryors did not get much help—just a short list of lawyers licensed to practice on both sides of the wall. Vogel's name was second on the list. They called him and met with him several times in September. If there was a cultural chasm between them, Vogel bridged it effortlessly. He impressed Mary Pryor in particular with his expressions of religious faith; his claim to suffer ulcers because of his devotion to his clients; and his willingness to believe her son was not, in fact, a spy. The Pryors hired him.

It was a first step, but a first step into a morass. For all his apparently good intentions, Vogel was only a go-between, and he was hard to get to. His office was deep into East Berlin along an S-Bahn line that, since August, had been accessible only by braving a cordon of stone-faced *Vopos* in the Friedrichstrasse station.

They would let the Pryors in, but there was no guarantee that they would let them out. Outside the Eastern Bloc, East Germany was a pariah state that was ready to demand official recognition by taking hostages and forcing foreign governments to negotiate for their release. That was one reason it was holding on to their son. It was also the reason, all diplomatic niceties apart, that the U.S. mission could do so little for them.

So the Pryors acquired a go-between to maintain contact with their go-between. His name was Duane Bruce. Where he came from, what he did after 1962, and whether Duane Bruce was his real name all remain mysteries, but thanks to the Stasi's meticulous record keeping this much is clear: on November 26, Bruce visited Vogel at his apartment in Prenzlauer Berg in East Berlin on the Pryors' behalf. He arrived in a VW bug, license plate B-ND 596, and stayed for two hours. Their discussion of the Pryor case was recorded in full by Vogel's Stasi handlers; the transcript ran to twenty-five pages. Bruce started by claiming that he worked in the American sector as an insurance salesman but, business being slow, had answered a small ad published by the Free University seeking a German-speaking American. Having imagined the work would be of the tour guide variety, he was surprised to find himself being briefed by the Pryors on their search for their son. When hired to help them, he was still more surprised—as, presumably, were Vogel and his eavesdroppers when he volunteered the information—to be commandeered by the CIA for a six-week course in basic espionage. He said his training included recognition drills on Soviet Army handguns, shoulder stripes, and tank types.

Having introduced himself with such expansive and unsolicited candor, Bruce asked how bad it looked for young Fred Pryor. Vogel gave a reply he had not given Pryor's parents: "Well, Herr Bruce, it depends what you think is spying and what is not. According to our understanding of the law, Pryor's actions probably qualify." (This was undoubtedly true. Under East German law the fact that no one had actively prevented Pryor reading dusty theses on the price of Russian corn at Rostock did not mean he was allowed to read them. Quite the reverse: anything he was not explicitly permitted to read, he was not permitted to read. And reading economic literature that he was not permitted to read amounted to economic espionage. Ergo, he was a spy.)

This being so, Vogel continued, Pryor was in big trouble if his case came to trial. He had not been allowed to see the evidence being gathered against the prisoner, he claimed, but the fact that they had been amassing that evidence for three months at the Hohenschönhausen Investigation Prison showed how seriously they were taking it.

"They undoubtedly have some proof," he said. "We have to assume the worst once a prosecution gets started. The only choice then for the judge will be between fifteen years and life."

And there it was, hanging above a sofa in an East Berlin apartment on a chilly autumn evening in 1961, floating onto the spools of a hidden Stasi tape recorder and into the receptive short-term memory of a freelance American spy: five words of pure political blackmail, "between fifteen years and life."

Bruce, who according to the transcript expressed no surprise, was probably exactly what he claimed to be. As Donovan would find, neither the U.S. mission nor the CIA's Berlin station were sending staffers across the wall for fear that it would swallow them up. So they were sending greenhorns like Bruce instead, and in this case were asking him to wear two hats. He was sounding out Vogel for the Pryors but also for the Agency, which was nervous about having to trust Vogel with the much bigger prize of Gary Powers.

Vogel was wearing not two hats but three. He spoke for the KGB via "Mrs. Abel." ("When they tell me they are ready to do an exchange, I will be able to do it," he assured Bruce.) He spoke for the Stasi when calmly threatening a life term for a noncrime, and he spoke for Pryor's parents in the same breath—because his solution to the problem served both parties equally.

"The parents must be convinced that there is a massive case against their son," he told Bruce. "Otherwise there is no reason to do anything for him in Washington." If the Americans wanted to add Pryor to the Abel-Powers deal, in short, they needed to ask nicely. The way things stood the only people who could make that happen were Pryor's parents, but in return they would get their son, and East Germany would get a little respect.

Bruce said he thought the Pryors would get the message. As he got up to leave, Vogel asked him to deliver a letter to a car dealer in West Berlin. He wanted to upgrade from an Opel Rekord to a Kapitän.

The Pryors did get the message. In the month before Christmas, Millard went into overdrive. He lobbied the State Department through his congressman and his Washington attorney. He solicited telegrams to the East German government from the president of Yale. He crafted an elaborate scheme whereby in exchange for his son's release the mighty Krupp steel and manufacturing combine would exhibit for the first time at the Leipzig Trade Fair. And he said something to the U.S. mission—what exactly is not clear—that made it assign, at last, a real person to his case.

That person might have been vaguely familiar to the Moscow policeman at the head of the queue to view the wreckage of Gary Powers's plane in Gorky Park the previous year. It was the amiable Frank Meehan, who knew little about spy planes but enough about Communists to have been reposted to Berlin, where America urgently needed to understand them better.

Meehan was born in New Jersey but grew up in Scotland and spoke English, German, and Russian with the same soft Celtic inflection. Looking back, he was modest about his role in springing Pryor, not least because in the great scheme of ideological empire building and nuclear deterrence that had trapped him, it was a modest task. But it meant a lot to the Pryors, and he was perfect for it.

"We heard in the mission that there was some political steam building up at home, and I was told to get into the case and start handling the family right," he says. "We had to deal with this, and we didn't have anyone to deal with. There was no one I could go to [in East Berlin] and say, 'I'm a representative of the American mission.'... I couldn't go to anybody. But I could go to Vogel."

Meehan and Vogel found they could trust each other. They were both Catholics, serious about faith but less so about doctrine. They actually looked similar, and they got along.

"He just didn't behave like an East German," Meehan remembers, sitting on a terrace beside a lake in the Bavarian Alps, having traveled there forty-seven years later to attend his old friend's funeral. "Here was one of the most ideological regimes going, totally devoted to the Soviet Union, a hard, militant, difficult pain in the arse, and here was a guy that you could talk to. He wouldn't read the leading article in *Neues Deutschland* to you. He would think and speak on his feet. That was certainly the impression that I got, which I reported, of course, so at that point I became a sort of channel."

The existence of the channel may have been the clincher. Millard Pryor's efforts in Washington and Berlin created a gratifying fuss on the American side. Vogel, as "Eva," duly reported it all to the Stasi, but his own connection with Meehan was more valuable. Here was a political officer from the U.S. mission cultivating the next best thing to diplomatic relations. From the point of view of the German Democratic Republic, it was not a bad reward for trading in a perfectly innocent economist.

Once Vogel had made this argument to his Stasi handler and his handler had made it to the East German attorney general, Vogel visited Pryor in prison at Hohenschönhausen. He made no promises, but for Pryor's remaining nights in prison his interrogator stood guard to make sure he didn't kill himself.

* * *

James Donovan kissed his wife and children and left for the airport.

It was January 29, 1962. For paying passengers, transatlantic travel was already a miracle of nonstop great circle routes over Gander and the Icelandic fishing grounds, only marginally subsonic. His Pan Am 707 had him in Heathrow in time for breakfast.

A cab took him to Claridge's. The Agency was ready to deny him if the operation turned sour, but he was not alone. On British soil, he was the guest of MI6. Soon after he checked in, a Mr. White knocked at his door, handed him an envelope of West German currency, and asked if he would mind being called Mr. Dennis while in London. Donovan said he didn't mind. He invited Mr. White in for a morning bracer of the hotel brandy, then lay down to snooze off his jetlag.

His mind drifted back to the war, when Claridge's soot-blackened bricks hid an oasis of expensive comfort and the OSS kept a suite on the same floor as the exiled kings of Yugoslavia and Romania. When steak could not be obtained anywhere else in Europe, it could generally be obtained at Claridge's.

Donovan was in no rush. It was a Tuesday. Not expected in East Berlin until the weekend, he indulged himself over the next two days browsing the shelves of rare-book shops in Mayfair. He left his purchases with a favorite bookbinder, together with his Brooklyn address; if all went well, he would not be coming back through London. On Thursday he dined at the hotel with old friends, telling them he was leaving for Zurich the next morning. From the front desk he sent a cablegram to his wife with the delightful news that he had been invited to Scotland for a short break.

On Friday, Mr. White was at Claridge's before dawn. He drove Mr. Dennis out of the sleeping city for two hours, through driving rain, to an RAF base where a U.S. Air Force C-45 was waiting for him. It took off immediately, with Donovan the only passenger. Coffee and doughnuts were served over the English Channel, sandwiches and more coffee while refueling at Weisbaden. Darkness was falling when they landed at Tempelhof, and so was snow.

There were no formalities. Donovan was met airside by Bob "El Supremo" Graver, the CIA's Berlin station chief, a man of mythic stature in intelligence circles whose all-knowing aura and confidence in dealing with the Agency's top management had saved him from disgrace when he completely failed to predict the building of the wall.

Graver took Donovan to a darkened safe house in the American sector and showed where stashes of American cigarettes and cask-aged Scotch had been left for his convenience. A maid would let herself in each morning to cook breakfast and clean the house. Otherwise he would be on his own there. Donovan unpacked, missing London already. Graver picked him up again for dinner at the Berlin Hilton, where he pointed out a public telephone at the Golden City Bar. He gave Donovan a number he was to call from there with his report the following and subsequent evenings, explaining that the number would be manned continuously "for this sole purpose" while he was in Berlin.

It was still snowing the next morning, only harder. Donovan ate breakfast in the safe house with Graver, studying the Agency's latest maps of the wall and its crossing points. He was running late by the time he reached the Friedrichstrasse crossing point. Marching to the front of a long line, he announced his appointment at the Soviet embassy and was let through at once. For a brief moment he could imagine himself as the spy who went out into the cold.

The heart of Berlin was a freezing lattice of ruins under snow—a monument to war. Donovan had last seen it in 1945, when Allied bombs and Soviet artillery had reduced Wilhelmine Germany's architectural showpieces to rubble and Mongolians in Red Army uniform terrorized those with nowhere else to flee to. He found it little changed. "As far as one could see in any direction, the buildings were in ruins or disrepair," he wrote in his diary.

> *Shell holes were still in the sides of crumbling walls. The streets were strangely deserted and seemed filled with an oppressive fear. It was as though the Russians had decided in 1945 that East Berlin should continue a living death so the Germans would never forget.*
>
> *Through the falling snow I made my way to Unter den Linden. As I rounded one deserted corner, there suddenly appeared a group of ten or twelve youths, in shabby trench coats or heavy turtleneck sweaters and without hats. Some had cigarettes dangling from their lips. They looked like a pack of wolves.*

Only the giant Soviet embassy was intact and lit; a beacon of socialist hope on the boulevard of tears. In the foyer of the consular section Donovan shook the snow off his coat and came face-to-face with the cast of amateur players that the KGB had assembled to maintain the pretense of disinterest in the case. Donovan's reception committee introduced themselves as Frau Abel, her daughter, and her cousin Drewes. Only their real names and a printed program were missing.

Drewes, played as ever by Yuri Drozdov, said nothing—just "kept opening and closing powerful hands," Donovan noted. But the woman playing Mrs. Abel took the trouble to ask after her husband. When Donovan replied that he was fine, she actually sobbed for several minutes. It was quickly clear to him that none of these characters was a principal. He had no way of knowing how much spadework had been done by "Drewes," he of the powerful hands, but his instincts were right. He had yet to meet his opposite number. They all waited. As they waited, he smoked. When the "daughter" asked for a cigarette, he ignored her.

At noon exactly, a door behind them opened and a tall, good-looking apparatchik in a suit and rimless glasses introduced himself as Ivan Shishkin, second secretary at the embassy.

Shishkin was in fact the most senior KGB officer in Europe. He was the summiteer to Drozdov's Sherpa, sent to Berlin in 1959 expressly to find and groom the intermediaries, Vogel among them, needed to bring in a spy the Kremlin did not recognize through a country the Americans did not recognize. He was fluent in four languages, including English, with a quick mind and a bone-dry sense of humor. He took one look at the big man from Brooklyn and decided he could have some fun with him.

He ushered Donovan and his retinue of unfortunate "East Germans" into a conference room and asked how he could help.

To begin with, Donovan played along. He presented his credentials, stated his business, and assured Mr. Shishkin that he could deliver Rudolf Abel, together with a pardon signed by President Kennedy, within forty-eight hours of an agreement being finalized to release Powers and Pryor in return. Shishkin said he knew all about the Powers-Abel plan; he had been empowered to seek the release of Abel out of socialist concern for the poor man and his East German relatives. But he knew nothing about the Pryor matter. On this he would have to seek separate instructions. Could he wait till Monday? Donovan was tired and his back was hurting. He rounded on the mute actress playing Mrs. Abel and accused her and Vogel of dragging him all this way from New York under false pretenses. Then he stomped out into the snow.

Abel's "daughter" followed him.

"Don't you wish to see Herr Vogel?" she asked.

It was an important cue, and Donovan missed it. He said that whether or not he saw Vogel was up to the Soviet authorities. He had never liked the sound of Vogel, and the latest Agency intelligence on the man, conveyed to him at the Harvard Club, had strengthened his own hunch that the East German could not be trusted. He said a curt good-bye and trudged back to Friedrichstrasse.

That evening Donovan had a long talk with Bob Graver, the CIA station chief, at the West Berlin Hilton's Golden City Bar.

He didn't know it, but he had almost blown the operation on day one. By failing to call on Vogel he had shown his contempt for the fiction that the East Germans had an important role in the exchange. To Vogel's Stasi controllers it was an important fiction, and they had Pryor. It took all of Vogel's diplomatic skill to repair the damage, especially to the vanity of his most important patron, a former Nazi concentration camp inmate named Josef Streit who only a week before had been appointed East Germany's attorney general.

For the next two days Vogel worked the phones from his office in the backstreets of East Berlin, mollifying Streit and waiting for a visit from Donovan. At last it came. Donovan drove out to Vogel's shabby three-story building on Alt-Friedrichsfelde in a cab with Drozdov. It was a significant test of the worldliness on which he so prided himself. Bearing in mind that whatever was said would inevitably be closely analyzed by those listening in, he needed to be courteous and grateful without being gushing. A little flattery might even have helped. But he was nervous. Outside, climbing the steps to Vogel's reception room in the gathering dusk, he was acutely conscious of Drozdov ("Otto the Strangler") behind him and thought he might actually be attacked. Inside, Vogel was charm itself and confirmed that as far as the East German government was concerned Pryor could be added to the Abel-Powers deal. But Donovan radiated mistrust. He refused to take the East German's word for anything or to confirm that he could deliver Abel on the basis of what had been promised so far. That depended on whether the promises were in good faith, which was for his government to decide. He would have to report back to Washington. Later he wrote that Vogel looked like an insurance salesman.

Streit was livid. Who was this jumped-up elitist to doubt Vogel's word, or his? He might have been at Harvard and Nuremberg, but Streit had been at Dachau and Mauthausen, and not as a guard. If Donovan wanted Pryor so badly, he could have him for Abel and no one else. Otherwise the deal was off.

Streit summoned Vogel to his office to remind him he could have Pryor shot, never mind locked up for life. Again Vogel soothed Streit's fragile ego and made the case that East Germany had more to gain by letting Pryor go—the Krupp steel exhibit at the Leipzig Trade Fair, the gratitude of sensible Americans like the young diplomat Frank Meehan—than by putting him on trial.

It is not clear what changed Streit's mind, but it was probably a combination of Vogel's common sense and Donovan's return to the fray the next day. He did not soften his act. He toughened it up. On his second visit to Vogel's office he listened stonily as Vogel tried to insist that his attorney general had taken "a firm position in the matter."

"Nonsense," Donovan said. "If Shishkin told the attorney general of East Germany to walk across this floor on his hands he'd get down and try.... I have no time for childish games."

Donovan then demanded to be directed to a good hotel for lunch, and left. Drozdov recommended the Johannishof on Friedrichstrasse and asked if he could come along. By the time the coffee was served, Streit had caved.

Even then it wasn't quite over. After lunch, the ersatz Abel family, together with their lawyer and their American associate, repaired once more to the Soviet consulate. All that remained was for Shishkin to repeat his original offer of Powers for Abel, and to approve the East German side deal. Shishkin chose not to. Possibly because of last-minute second thoughts in Moscow, probably for the sheer sport of seeing Donovan explode, he pointed out that since Powers was hardly a national hero at home, a more appropriate swap would involve Abel and Marvin Makinen, the student-spy arrested in Kiev the previous summer.

Donovan duly exploded. He issued his own Berlin ultimatum: if Moscow did not approve the deal in twenty-four hours, he would fly back to New York and tell Abel it was time to start cooperating with the United States since his family had cut him loose. "I left Shishkin in considerable heat and without shaking hands," he cabled Washington that night.

Shishkin let Donovan stew in his safe house for most of the next day. As darkness fell, he sent a message asking for more time. At dawn on Thursday, February 8, he sent another: "I got a favorable reply." They met that afternoon in Shishkin's office to toast the plan for a three-way swap with four-star Armenian cognac. Pryor would be handed over to his parents at Checkpoint Charlie; Powers and Abel fifteen miles away on Glienicke Bridge. It would be nice and quiet there if anything went wrong. Even if everything went right, there was to be a news blackout until the principals were airborne, and Shishkin had requested that press releases speak of humanitarian gestures, not spy swaps.

When Donovan crossed back to West Berlin, he met the CIA's Bob Graver again at the Hilton and told him it was time to send the package waiting in New York. Word reached Abel's handler, Fred T. Wilkinson, that evening.

***

Prisoner 80016-A knew he was going home, even though no one had told him. If he had been going anywhere else he would have heard from his lawyer—and his lawyer, James Donovan, had been conspicuously out of contact.

The clothing officer at the Atlanta federal penitentiary had been told to retrieve Abel's civilian clothes from storage at the beginning of the week. After the midnight prisoner count on Tuesday, February 6, the Soviet master spy who had posed a threat to Western civilization and stayed late at Burt Silverman's wedding party walked out of his cell carrying two brown suitcases. Leaving Atlanta at two in the morning, he was flown to New York on an almost empty Delta Airlines jet. He was put in a federal holding cell until Donovan's message reached Wilkinson, the deputy director of prisons assigned to take Abel to Berlin, thirty-six hours later.

On the onward journey there would be a party of three: Abel, Wilkinson, and Noah Alldredge, supervisor of custodial services for the U.S. Bureau of Prisons. Fisher was the package. Wilkinson would carry the pardon, signed by both Kennedys—John F. and Robert F. He would countersign it on the bridge in Berlin. Alldredge would carry handcuffs and a gun.

They drove into New Jersey to McGuire Air Force Base and down the runway to a waiting Lockheed Super Constellation. It was luxuriously equipped with just eight seats, curtains on its windows, and a good-sized kitchen. At 6:00 p.m. it took off and flew into the night. Once it was over the ocean, the captain was told to head for Germany.

Fisher slept fitfully and talked about prison reform with Wilkinson to pass the time. On Friday afternoon he stared uneasily at the MiGs that shadowed the huge Lockheed down the air corridor to Tempelhof. He spent that night in the U.S. Army brig in Dahlem.

As promised, Powers caught a train to Moscow on Thursday, with the colonel from Vladimir but without guards. He spent that night back in the Lyubianka, but they drank brandy from tin cups before turning in. It was Powers's first alcohol since Adana. On Friday he was flown by military transport to East Berlin and put up in a KGB guesthouse where dinner was served on bone china and the brandy was several grades better than in Moscow. Afterward, drawing on coaching he had received from his cell mate Zigurd Kruminsh, he beat his interpreter at chess.

That afternoon the East German attorney general's office signed Fred Pryor's release papers. There would be no trial. Vogel was authorized to pick him up from Hohenschönhausen at eight o'clock on Saturday morning.

# 13
# THREE MEN AND A BRIDGE

The news blackout was holding, but only just. By dawn on February 10, 1962, a Powers-for-Abel trade had been a media proposition for twenty months, because it seemed a sensible idea and because it would make a cracking story: the summit wrecker and the master spy, all in one headline.

But there were also some generalities that made it seductive: a spy swap was an admission by everyone involved that they really did spy. It was an admission that spies got caught and that when they did, their spymasters needed them back—to debrief, punish, perhaps reward, and to persuade those still working the dead drops that someone was looking out for them. It was an admission by the spy traders that despite the wall and the codes of silence by which they lived, they could put their shadow war on hold long enough to hammer out a deal. In a way this was reassuring. But a swap was also a fleeting chance for the disclosure people—the best-connected reporters, or the luckiest—to glimpse the secrecy people in action and photograph the hell out of them and study the creases on their foreheads and then hold the evidence up to the light and ask: do these people make us safer, or are they as dangerous as the H-bomb secrets they supposedly try so hard to steal?

First, though, they had to know where it was going to happen.

"There were rumors that it was imminent," Annette von Broecker remembers. Where they came from nobody would say, but by Friday night the list of people with useful knowledge on the west side of the wall was long. At the U.S. mission General Clay knew everything, as did Allan Lightner, the head of mission, and Meehan, the newcomer from Moscow. They could be relied on to keep their counsel. Duane Bruce was another matter. Who knew how deep his loyalty to the Agency ran after just six weeks' training? Then there were the Pryor parents, who had moved out of the Kempinski to an apartment in Wilmersdorf and after five months in the city had made some useful contacts. They had been sworn to secrecy for fear that a leak would wreck the deal, but Millard Pryor was, as his son knew, a take-charge type of person. He knew that if Meehan and Vogel failed to deliver he might need the sort of leverage that only the press could provide. How much had he told his DC lawyer and his congressman? How much did Berthold Beitz know, for that matter? He was the chairman and chief executive of Krupp, and from what Fred Pryor could establish afterward the initial plan for his release had Beitz greeting him in person at the Friedrichstrasse crossing point.

And Bob Graver, "El Supremo"? No network correspondent worth his earpiece—and there were a few in Berlin in 1962—did not at least recognize the CIA station chief, and he'd been staying up late all week in the Golden City Bar with a big out-of-towner in well-cut suits with a Brooklyn accent who looked awfully familiar from a big New York story a few years back. It was probably worth asking the picture library to wire over a few head shots of Abel's lawyer, James B. Donovan, just to compare.

Small wonder there were rumors. Small wonder the entire West Berlin staff of the Reuters news agency had gathered at the bureau on Savignyplatz in West Berlin soon after dawn on the tenth, or that Alfred Kluehs, the Reuters bureau chief, was already into his second pot of coffee by then. Or that "correspondents from radio and newspapers who shared our building had dropped by," as von Broecker recalled.

"Everyone had picked up the same rumor."

Still, no one knew where it was going to happen. Covering himself as best he could, Kluehs sent his two correspondents to Checkpoint Charlie—one to the east side, one to the west. It was not an original strategy, but it was the obvious place. If an exchange happened, both sides would surely use cars, and Checkpoint Charlie, four blocks south of the Friedrichstrasse S-Bahn station, was the only place in the city that foreigners could use cars to cross the wall.

Most news bureaus took the same view, but only Reuters had von Broecker. She was a native Berliner who chafed at her copy-taking duties as a mere editorial assistant, and who, after Kluehs's two staff reporters had left, had little to do but stare at a giant wall map of the city and wait for the phone to ring.

Kluehs had stuck pins in the map along the wall to mark each crossing point. "He sat with his back to it," she recalls. "My eyes wandered about, [then] stopped suddenly, in the southwest corner of Berlin. There was a border. There was a bridge.... I said nothing for a while. But then I could not hold back. 'Herr Kluehs,' I coughed. 'What about Glienicker Brücke?'" She was staring at the pin that marked the Glienicke Bridge over the River Havel. "Alfred looked around, then a bolt of lightning seemed to hit him."

* * *

Donovan's day started at five thirty. He packed, made coffee, and waited in the darkened house for Graver. By seven o'clock they were at the Dahlem army base, where he asked for a final moment alone with his client.

Fisher had been under suicide watch, not because he seemed depressed but because the Bureau of Prisons thought he might have something to fear on his return to Russia, and there could be no exchange without a live body.

He was not suicidal, but Donovan, seeing him for the first time in months, thought he looked suddenly old. Fisher accepted a cigarette and said he would miss the American brands. Then he took Donovan's hand and thanked him gravely for his efforts as his lawyer. He promised to send some rare books from home as a token of his gratitude. (Six months later, a Soviet courier came to the Friedrichstrasse crossing point and handed over a package for delivery to Donovan's Manhattan offices. It contained two vellum-bound commentaries on the Justinian Code, in Latin, each about five hundred years old.)

A small convoy formed outside the army cell block: Donovan in Graver's car with Alan Lightner; Fisher with Wilkinson and a hulking U.S. Army security guard; Alldredge with Jim Murphy, the former Detachment 10 security officer from Watertown, Adana, and now Washington. He had been flown in to identify Powers on the bridge.

By the time the American cars headed out of the base and turned west toward the Grünewald forest, a KGB convoy was already on the road. It had a longer drive, looping south of Berlin from the Soviet sector to approach the Glienicke Bridge from Potsdam and the west. For the second time in two days, Powers had washed down breakfast with brandy left over from the night before. He sat in the back of a Wartburg sedan with the colonel from Vladimir and worried that they were driving through countryside. At around seven thirty they reached Potsdam. Shishkin appeared as if from nowhere and climbed in. He explained the plan in perfect English, and they continued to the bridge.

Punctually at eight o'clock, Vogel pulled up outside the Hohenschönhausen prison in a Mercedes borrowed from a butcher friend. This was no day to be seen in an Opel. He was let into Pryor's cell and told the prisoner he was being released. Pryor was completely unprepared for the news, still contemplating a choice between suicide and a show trial and still digesting what Vogel had said as he packed hurriedly and walked with him to the car. He would return to Hohenschönhausen, but not for more than thirty years.

After four years Yuri Drozdov must have been tired of having to play the role of Rudolf Abel's cousin. He overslept. He reached the bridge unshaved but on time and in character. He introduced himself to the bemused colonel from Vladimir as Cousin Drewes.

In the end it was all so much easier than dismantling nuclear missiles—though one still wonders whether Shishkin and Donovan might not have made a better job of the Paris summit than Khrushchev and Eisenhower.

They left nothing to chance. Shishkin's underlings threw a vast, silent security net around the whole operation that they code-named Lyutentsia. Armed KGB operatives were posted overnight in the East German customs house at the west end of the bridge. More of them mingled with the regular Soviet troops guarding the barrier on the Potsdam side, and still more hid in the woods around the summer palace of the Prussian kings, across the water to the south.

Not to be outdone, the U.S. Army provost marshal for West Berlin gave most of the West German police unit at the American end of the bridge the day off and replaced them with U.S. military police. From the U.S. officers' club to the north of the bridge on the east side he dispatched two rowboats to drift downstream and loiter under the girders, each carrying a fisherman with a shotgun instead of a rod.

Drozdov is scornful of the American flotilla. "Why would we need such precautions? We had the agreement of two presidents," he points out, unwilling to admit the scale of Operation Lyutentsia five decades later. The truth was that the Soviet side could not have launched boats even if it wanted to. Since the previous August the western shore of the Havel had been mined and concrete barriers sunk into the water to deter anyone hoping to swim to freedom.

Joe Murphy remembered a big Soviet bomber flying low over the bridge and shattering the calm shortly after his arrival at the American end. Otherwise, silence reigned. Even on a normal day, no civilian traffic was allowed on what the East Germans called "the Bridge of Socialist Unity." Today, even diplomatic traffic was being turned back before it could get close.

All the principals were in place by eight o'clock. By eight fifteen they were out of their cars and huddled around the barriers at each end of the bridge. It was cold and overcast but not snowing. There was time for a cigarette, and wisps of smoke hung in the air above the clusters of winter coats. Donovan looked at his watch. At exactly eight twenty two groups of three detached themselves from the larger groups and began walking toward each other and the center line. The trio from the Potsdam side was led by Shishkin. From the American end came Donovan, Murphy, and Lightner. Each group paused, with a few feet to go, to let Shishkin and Donovan step forward alone and shake hands at the border. Then the others joined them for introductions and a moment's small talk.

Shishkin had drawn a sketch of the bridge at his last meeting with Donovan the previous day and choreographed the next moves minute by minute. Two more groups stepped onto the bridge: at one end, Abel carrying his suitcases, flanked by Wilkinson and the hulk from army security; at the other, Powers and the colonel from Vladimir and another KGB man whom Shishkin introduced as a Mr. Pryzov. Powers had one suitcase and a rolled-up rug he'd made in prison.

Pryzov crossed the line and asked Fisher to remove his glasses. He turned smartly and told Shishkin they had the right man. Murphy identified Powers.

"He obviously was nervous. He didn't know my name, which he should have," Murphy says. Powers had confused him with his security officer from Peshawar. Murphy didn't doubt that the man in front of him in the too-big Russian greatcoat, flanked by Russian goons, was the proud young pilot he'd first met in the canteen at Paradise Ranch in the middle of the Nevada desert. But he had come a long way to make sure the KGB hadn't produced a look-alike.

"Look, I want to ask you a couple of questions. . . ."

As the others on the bridge looked on and the personnel of Operation Lyutentsia waited in their hiding places, Murphy asked Powers the name of his high school football coach. Powers couldn't remember. "Then I asked him the name of his dog," Murphy says. "He got that right."

Wilkinson took the presidential pardon from an inside pocket, signed it, and told Fisher he was free to go. The colonel from Vladimir shook Powers's hand and gave him a box of souvenirs (including several Sputnik paperweights) bought in Moscow with the money left in his prison account. Powers and Abel walked past each other and across the line. No one died. No one took a picture. Both men looked straight ahead and kept walking until they were back among their own people, out of the onrush of the cold war.

Shishkin was anxious to go, but both sides had agreed to stay on the bridge until word came from Checkpoint Charlie that Pryor had been freed. No message had come through. Shishkin tried bluffing. He said that as far as he knew Pryor had already been handed over.

Donovan: "We wait right here until my people confirm he's been released."

And there they waited, as a hint of sun behind the clouds relieved some of the gloom over the bridge and Annette von Broecker, the Reuters editorial assistant, raced toward it in a taxi.

As they waited, Drozdov studied Powers and Fisher. Powers was wearing a good coat and a warm hat and looked well fed, he reckoned. Fisher looked awful, "as if he'd been on a real prison regime." The truth was that Fisher smoked too much but had never been more admired than in prison. Powers had lost a bit of weight, but by prison standards both had been pampered. It paid to be a real spy.

Pryor, the innocent, had suffered. At Checkpoint Charlie he was still having trouble taking in developments. "It was so unreal I couldn't allow myself to be anything but a passive observer," he says. "It was like participating in a stage play."

The play dragged on. As arranged, Frank Meehan and Millard Pryor were on the south side of the checkpoint waiting for the handover, but there was a delay. Meehan strolled across the border and approached the Mercedes. "Just get in the car, Frank," Vogel said. Meehan got in. Stasi men, unmistakable in their gray leather jackets, were more in evidence than usual on the East German side. Vogel made light of them by asking Pyror if he recognized any from prison, but he did not appear to understand the holdup.

On the bridge, Donovan felt the need to say something. He tried a joke. Maybe Vogel was arguing with Pryor over his fees, he said. "This could take months." Shishkin loved it, which was a good thing. He had Abel now and could have marched him off the bridge at any moment. If he had, there would have been little the Americans could have done for Pryor if the Stasi decided to hold on to him. For the next few minutes the only thing keeping Shishkin on the bridge was what Tolstoy might have called his honor. That and the sense that Donovan might have come after him with his fists, and perhaps the strange pleasure of being suspended above the water, between two worlds, in a moment of history.

Powers began to worry again. "I'm not going back," he told Murphy. The Russians had told him that if anything went wrong he was to return to their side, but he wrote later that he had resolved to run—or jump—instead, even at the risk of a bullet.

Meehan sat in the Mercedes with Vogel and Pryor at Checkpoint Charlie and thought, "Oh Jesus, what to do?" Each handover point seemed to be waiting for the other, unless Vogel knew something he wasn't saying.

At about eight fifty a Stasi man approached Vogel in the driver's seat and muttered something in his ear. Vogel listened, then told his passengers: "We can go now."

Meehan and Fred Pryor got out and walked the few yards to the sign that said they were entering the American Sector. Millard Pryor was waiting.

An army signalman radioed from his Jeep and a shout went out across Glienicke Bridge from the American end. Pryor was free. It was time to move.

Who made them wait? It might have been an unnamed Stasi officer, fond of protocol but in over his head. More likely, it was Josef Streit, the East German attorney general whom Donovan had pictured walking on his hands for Shishkin. Donovan was right that Streit had no real power, but for those few minutes he could know how it felt to have a finger on the pause button of world affairs. For those few minutes time stood still on the bridge and only Streit could restart it. He took his time, and Annette von Broecker was forever grateful. She arrived in time to drag a friendly witness behind the bushes at the American end and to extract from him enough detail for the first scoop of a long career.

In the meantime the convoys vanished. One took Fisher to see his real wife and daughter for the first time in seven years. The other took Powers to Tempelhof, where he, Donovan, and Murphy took off in the C-45 that eight days earlier had brought Donovan from London. Powers was given a medical examination in the cargo area. In Frankfurt they switched to the plane that had brought Fisher from New Jersey the day before. It was equipped for the personal use of the commanding U.S. Air Force general in Europe, and as it soared over the Rhine the steward came aft to take orders for cocktails. Murphy and Donovan had Scotch. Powers ordered a martini.

* * *

In Washington, after a long White House party, President Kennedy's press secretary called an impromptu 3:00 a.m. meeting to announce that Powers was free. In Berlin, the press corps scrambled to catch up with a wire report from the Glienicke Bridge that confirmed the dawn of the age of cold war spy swaps but carried no byline. By way of compensation, von Broecker's colleagues took her out to a local café, though not for lunch or champagne. Half a century later she looks out over the River Havel from the spot where she scribbled the notes for her first scoop. She shivers at the memory of the cold and the excitement and remembers very clearly. "They bought me a hot chocolate."

# EPILOGUE

After his martini, Powers enjoyed a steak, medium rare, with a green salad and a baked potato. He ate it with Donovan and Murphy at a table laid as if in a restaurant, thirty thousand feet over the Bay of Biscay. Afterward they talked. Donovan knew very well that Powers had been pilloried in the press for his trial performance but could only admire his nerve as a man willing to "sail a shaky espionage glider over the heart of hostile Russia at 75,000 feet . . . [who] as he passed over Minsk would calmly reach for a salami sandwich."

When Powers joked that he might need a lawyer back home, Donovan told him his fee would be one Virginia ham a year. He received one in the mail the following Christmas.

The rest of Powers's homecoming was less pleasurable. The CIA was not proud of him or done with him. In case anyone saw him, he was told to stay aboard the Super Constellation when it stopped to refuel in the Azores. From Dover Air Force Base he was taken for debriefing to Ashford Farms, an Agency compound in Maryland. Donovan continued to Andrews Air Force Base and was met there by a Powers body double who ran with him to a waiting helicopter to put the press off the scent.

On his first morning in Maryland, Powers enjoyed an emotional reunion with his parents and learned for the first time of his father's efforts to get him released. As he wrote later, he had underestimated his dad. Then the debriefing team arrived. Their questioning lasted eight days and gave him the strong impression that the Agency was more interested in covering its own back than in finding out what had happened to him. But there was one set of operational details to which they kept returning: his altitude when hit and how he descended. They referred to intelligence that conflicted with Powers's version, and that baffled him, as the declassified transcript shows:

> *Interrogator:* Can you say with certainty that...you didn't come down in stages?
> *Powers:* No, I came straight down, straight down. This is something that was mentioned to me on the way over [from Berlin] and I don't understand....At 70,000 feet the airplane fell apart and came straight down as far as I know. I don't know what kind of a shine it cut through the sky as it was falling, but it seemed to me straight down.

A minute later the interrogator picked up on Powers's reference to what he had been told on the flight from Berlin:

> *Interrogator:* Now of course I have access to the same information....And there is some information to indicate that you may have been in the vicinity of 69 or 70,000 and then for some reason unexplained went too close to 74,000.
> *Powers:* No. I didn't climb.
> *Interrogator:* After which you came down to approximately 60,000.
> *Powers:* Nope.
> *Interrogator:* And then with a fast descent, about 3,500 feet a minute, came down to 37,000 and leveled off. There was absolutely none of that at all?

There was, of course, but it did not involve Powers's plane. The interrogator was describing in remarkable detail the flight profile of Igor Mentyukov, the Sukhoi pilot ordered to ram the U-2, who was then ordered to cut his afterburner and whose "fast descent" thereafter was followed by Russian radar operators and by NSA eavesdroppers listening to their communications from Iran.

The NSA had also reconstructed the last moments of Sergei Safronov in his MiG and added them to the confusion. John McCone, who had succeeded Allen Dulles as director of Central Intelligence after a career in business (and was as impressed by "data" as he was cynical of people) chose to believe the NSA, not Powers. He made this clear to Congress and to handpicked journalists, at untold cost to Powers's reputation and career. Diligent historians were still affording McCone's view as much credence as Powers's nearly a quarter of a century later, even though McCone had been an intelligence novice at the time, while Powers's account had the great merit of being based on firsthand experience.

It was flat wrong to say that Powers descended slowly to somewhere near thirty thousand feet before bailing out. It was also flat wrong to say he was under orders to kill himself. Not that the editorialists cared much. *New York Newsday* said he should forgo his back pay because he had "flopped at his job." The *Dallas Morning News* refused to call him a hero because the term should be reserved for the two U-2 pilots who, "it has been reported," had blown themselves up with their planes when their covert missions went wrong. No U-2 pilots ever blew themselves up with their planes.

The most misled and misleading commentator of all was William Tompkins, the prosecutor at the Abel trial, who still had a professional interest in the myth of the Soviet master spy. The exchange on Glienicke Bridge, he said, was "like trading Mickey Mantle for an average ballplayer. We gave them an extremely valuable man and got back an airplane driver." Never mind that the average ballplayer in this case had been trained, deployed, and sent to photograph the Soviet Union's most sensitive nuclear sites in less time than it had taken Willie Fisher to unpack his paintbrushes in Brooklyn.

At a packed Senate hearing in March 1962, Powers had a chance to explain his apology at his Moscow trial: "It was easy to say I was sorry because what I meant by saying that, and what I wanted them to think I meant, were quite different," he said. "My main sorrow was that the mission failed, and I was sorry that I was there."

The hearing ended with an ovation for the pilot, and he was exonerated by the official inquiry that preceded it. But his account of the shoot-down was considered suspect until long after the end of the cold war. In the meantime he was rehired by Kelly Johnson as a Lockheed test pilot and peppered with offers for his memoirs. In deference to the CIA, he did not write his memoirs until 1970 and even then submitted them to the Agency's censors before publication. He knew he could have sold more copies by going straight into print and picked up sales where he could.

"He was flying U-2s out of Palmdale [California], where they did heavy maintenance," his old friend Tony Bevacqua remembers. "He'd bring them up to Beale Air Force Base, near Sacramento, where I was flying SR-71s." After the memoirs came out, he would sign a few dozen copies at a time and bring them with him on his delivery flights to Beale for Bevacqua to distribute in the spy plane fraternity. "I must have sold hundreds of copies for him that way," Bevacqua says.

Soon after publication, Lockheed let him go. The CIA had, in fact, been paying his salary, but Johnson was loyal to his client and didn't bring the Agency into it. He just told Powers there was no more work.

Before moving to California, Powers had divorced Barbara and married an Agency psychometrist, Sue Downey, with whom he built a new life, raising her daughter and a son born to them in 1965 in Burbank, at the foot of the Verdugo hills. Told he could no longer fly for Lockheed, he flew for another big local employer, the local NBC News affiliate. He crashed and died in 1975 while flying the station's helicopter back to the San Fernando Valley after covering a brush fire up the coast near Santa Barbara. He ran out of fuel. Bevacqua asked around after the crash and was satisfied that there was no foul play. "That helicopter had a history that Gary was aware of of showing empty when in fact it still had fuel," he said. "They'd fixed it, but they didn't tell him. What a way to go."

The banality of it was almost as shocking as Powers's first crash, which continued to reverberate. Two years earlier, James Nathan, a young historian at the University of Delaware, had published an article in the journal *Military Affairs* entitled "A Fragile Détente: The U2 Incident Re-examined," in which he assembled all the available evidence to support his view that the shoot-down had been "contrived" by the CIA to nip détente in the bud. Khrushchev, of course, would have agreed. His son still does, citing unnamed CIA sources who he says concur with the view that Powers was never meant to get through to Norway.

It was not hard in 1975 to identify powerful groups with an interest in torpedoing the Paris summit, chief among them the missile builders on both sides. Details that have emerged since the cold war actually make it possible to construct a narrative in which decision makers at the heart of the U-2 program achieve precisely this goal. It starts in Adana in 1959: Stan Beerli, the Detachment B commander with the strongest record in maintaining U-2 secrecy, is moved from Turkey back to Washington. His replacement, Colonel William Shelton, is an air force man unversed in CIA lore and disinclined to respect the niceties of Operation Quickmove. As the end of April 1960 approaches, Beerli is moved again, on a brief assignment to northern Norway that he is assured requires his personal touch (and will keep him out of Washington). In his absence, the go/no-go decision for Operation Grand Slam will be taken by General Bill Burke, another air force man, because Richard Bissell will be out of town for the weekend.

In the tense weeks preceding the final U-2 overflights, Bissell has asked Burke for his assessment of the likelihood of a shoot-down by Soviet surface-to-air missiles. Burke tells him there is a high probability of a successful intercept "provided the detection [of the U-2 by Soviet air defenses] is made in time." This means that anyone hoping for Powers to get through must ensure that he is not detected early. Conversely, anyone hoping for him to be shot down would be wise to do everything possible to advertise his mission in advance.

Beerli leaves for Oslo believing May 1 is the target date for Powers's flight. "As far as I knew, May 1st was the only day," he says. "When I left Washington, that was the plan." If so, there was no need for Powers or the Quickmove team to arrive in Peshawar before the night of Saturday, April 30. Yet by this time Powers has been waiting in the hangar there for three days, his earlier departure dates ostensibly scrubbed because of bad weather over Russia. U-2s have shuttled between Adana and Peshawar five times. Because of the mileage accumulated in those flights, the most reliable plane in Detachment 10's inventory has been replaced with the least reliable. Worse still, according to the then U.S. ambassador to Kabul (briefed later by the Afghan foreign minister), the entire Pakistani Air Force officers' mess in Peshawar knows about Powers's mission in advance. In case it has not been adequately telegraphed to Soviet forces, the final go code is transmitted from Turkey to Pakistan over an open radio channel. Powers is indeed detected "in time."

The makings of a conspiracy are strewn across the historical record. In practice, as ever, mismanagement is the more plausible explanation. Even if Burke "screwed the whole thing up," as Beerli maintained when he learned about the myriad security lapses much later, he appeared genuinely distraught when news of the shoot-down broke.

Joe "Wonderful News" Alsop was less distraught. The same was presumably true of his friends and sources in the missile-gap lobby, including Colonel Thomas Lanphier (retired) of the Convair division of General Dynamics. At the time of the shoot-down each superpower had approximately ten operational nuclear warheads. Two months earlier Lanphier had argued before Congress that if Convair had been allowed to start building Atlas missiles in 1957 it would have four hundred of them by now. One month before the shoot-down he made a specific plea for an order for one hundred Atlases and twenty Titans. After May 1, he never had to plead again. A contract with Convair was signed and by 1963 the Air Force's Strategic Air Command had thirteen Atlas missile squadrons with one hundred thirty-seven ICBMs between them. Twenty-six years later, each superpower had roughly nine thousand warheads. Harold Macmillan called the U-2 affair "a very queer story." For the defense industry, it was also a very happy one.

* * *

Fisher flew home with his wife, Elena, and daughter, Evelyn. They had enjoyed a few days' shopping in the relative abundance of East Berlin and could now enjoy the company of their beloved, stoical Willie.

He was officially revered by the KGB but was too famous to be of any more use as a spy—or for his employers to admit he had never been much use in the first place. He gave speeches, lectured schoolchildren on the patriotic glories of intelligence work, and moped occasionally that he had not been able to give his life to art.

In 1967 Burt Silverman came looking for him in Moscow, to write a book and to apologize for failing to write to him in prison. A meeting was almost arranged through a series of intermediaries but was canceled at the last moment when a reporter got wind of it. So Silverman left him a letter, in which he made his apology and wrote: "I can only say that they were different times, and I was not above fear.... Maybe the reason I'm here now is to make up for that.

"It is almost ten years to the day since your trial started back in Brooklyn. Many things have happened to all of us since then—to me, my friends... and to you as well. I had hoped to talk to you about all of it. I had also fantasized a trip to the Hermitage to talk about art and painting once again. I also thought we could talk about your feelings about America and the people you met there. Apparently, this is not to be. Some other time perhaps—when the two of us can meet simply as old friends."

They never did. Fisher died of lung cancer in October 1971. His ashes were interred at the Donskoi cemetery under his real name, and a few Western correspondents were taken there to see for themselves the true identity of the master spy who never broke. They were even told that he was British.

His art outlived him. The Soviet embassy in Washington declined a request for one of his paintings from Robert Kennedy, but a book of reproductions of his Russian landscapes was published by the KGB in 1999, and two of his American canvases are still in the possession of the Federal Detention Center in Manhattan.

***

Fred Pryor did his best to forget what his friends called his Rip Van Winkle experience in Berlin, because it was easier to forget than forgive.

The family flew straight home, pausing only for a short press conference at Idlewild Airport in New York. Millard and Mary, who had spent an estimated $25,000 to free their son, were described as "beaming with happiness." Fred was brisk and serious, in a pressed white shirt, jacket, and striped tie. "I would like to resume a normal life," he said.

"Resume" was perhaps misleading given his extensive wanderings since college, but he was determined to knuckle down and join his brother among the gainfully employed. He found a teaching job at the University of Michigan and soon published his first book. It was called *The Communist Foreign Trade System* and referred briefly in the preface to his imprisonment: "The reader can judge the nature of my 'spying' for himself; for this book is essentially the 'spy document' which was found in my car upon my arrest."

It was not a bestseller, but for many years it was definitive.

In 1992 Pryor applied for permission to read his Stasi file. In 1994 it was granted, and he returned to a reunified Berlin. In the reading room established by then for victims of the secret police in the former Stasi headquarters on Magdalenenstrasse, the sheer heft of his ten-thousand-page file gave him what felt momentarily like special status. Then someone appeared with fifteen thousand and he took his place among the mortals.

He was interested chiefly to know whether any of those he had interviewed had joined the Stasi in accusing him of spying. None had, though some had been denounced by their colleagues for their contact with him. That knowledge distressed him, but not as much as the circumstances in which he found the man he credited with his release.

Wolfgang Vogel was by then in jail, accused of blackmail by the reunified German state and by some of those whose freedom he had negotiated. When they had first met, Pryor wrote, "I was on one side of the bars, he on the other.... [Now] our positions were reversed. Although he seemed able to bear up under the situation, I had a hard time maintaining my composure. He had been able to help me get out of prison in a totalitarian state; but now, I could not help him get out of prison in a democratic state."

Vogel served only a short term and retired comfortably to Schliersee, an hour south of Munich. His funeral there was attended by a fabulously retro cast of Berlin luminaries including Egon Krenz, the last East German Communist leader, and the last U.S. ambassador to East Berlin—Francis J. Meehan.

Having faced down the flood of memories brought on by reading his file, Pryor returned to the United States and lived with them for five more years. Then he took the next step. The file identified his interrogator by name. He went back to Berlin and looked the name up in the phone book. "I went to his house," he recalls. "His wife stuck her head out of the window and asked what I wanted. I said I wanted to talk to her husband. I explained who I was, and she retreats and says to come back that evening."

The two men went to a bar and drank beer for three quarters of an hour.

"We walked there and we walked back. I didn't taunt him about the fall of Communism, didn't ask him about his life," Pryor says. "I wanted to know what they planned to do with me if I hadn't been exchanged, what they were really going to try me for. He was not forthcoming. It was a meeting of two people who didn't like each other. But he made no apologies. He still believes I'm guilty. He said, 'You were spying. We did our duty.'"

# A NOTE ON SOURCES

Most of the original material for this book comes from face-to-face interviews that I conducted from 2007 to 2009 in Russia, Germany, and the United States with participants in the story and people who knew them. These interviewees included, in alphabetical order: Nikolai Batukhtin, Stan Beerli, Tony Bevacqua, James Bozart, Yuri Drozdov, Jack Goff, Jean Goff, Marvin Makinen, Carl McAfee, Frank Meehan, Joe Murphy, Alexander Orlov, Gary Powers Jr., Frederic Pryor, Burt Silverman, Annette von Broecker, and Mikhail Voronov. Eileen Cline, Carolyn Cooper, Richard Cooper, Sergei Khrushchev, and Martin Skala, among others, were interviewed by telephone. Igor Mentyukov was traced to his home in Belarus and interviewed for me by Olga Sorokina.

Among the most important primary and online sources were White House and other official papers relating to the U-2 affair made available by the CIA at the Center for the Study of Intelligence and by the Eisenhower Presidential Library. More declassified documents on the U-2 shoot-down, including a transcript of the Prettyman Enquiry conducted upon Powers's release, are available at the National Archives in College Park, Maryland. Yet others have been released as a result of Freedom of Information Act requests by Chris Pocock. I used newspaper and magazine accounts in the archives of the *New York Times*, the *Times* (London), and *Time* magazine for contemporary views of Abel's arrest and trial, the aftermath of the shoot-down, the failure of the Paris Summit, Powers's trial, the building of the Berlin wall, and the Glienicke Bridge exchange. Recollections in the Russian media of the events of May 1, 1960, were also valuable, although most were not published until after the fall of the Soviet Union.

The best research conducted since the cold war on Khrushchev's desire for détente in 1960 is contained in *Khrushchev, the Man and His Era* by William Taubman, and *Khrushchev's Cold War* by Timothy Naftali and Aleksandr Fursenko. *Like Father, Like Son* by Vin Arthey and *The U2 Spyplane: Toward the Unknown* by Chris Pocock are definitive studies of William Fisher and the U-2 respectively. While any errors in this book are mine alone, I also turned for detail on Fisher to *Bombshell* by Joseph Albright and Marcia Kunstel, *The Mitrokhin Archive* by Christopher Andrew and Vasily Mitrokhin, *Abel* by Louise Bernikow, *By Any Means Necessary* by William E. Burrows, *My Silent War* by Kim Philby, *The Shadow Network* by Edward Van Der Rhoer, *Sacred Secrets* by Jerrold and Leona Schechter, and *Special Tasks* by Anatoly Sudoplatov. For perspectives on the U-2 affair I drew on *The Man Who Touched the Sky* by Johnny Acton, *Mayday* by Michael Beschloss, *Reflections of a Cold Warrior* by Richard Bissell, *Remembering the Dragon Lady* by Linda Rios Bromley and Gerald E. McIlmoyle, *Red Moon Rising* by Matthew Brzezinsky, *The Craft of Intelligence* by Allen Dulles, *Waging Peace: The White House Years* by Dwight D. Eisenhower, *Spyplane* by Norman Polmar, *Spy Wife* by Barbara Powers, and *Skunk Works* by Ben Rich. For the context and mythology of the Glienicke Bridge exchange I made use of *Negotiator* by Philip Bigger, *K Blows Top* by Peter Carlson, *Strangers on a Bridge* by James B. Donovan, *Stasiland* by Anna Funder, *Nikita Khrushchev and the Creation of a Superpower* by Sergei Khrushchev, *Spy Trader* by Craig R. Whitney, and *Joe Alsop's Cold War* by Edwin M. Yoder Jr.

ACKNOWLEDGMENTS

Half a century is more than half most lifetimes. I was lucky to find survivors of the stories told here and I am grateful to those who agreed to tell them, especially when it meant throwing off the secrecy that bound them during the cold war. Most are acknowledged in the Note on Sources, but I am particularly indebted to Frederic Pryor, the only survivor of the prisoner exchange of February 10, 1962, for reaching back into his memories of a unique and painful episode.

Scores of others helped with the research and writing of this book, chief among them Chris Pocock and Vin Arthey. Both are experts without whose unstinting advice the project might well have imploded. In Russia, I would have been at a loss without the irreplaceable and irrepressible Olga Sorokina. For their willingness to answer e-mails, give out numbers, or tolerate long absences or sudden impositions I would also like to thank Christopher Andrew, Joseph Albright, Tom Baldwin, Stan Beerli, Tony Bevacqua, Grace Blundy, Linda Rios Bromley, David Chappell, Daniel Finkelstein, Thomas Fuchs, Tim Hames, James Harding, Yuri Kobaladze, Margarita Kondrasheva, James Nathan, Rebecca Nicolson, Norbert Potzl, John Ray, David Reynolds, Laura Swanson, Alla Vareldzjan, Konstantin Yershov, and Lyudmila Yershova.

My thanks to Bill Hamilton for his unfailing support and wisdom, to Bill Thomas for taking the plunge, to Charlie Conrad for making sense of the result, and to Jenna Ciongoli, Rachel Rokicki, Julie Cepler, and the rest of the team at Broadway Books for their astonishing patience. I am grateful also to George Lucas in New York for lunch and Mike Jones in London for whatever lies in store. In Wiltshire, Jon and

Hilary Stock let me use their house. In Chelsea, Matthew and Kate Whittell let me use their boat. In Putney and Marblehead, Jim, Jane, Fran, and Ted helped to look after Bruno, Louis, and Enzo, but my deepest thanks and love are for Karen, who looked after everyone, all the time.

# INDEX